SOUTHERN EUROPE AND THE NEW IMMIGRATIONS

Southern Europe and the New Immigrations

Edited by

Russell King and Richard Black

sussex
ACADEMIC
PRESS

2 4 6 8 10 9 7 5 3

First published 1997, reprinted 2008, in Great Britain by
SUSSEX ACADEMIC PRESS
PO Box 139
Eastbourne BN24 9BP

and in the United States of America by
SUSSEX ACADEMIC PRESS
920 NE 58th Ave   Suite 300
Portland, Oregon 97213–3786

British Library Cataloguing in Publication Data
A CIP catalogue record for this book is available from the British Library.

Library of Congress Cataloging-in-Publication Data
Southern Europe and the new immigrations / edited by
   Russell King and Richard Black.
   p.   cm.
   Papers presented at a workshop held Dec. 6–7, 1996,
      Sussex European Institute.
   Includes bibliographical references (p.   ) and index.
   ISBN 978-1-898723-61-5 (h/c : alk. paper)
   1. Europe, Southern—Emigration and immigration—
   Congresses. 2. Immigrants—Europe, Southern—
   Congresses. I. King, Russell. II. Black, Richard, 1964–
   JV7590.S68   1997
   304.8′4′0091822—dc21   97–38086
   CIP

Printed by TJ International, Padstow, Cornwall.
Transferred to digital printing 2008.
This book is printed on acid-free paper.

Contents

Preface and Acknowledgements

This book is a product of the newly-formed Sussex Centre for Migration Research, an interdisciplinary grouping of some 25–30 faculty and research students working on various aspects of migration research. The University of Sussex was founded on the ethos of interdisciplinarity, and remains committed to that philosophical ideal. Within the social sciences and the humanities, there can be few research themes which are so open to interdisciplinary work than the study of human migration. Hence the new Centre comprises scholars from a wide variety of academic backgrounds: anthropologists, geographers, sociologists, economists, historians, specialists in international relations, cultural and literary studies and others who share a common interest in migration and economic, social, cultural and political change.

With the help of a grant from the University of Sussex Research Development Fund, one of the first activities of the Sussex Centre for Migration Research has been the organisation of a series of workshops on specific themes in migration research. This book collects together revised versions of papers presented and discussed at the first of these workshops, held in the Sussex European Institute on 6–7 December 1996. Focusing primarily on the theme of links between migration and economic development, this workshop was devoted to the study of Southern Europe as a major region of immigration in the late twentieth century.

The workshop itself attracted lively interest in particular from a number of young researchers who were completing, or had just completed, their doctoral theses. This provided an immediacy to the discussions and presentations which in most cases were based on recent and extended periods of field research in Southern Europe, investigating the evolving character of immigration phenomena in some detail. Some of this research was funded by European Union mobility grants.

Finally, we thank the chapter authors for adhering to the rather stringent timetable we set for the preparation and revision of their contributions, we gratefully acknowledge the interest and support of Tony Grahame at Sussex Academic Press in proceeding to publication so quickly, and we thank Jenny Money for help in preparing the manuscript for publication.

Russell King and Richard Black

1

The International Migration Turnaround in Southern Europe

Russell King, Anthony Fielding and Richard Black

Amongst the self-indulgent and trivial news that dominated the British media over Christmas 1996 and New Year 1997, one tragic news item was all-but completely overlooked: the horrific drowning of 289 illegal immigrants in the Mediterranean south of Sicily. Those who perished – mainly Indians, Pakistanis and Sri Lankans – had each paid up to $10,000 to be smuggled into Europe. Off-loaded into a small fishing-boat which had been stolen a few days earlier from a Maltese harbour, they were abandoned to die in rough seas when their over-crowded craft was in collision with the larger boat from which they had just been transferred.

In the long term this tragic event will probably only be a footnote in the history of immigration into Europe. Here we wish to highlight it for a number of reasons. First, and most obviously, in order to expose the sometimes terrible human consequences of a migratory movement which seems to have its own logic of push and pull factors (above all push factors), its own momentum and its own economic code. Second, the location of the tragedy was significant. The migrants were trying to gain clandestine entry to Italy, now one of the richest countries in Europe and a destination widely regarded as the new European *eldorado* for migrants coming from poor countries because of its perceived wealth, ease of entry and access to employment. Once they have landed on Italian soil they have, literally, gained a foothold in the West, for Italian law prevents them from being immediately expelled or repatri-ated. Third, the incident above shows how very different is the informal and partly-criminalised organisational structure of this 'new immigra-tion' when compared, for example, to the colonial and post-colonial immigrations into Britain in the 1950s and 1960s, or the 'guestworker' migrations into Germany in the 1960s and early 1970s, both of which were quite tightly regulated according to the quantity of labour demand. There are other differences too. Unlike the large homogeneous groups of industrial labour migrants entering Europe between the 1950s and the mid-1970s, the more recently-arrived groups in Southern Europe are characterised by ethnic diversity, high mobility, often informal economic activity and the tendency for ethnic groups to carve out 'niches' for themselves in host countries. Indeed the complexity of the migrant footprint in southern Europe has confounded many of our traditional perceptions about immigrants and migration and has forced us to seek new ways of examining and understanding the phenomenon. This is what this book tries to do.

This chapter is organised in the following way. First we will note the small amount of literature that has looked at immigration into Southern Europe as a unified region – as opposed to the much larger numbers of studies on individual destination countries or localities, or on individual migrant groups. Based on a review of literature, we will describe the general contours of the 'new immigrations' – their timing, origins, numbers involved and some suggestions regarding processes and mechanisms. Following on from this largely factual outline we will then present a simple scheme explaining some of the causes of the migration turnaround in terms of the changing labour needs and opportunities in the destination countries. Based on this economic rationale, and on the premise that most migrations are fundamentally economically determined, we will then examine in more detail how the new immigrants are becoming embedded in the economic and social geography of Southern Europe, drawing examples from all four countries and pointing to the case studies presented in the succeeding chapters.

Literature review: documenting the new immigration

Although individual country studies had identified the emerging immigrant flows into Southern Europe in the early 1970s (see Nikolinakos 1973 for an interesting early study of the Greek case), the first overall treatment of the phenomenon of the new immigrations into Southern Europe was a lengthy paper by the French geographer Gildas Simon published in 1987. Simon pointed out that the switch from net emigration to immigration in Southern Europe was the product of a complex interaction between several pre-existing and new migration flows. Looking at the period between the early 1970s and the mid-1980s, he identified four migratory processes:

- a substantial potential for continued emigration, above all from the poorer regions such as northern and eastern Portugal and adjacent districts of interior Spain;
- significant return migration of Southern Europeans from a variety of countries, mainly in North-West Europe;
- a continuous shuttle migration or to-and-fro movement between villages in Southern Europe and their emigrant communities abroad, reflecting the maintenance of strong economic and cultural ties between origin and destination;
- the appearance of new immigrant flows of workers and refugees, many clandestine, coming from countries to the south and east of Southern Europe and (especially in the case of Portugal and Spain) from former colonies.

Hence although the official statistics tell us that the change from net emigration to net immigration occurred in Italy in 1972, in Spain and Greece in 1975, and in Portugal in 1981, it is important to realise that these shifting balances are based on the interrelation of a number of different types of flow, that the statistical 'hold' over some migrations (such as return migration, temporary movement and recent immigration) is very weak (and so the real dates may be somewhat different), and that finally there is, of course, no such creature as a net migrant!

Simon went on to review some of the key characteristics of the 'new immigrants' in Southern Europe, namely their often clandestine nature, the great variety of migrant nationalities, the fundamental role of the 'new underground economy' (Simon 1987, p. 287), and the lack of national policies to cope with the uncoordinated influx.

Although he does not reveal the basis of his figures, Simon (1987, p. 284) estimated a total of 2 million immigrants in Southern Europe, including 1 million in Italy and 650,000 in Spain; only a minority were regarded as legally present and most of this category were North European professionals, retired persons and students.

After Simon's initial overview of the phenomenon, a more detailed analysis was prepared by ISOPLAN of Saarbrücken in 1989, and published in the Commission of the European Communities' bulletin *Social Europe* in 1991 (Werth and Körner 1991). This analysis considerably extended and deepened scholars' and politicians' understanding of the still relatively new phenomenon of immigration into Southern Europe, and also provided new estimates on the size of the rapidly-developing immigrant populations in the four southern EU countries. It remains a fundamental source, despite the gradual obsolescence of its data.

After noting the abundance of literature on the emigration of

Southern Europeans towards Northern Europe (and overseas) during the 1950s and 1960s, the ISOPLAN study sets out three important reasons for interest in the new immigrations to Southern Europe:

- the quantitative dimension of the phenomenon, greatly underestimated in previous commentaries;
- the 'surprise element' of the migration turnaround, so that South European governments were unprepared for the influx and unsure how to cope with its social impact;
- the '1992 perspective' of the Single Market, with the attendant fear that immigrants would use Southern Europe as a 'waiting room' in anticipation of an onward move to the north.

Following a simple threefold typology of regular, irregular and refugee migration, Werth and Körner assembled data from a variety of national and international sources to demonstrate that previous estimates (for instance that of Simon) had significantly underestimated the scale of irregular migration. This underestimation was partly explained by the variety of mechanisms and states of irregularity: 'the tourist who decides to stay longer than permitted, the student who accepts a job without having a work permit, the Tunisian seasonal worker in agriculture in Sicily, the Moroccan peddler in Spain, the illegally-employed construction worker in Portugal, the Filipino domestic servant in Athens, or the refugee whose application for asylum has been refused and who remains in the country' (Werth and Körner 1991, p. 12). Differences also existed – and continue to exist – regarding the amount and quality of data across the four countries. The immigration issue has been most thoroughly analysed in Italy whereas the standard of data available and the level of associated research are probably lowest in Greece. Even in Italy, however, the information base leaves much to be desired (King 1993).

Table 1.1 Foreigners in Southern Europe, 1988–9

	Regular ('000)	Irregular ('000)	Refugees ('000)	Total ('000)	% of total population
Greece	200	70	5	275	2.8
Italy	645	850	10	1,505	2.6
Portugal	94	60	1	155	1.5
Spain	475	294	9	778	2.0
Totals	1,414	1,274	25	2,713	2.3

Source: ISOPLAN estimates in Werth and Körner (1991, p. 38).

ISOPLAN's total for 1988-9 is a minimum of 2.7 million and a 'more likely' estimate of 3 million. The bases behind the lower estimate are set out in table 1.1, whilst table 1.2 presents some analytical aspects of the immigrant totals: the proportions who are 'irregular', who come from outside the EU, and an indication of the diversity of source countries. In broad terms, the 1.4 million regular immigrants are drawn in roughly equal proportions from EU and non-EU countries, whilst the 1.3 million irregular immigrants come mainly from outside Europe.

The ISOPLAN data provide a credible basis for an understanding of the evolving character and structure of immigration into Southern Europe at the end of the 1980s. They represent a 'best compilation' of available sources on both documented and undocumented migrants. Two important qualifying statements should be made, however. First, the balance between regular and irregular is constantly shifting, due above all to the periodic amnesties and regularisations instigated in Spain and Italy since 1985. Secondly, the data presented in tables 1.1 and 1.2 chronicle the situation just before the exodus from Eastern Europe in the early 1990s. For Southern Europe the most important effects were the rapid installation of mostly illegal Albanian immigrants in Greece and a broader distribution of Poles in Spain, Italy and Greece.

Table 1.2 Some characteristics of the structure of immigration in Southern Europe, 1988-9

	Irregular (%)	Non-EU (%)	No. of countries supplying 50% of total immigrants	No. of countries supplying 75% of total immigrants
Greece	25	70	4	10
Italy	55	61	10	28
Portugal	39	73	4	8
Spain	38	48	5	14

Source: ISOPLAN estimates in Werth and Körner (1991, p. 79).

Following the conventional framework for analysing international migration, Werth and Körner (1991, pp. 25-7) listed several push and pull factors for the new immigration. Amongst push factors two were thought to be particularly important: growing poverty and unemployment in the world's underdeveloped countries; and an increase in the number and intensity of political, religious and ethnic conflicts. Amongst pull factors Werth and Körner followed Sassen's (1988) analysis of changing labour demand in Western economic systems and stressed that the qualitative polarisation in the demand for labour described by her also applied to Southern Europe, giving rise to two immigration trends: an increasing demand for highly qualified manpower, creating an elite flow of professionals; and a numerically much larger flow of unqualified workers who are drawn into low-status, low-wage activities, primarily in the burgeoning informal economies of Southern Europe. We shall return to this key relationship between immigration and the informal economy later in this chapter, and it is also the focus of specific analysis in several other chapters of the book.

Table 1.3 Southern Europe: foreign population by country of origin (regular migrants only), 1987–8

	no.	% of total
Great Britain	128,922	9.8
Germany	117,945	8.9
USA	112,475	8.5
France	72,028	5.5
Morocco	50,926	3,9
Portugal	37,647	2.9
Switzerland	33,848	2.6
Cape Verde	33,293	2.5
Greece	32,240	2.4
Turkey	30,347	2.3
Argentina	26,003	2.0
Philippines	24,723	1,9
Spain	24,059	1.8
Venezuela	23,757	1.8
Italy	22,716	1.7
Netherlands	20,772	1.6
Yugoslavia	20,210	1.5
Brazil	19,486	1.5
Cyprus	19,338	1.5
Jordan	18,706	1.4
Belgium	17,302	1.3
India	16,642	1.3
Poland	15,095	1.1
Canada	14,006	1.1
Egypt	13,832	1.0
Tunisia	12,329	0.9
Sweden	11,063	0.8
Ethiopia	10,781	0.8

Source: Werth and Körner (1991, p. 48).

Consolidated data on migrant origins for the four South European countries reveal the dual structure of migration flows. Table 1.3 is a rank ordering of immigrant nationalities (note for *regular* migrants only) and clearly differentiates between what Werth and Körner call 'expert migrants' from developed countries (Europe, USA) and 'poverty migrants' from underdeveloped countries (Werth and Körner 1991, pp. 44–52). The table lists the top 28 migrant nationalities, down to the threshold of 10,000. A more detailed examination of table 1.3 reveals the following types of flow:

- a high-status immigration from Northern Europe and North America composed both of working professionals and business-owners, and of retirement migrants (see Williams et al. 1997 for a detailed analysis of this latter group);
- migrations amongst the Southern European countries themselves, for instance Portuguese to Spain, Cypriots to Greece;
- immigration from former colonies, where socio-cultural and linguistic ties have played a key role, e.g. from Brazil and Cape Verde to Portugal; Argentina to Spain;
- immigrations from within the Mediterranean Basin based on geographic proximity and other ties (e.g. Tunisians to Sicily, Egyptians to Greece, Moroccans to Spain); indeed Werth and Körner suggest the de facto creation of a 'Mediterranean labour market' (1991, p. 80);
- immigrants from other 'Third World' countries: a diverse range of long-distance migrants (India, the Philippines, Senegal etc.);
- Eastern European immigrants, notably Poles and Yugoslavs who were the harbingers of more massive movements both from these and from other East European states after 1989.

In the final section of their report, Werth and Körner (1991, pp. 113–29) develop a series of hypotheses and scenarios concerning the future of immigration into Southern Europe, looking both to the (then) immediate agenda of '1992' and towards the longer-term future. Their first scenario was already coming to pass in the late 1980s: the conversion of the 'waiting room' into a 'terminus' as migrants, unable to move to northern EU countries, stayed on and developed their livelihoods and formed communities in Southern Europe. The second scenario is the quantitative prediction of a growth in immigrant numbers to around 5 million by the year 2000, made up of 3 million regular and 2 million irregular immigrants. This forecast, based on the accelerating trends of the late 1980s, is proving to be an overestimate, despite new and unforeseen migrations of the early 1990s, such as the Albanian exodus to Greece and Italy. The ISOPLAN authors also do not make it clear how the figure of 5 million is related to the alternative hypotheses of future migration behaviour which they make: the 'catastrophe scenario' of uncontrolled irregular immigration, the 'zero immigration' scenario, and the scenario of continued steady immigration.

In the early-mid 1990s, a number of studies appeared which aimed at a more holistic and analytical interpretation of Southern Europe's new immigration. Montanari and Cortese (1993) concentrated on the 'Mediterranean Basin' perspective and stressed the demographic context. The Mediterranean, for them, was Europe's Rio Grande separating two entirely different demographic and economic systems: the 'First World' on the one side and the 'Third World' on the other. The fault-line nature of this divide had become much sharper after the early 1980s as South European prosperity rose to more-or-less European levels and the birth-rate collapsed. Meanwhile, on the southern flank of the Mediterranean, populations were increasing at such a rate that there was no way that the various national economies and labour markets could absorb the escalating numbers of new labour market entrants.

King and Rybaczuk (1993) stressed the changing role of Southern Europe in the global division of labour. In addition to the straightforward migration factors of ease of entry, geographical location, and the 'diversion effect' caused by the near-impossibility of gaining direct access to Northern Europe, particular emphasis was placed on the transformed economic context of Southern Europe within the European and global economies. King and Rybaczuk (1993, pp. 178–82) specified the following causes of the new immigrations:

- ease of access because of relatively open borders and channels of entry: geography makes the complete sealing of Southern Europe's long coastal borders virtually impossible, whilst tourism, fishing and shipping provide channels of entry which are likewise difficult to monitor;
- geographical and cultural proximity: geographical closeness for Mediterranean countries like Morocco, Tunisia, Turkey or Albania where migration is only a short sea or mountain trip; cultural proximity for former colonial states and countries where there is a linguistic or religious link (Brazil, Cape Verde, Colombia, the Philippines etc.);
- the demographic push pressures of overpopulation, rapid population increase and unemployment in the source countries of the developing world, whose average fertility rates range from four or five children per woman up to seven or more, compared to sub-replacement fertility levels throughout most of Europe including the lowest levels of all (1.2–1.5 children per woman) in Southern Europe;
- the marked economic differences between the rapidly modernising

and newly prosperous economies of Southern Europe and the still-backward economies of the various migration-supply countries which were not only suffering from traditional supply-push factors of poverty and unemployment amongst the rural and urban proletariats but also overwhelmed by intellectual unemployment as educational standards rose faster than the availability of high-status jobs;

- the transformation and restructuring of Southern European economies and societies, which provided a context for immigration linked to dynamic processes of informalisation of the economy and the replacement of an indigenous labour force increasingly unwilling to engage in low-status and precarious work.

The specific labour market context was further analysed by King and Konjhodzic (1995; abridged version 1996) and Iosifides and King (1996). Following important earlier work by Venturini (1988), Pugliese (1993) and Mingione (1995), this line of analysis challenged the concentration on the explanatory power of push pressures from the countries of origin and sought instead to explain the existence of a *demand* for immigrant labour by analysing the specific socio-economic formation of Southern Europe. Key features of this formation are the strongly represented processes of modernisation, urbanisation and tertiarisation, the dynamism of the informal sector, the importance of small-scale enterprises, an enhanced level of education for most young people leading to a rejection of manual work, and a sharply defined conception of social and family prestige reflected in attitudes towards 'acceptable' and 'unacceptable' types of work.

Hence recent thinking has focused attention on the internal market structures of Southern European countries as both a setting and an incentive for immigration. This analysis is not without contradictions, for example the coexistence of high unemployment with high rates of immigration. However there are some clear answers to this paradox, as the next section will show.

Modelling the migration turnaround in Southern Europe

In this section we offer a relatively simple scheme which seeks to answer the question: 'why did Southern Europe experience a turnaround from net emigration to net immigration in the 1980s?' It will be shown that, although external push factors operating from the new source countries were important (as stressed in our previous account), the question cannot be divorced from internal migration trends and from the supply and demand for labour in what has become an increasingly differentiated economic structure in the four destination countries.

Three preconditions lie behind the model. These preconditions are fairly specific to Southern Europe and do not, in general, apply to Northern Europe, at least during the period in question – the 1950s to the 1990s. Clear evidence of these preconditions can be found in studies of Southern Europe's postwar economic and social transformation (see Hadjimichalis 1987; Hudson and Lewis 1984 and 1985; Sapelli 1995). The first precondition is the coexistence of high and low productivity sectors. Although in broad terms this dualism corresponds to the contrast between urban, industrial activities on the one hand and rural, agricultural pursuits on the other, there is also an intra-sectoral dualism to be observed: the large capitalist farm and the peasant smallholding, the modern factory and the artisan workshop. On the whole, low productivity sectors have either disappeared from North European countries, or form only a small part of the economy. The second background element is the rapid transfer of indigenous workers from low to high productivity sectors as the Southern European economies developed during the postwar decades. Often this was facilitated by short or long distance internal migration. For instance the growth of high-productivity industry in North-West Italy drew first on local supplies of rural surplus labour, then on migrants from Veneto in North-East Italy, and finally on long-distance migrants from the Italian South (King 1985, p. 238). Thirdly, Southern Europe experienced a very rapid decline in the rate of rural depopulation in the 1970s. In other words, freely available supplies of indigenous labour were suddenly closed off. Again, this is unlike Northern Europe where rural depopulation had started much earlier and had largely run its course by the postwar period. This last fact explains the keenness with which the industrial economies of North-West Europe recruited new supplies of labour via guestworker migration from Southern Europe during the 1950s and 1960s: according to Kindleberger (1967) this Mediterranean migrant workforce was the key factor sustaining high rates of industrial growth in North European economies at this time.

Let us now examine more closely how these processes have worked themselves out over the period since about 1950, based on a graphical representation of the model (see figure 1.1). The schema proceeds in three stages. It should be stressed that the timings of these stages, and hence the positioning of the lines on the graph, are approximate and vary between Southern European countries (Italy being the 'leader') and even within them (e.g. Catalonia versus other regions of Spain, North versus South of Italy etc.).

During the 1950s, and in some regions during the 1960s as well,

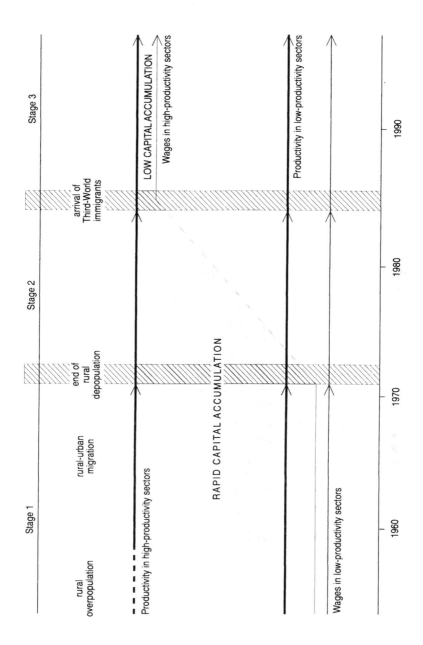

Figure 1.1   A model of migration trends in Southern Europe, 1950s–1990s

virtually all production was low in technology and productivity: peasant farming, craft activities and petty services were the dominant productive forms. Progressively during the late 1950s, 1960s and early 1970s, the co-presence of high productivity and low productivity sectors emerged as some sectors incorporated the latest North European and American technologies to produce for the home market and for export. Examining the industrial development of Southern Europe over these decades Hudson and Lewis (1984, pp. 194–7) identify three forms of industrialisation: import-substituting (cement, steel), export-processing (agricultural industries, processed minerals), and export-platform (petrochemicals). Because of 'unlimited supplies of labour' (cf. Lewis 1958), labour costs were held close to subsistence level, even in high-productivity sectors. In Spain, Portugal and Greece political suppression of trade union activities also helped to depress wages for much of the period preceding the mid-1970s. As figure 1.1 shows, this situation leads to very high rates of capital accumulation, leading in turn to further domestic and foreign capital investment, and to high GNP growth rates. Throughout this period of rural overpopulation and rural-urban migration, indigenous workers experienced high (but falling) unemployment, partly also due to high or steady rates of population natural increase.[1] Unemployment was also kept up and wages held down by the inability of Southern European producers to compete with the somewhat higher productivity industries in Northern Europe, with whom they came to be in direct competition.

In stage 2 of the model, during the remainder of the 1970s and the early 1980s, high GNP growth rates continued, but the sudden closing off of internal migration reduced the supply of labour in urban and industrial labour markets. This led to a transfer of labour from low productivity to high productivity sectors, where workers could make successful claims for higher wages. In Italy the 'hot autumn' of 1969, when industrial workers (many of whom were rural migrants from the South), went on strike and brought the economy of Northern Italy virtually to a standstill, was the defining moment in this process (Slater 1984). However, higher wages squeezed profits leading to a reduced rate of investment. As well as the cessation of internal mass migration, emigration abroad also faded away as indigenous workers enjoyed higher than subsistence wages while the beginnings of a welfare state helped those who were unemployed, allowing them to stay at home and receive benefit rather than being forced to emigrate to survive.

1   High unemployment, low wages and a desire to 'escape' also drove large numbers of Southern Europeans to emigrate abroad during these decades, moving to high-productivity work in North European countries or overseas in the Americas or Australia.

The third stage of the model comprises the late 1980s and the 1990s. A reduced rate of investment has combined with recession to produce a new phase of high unemployment for indigenous workers, who prefer to remain unemployed, receiving benefit, or to continue their education rather than revert to low-wage, low-productivity employment. Meanwhile the low productivity sectors cannot afford to increase wages, since to do so would price themselves out of business; low wages are the only means of retaining a competitive edge. Since they cannot recruit indigenous workers, who refuse to work for low wages in 'unseemly' jobs, employers therefore turn to immigrant workers from the 'Third World' to survive. Hence we have a structural explanation of how 'Third World' immigration is needed to fill the gap vacated by transfers of indigenous workers from low productivity sectors to high productivity ones. This explanation adds a new perspective to the prevailing orthodoxy that the new immigrations into Southern Europe are driven mainly or exclusively by push pressures and are 'unwanted' by the destination countries.

Immigrants in the changing social geography of Southern Europe

The previous account has given an economic rationale for immigration flows, based on labour market trends and on the interrelationship between internal and international migration. It now remains to examine in a little more detail the ways in which immigrant workers are incorporated into the workforce of Southern European countries; or, in some cases, how the migrants create an economic existence for themselves. It also needs to be pointed out that their economic integration is generally not accompanied by a parallel social integration. Indeed the lack of any serious measures for social integration, together with the widespread tolerance of the illegal status of many de facto immigrants, produces a situation of extreme marginality and social exclusion.

Taking our cue from Barsotti and Lecchini's (1994) analysis of the Italian case, the following economic types of migration can be recognised, each defined according to a different function and profile in the labour market and to a corresponding set of social relationships with the host population.

Production workers

First, we can identify workers employed in production, of which a variety of subtypes can be observed. Specialised Mediterranean agriculture has highly seasonal work regimes with a corresponding demand for a flexible supply of labour. Traditionally this was satisfied either by concentrated hard work by all members of the farm family or by local internal migrations, for example from overpopulated highlands to the intensively cultivated plains. Now farmers and farm business managers rely on immigrant workers from destinations as far apart as Senegal, Morocco, Albania and Bangladesh to perform harvesting and picking jobs. The work is unskilled and so requires virtually no training. Partly because of this, but also because most seasonal farm workers are undocumented immigrants, very low wages are paid, considerably below official contract or legal minimum levels, and with no social security. Immigrant farm workers do not complain because of their illegal status.

It is a moot point whether this influx of migrant rural labour causes labour market conflicts with local workers. In Southern Italy, for example, temporary farm work continues to be carried out on an often informal, non-contract basis by local workers, especially women. Here it is likely that migrant labour will have both driven down wages and worsened working conditions for indigenous workers. Overt conflict has rarely occurred, however; for the most part local workers increasingly reject agricultural employment, sometimes pursuing a strategy of internal migration to further their careers in jobs which carry better prestige.

Other productive sectors where immigrants are active include fishing and industry. North Africans have been important contributors to the fishing workforce in Southern Europe: mainly Egyptians in Greece, Tunisians in Italy and some Moroccans in Spain. In the case of Tunisians in Sicily this involvement is of long standing, traceable to the late 1960s (Guarrasi 1983). Industrial employment is generally much more recent, often resulting from upward socio-economic mobility of migrants already settled for some time in the host country, as Mendoza shows in Chapter 3 of this volume. In the more industrialised parts of Southern Europe such as Catalonia and Northern Italy immigrant workers are found in a range of industries, especially those where the work is heavy and dirty such as quarries, foundries, bricks, ceramics etc., as well as in small artisan workshops where they work as low-paid assistants.

Once again, there are a variety of knock-on effects and potential conflicts with indigenous labour. Barsotti and Lecchini (1994) acknowledge that, where immigrants are employed to overcome bottlenecks in the industrial process, they contribute to an overall increase in production and allow local workers to shift to higher positions in the occupational hierarchy. Where legally settled immigrant workers are employed on a more permanent basis in production roles where the work is tough and rejected by local labour, there is a clear complementarity between immigrant and indigenous employees – this is becoming a common situation in some North Italian industrial towns. On the other hand the counter-argument has been stated by Dell'Arigna and Neri (1987) that immigrant workers fuel the expansion of the informal sector of productive activity, slowing down structural change and impeding the adoption of modern technology. Hence 'the informal economy, "encouraged" by immigrants, might give rise to an element of pressure against the local labour force and supplant Italian nationals working in the formal sector of the economy' (Barsotti and Lecchini 1994, p. 89). This view may be true in certain situations, but it is based on an exaggerated dichotomisation between the formal and the informal sectors. In Chapter 2 of this book Iosifides explores some of the more complex inter-connections between the formal and the informal sectors in Athens and shows how the buoyancy of the informal sector also acts to shore up formal sector employment.

Domestic workers

In all four countries of Southern Europe, a strong demand has arisen for domestic helpers – an example of gender-specific immigration, as Chell's account of Filipino and Somalian women in Rome (Chapter 4) shows. Inasmuch as these jobs in domestic service would not be filled by indigenous workers even if offered to them for the legal minimum wage, it would appear that such work has been specifically created for immigrant workers, and therefore no competition with the indigenous labour force occurs (Barsotti and Lecchini 1994, p. 90). This statement is probably true, but it overlooks historical precedents and recent social and gender processes in Southern Europe. In Italy, for instance, domestic servants employed by wealthy households in mainland cities like Rome and Turin traditionally came from Sardinia where it was common practice for girls from poor families to work on the mainland for a few years to save for their trousseaux (Watson 1994). However the real stimulus to the employment of domestic helpers across a larger range of social classes in recent years has been the rapidly increasing participation of South European married women in the labour market (King and Konjhodzic 1995, pp. 4–11). Lack of childcare facilities combined with the reluctance of most South European men to share equitably in homecare and childminding responsibilities has opened the way for a massive demand for foreign domestic workers to help with, or take over, tasks such as house cleaning, cooking, babysitting, management of children, caring for elderly people etc. Whilst these practical considerations are the key factors, not to be ignored are the overtones of social prestige – where the employment of a foreign maid is a status symbol for middle-class *arrivistes*.

Self-employed workers

Most emblematic of this group are the Maghrebi and Senegalese street-vendors who are especially common in Spanish and Italian cities and tourist resorts, selling cigarettes, sunglasses, cheap jewellery, leather goods, tee-shirts and other low-priced goods (though prices are rarely fixed!). Many other nationalities are also involved in street-selling, including Egyptians in Athens (see Iosifides, Chapter 2) and Bangladeshis in Rome (Knights, Chapter 6). Nor is street-hawking the only casual self-employment amongst immigrants in Southern Europe. Washing car windscreens at traffic-lights is another common activity, practised by different groups (including immigrant children) in different cities of the region. Prostitution by women of various Third World and East European nationalities may be regarded as another form of self-employment, although often this activity is brutally controlled by male gangs operating regimes of mafia-like intimidation and terror.

Whilst street-hawking, windscreen-cleaning and prostitution are highly marginal and precarious forms of self-employment, other examples exist of more integrated and stable self-employment, often based on specific niches of ethnic/economic specialisation. In Chapter 5 Malheiros describes the settlement in Lisbon of Indian traders and entrepreneurs, Knights in Chapter 6 notes the transition amongst Bangladeshis in Rome from street-vending to stalls and shops, and Herranz Gómez (1991) has documented the rise of Latin American shopkeepers in Madrid. Some particularly thorough studies have been carried out on the Chinese in Italy where two sectors of entrepreneurial specialisation have evolved: in the restaurant trade throughout the country, and in the leather trade in and around Florence (Barsotti 1988; Campani et al. 1994; Campani and Maddii 1992). A final example of ethnic enterprise that can be cited is the import and sale of carpets by Iranians settled in Italy: a role considered by the host population as 'natural' for this group of immigrants. Carpet-trading has developed out of a mixture of the business talents of the immigrants, most of whom have a high level of education, and their privileged links to the source of the Persian rugs and carpets, often via family connections. The pioneers of this trade were exiles from the Khomeini revolution in the 1970s, and they have paved the way for successive waves of Iranian immigrants arriving as business associates or students. The successful integration of this particular group of immigrants is indicated by high rates of intermarriage with the Italian population (Barsotti and Lecchini 1994, pp. 87, 90).

Construction workers

This sector has common ground with the intra-European migrations of the early postwar decades which saw the building-sites of North-West Europe swarm with migrant workers: the Irish in Britain, Mediterranean workers in the northern countries of continental Europe. Now, as then, the building trades generate a fluctuating demand for labourers to work in an industry which is affected by strong seasonal and cyclical swings, and is characterised by tough, mainly outdoor work, insecure contracts and frequent mobility. Hence it is not surprising that the construction sector in Southern Europe has started to draw in its own supplies of migrant labour: in Portugal mainly from Cape Verde, in Greece mainly from Albania, and in Italy and Spain from a variety of nationalities in North Africa, Eastern Europe and beyond. Many if not most of the workers in this sector tend to be undocumented, and rates of pay and conditions of work are unregulated. Several subsectors of building work can be recognised: the construction of relatively small-scale buildings such as houses and blocks of flats; building maintenance work such as house decorating and repair; road-mending and public utilities construction (sewers, cables etc.); and large civil engineering projects such as tunnels, airports or motorways. Although the bulk of workers in the construction trades are dependent and insecure labourers, opportunities do exist for some advancement, as the growth of Cape Verdean subcontracting firms in the Lisbon construction sector demonstrates (see Malheiros, Chapter 5).

Service sector workers

Finally there is a diverse category of immigrants who work in the service sector. Some of these jobs overlap with one or more of the categories listed above, but the main types of employment to be considered here include work in the hotel and catering sector and jobs as care workers in hospitals and other institutions. The specific case of Moroccans who work in the partly-privatised garbage collection trade in Catalonia is briefly described by Mendoza in Chapter 3.

A wide range of nationalities are involved in these various service sector activities, with jobs open to both men and women. Inevitably, given the structural position of immigrants in the South European labour market, combined with high levels of illegality amongst some groups, these jobs are in the lowest grades in the various sectors.

Generally they are labour-intensive, demeaning and underpaid. They comprise washing-up in hotel and restaurant kitchens, chamber-maids, unskilled or semi-skilled maintenance staff, hospital orderlies etc. Opportunities for upward mobility in these petty service occupations are generally limited although some cases have been noted of immigrants rising to intermediate levels – for example Filipinas with nursing qualifications (see Chell, Chapter 4) or Moroccan foremen in the rubbish collection business (Mendoza, Chapter 3).

Ethnic and gender specialisation

Given the strong correlation between immigrant employment and the informal labour market, there are few comprehensive survey data on the employment parameters of the immigrant presence in Southern Europe. Those data that exist are mainly linked to legally-present immigrant workers or are based on smaller-scale qualitative studies which by definition are restricted to certain limited geographical areas and types of migrant. There is also a shortage of data which are cross-tabulated by nationality of the migrant.

These data shortcomings are particularly unfortunate since it is known from observational and other evidence that there are high degrees of ethnic, gender and regional specialisation within the economic and demographic characteristics of the population of immigrants. This complexity derives from the generally spontaneous way in which the various immigrant flows developed, the large variety of immigrant nationalities involved (especially in Italy and Spain), the multiplicity of different types of local and regional labour markets across Southern Europe, and the strong role of social networks in the reproduction of the migrant flows from particular origins to specific destinations. Hence there is a complicated mosaic of employment types and ethnic mixes in different localities, often further differentiated by gender assymetry.

The following chapters give some specific insights into the spatial and occupational patterning of individual immigrant groups in a number of South European regions and cities: Albanians, Egyptians and Filipinos in Athens (Chapter 2); Moroccans, Senegalese and Gambians in Girona (Chapter 3); Bangladeshis in Rome (Chapter 6); Moroccans in Bologna (Chapter 8). Some further brief examples were mentioned in the analysis of immigrant employment types given above. In the remainder of this subsection we present a more complete range of examples and data drawn from Italy, which undoubtedly has the greatest variety of immigrant nationalities and employment types.

Table 1.4 is a simple ranked listing of the 50 most important foreign nationalities in Italy according to the data on foreigners with 'permits to stay' (*permessi di soggiorno*) at the end of 1995. These data therefore exclude undocumented immigrants – the so-called *clandestini* or *irregolari*. The percentage data show that 14 nationalities have to be summed to reach half of the total immigrant stock of 991,419, and 32 to reach 75 per cent. These data illustrate the fragmentation of the immigrant population in Italy amongst literally dozens and dozens of different nationalities drawn from all parts of the world – Europe (North-West, South, East), North America, South America, North and Sub-Saharan Africa, various parts of Asia etc. – with each immigrant community tending to have its own social, cultural, demographic and economic characteristics.

Table 1.4   Immigrants in Italy: 50 main nationalities, 31 December 1995

Nationality	no.	%	Nationality	no.	%
Morocco	94,237	9.5	Bosnia Herzegovina	10,224	1.0
USA	60,607	6.1	Russia	10,197	1.0
Yugoslavia	51,973	5.2	Peru	10,025	1.0
Philippines	43,421	4.4	Ethiopia	9,895	1.0
Tunisia	40,454	4.1	Colombia	8,626	0.9
Germany	39,372	4.0	Dominican Republic	8,562	0.9
Albania	34,706	3.5	Japan	8,290	0.8
GB	27,694	2.8	Austria	8,110	0.8
France	27,273	2.8	Iran	7,956	0.8
Romania	24,513	2.5	Netherlands	7,378	0.7
Senegal	23,953	2.4	Mauritius	6,564	0.7
Brazil	22,053	2.2	Pakistan	6,535	0.7
Poland	22,022	2.2	Nigeria	6,343	0.6
Egypt	21,874	2.2	Bulgaria	6,181	0.6
China	21,507	2.2	Bangladesh	5,541	0.6
Sri Lanka	20,275	2.0	Hungary	5,511	0.6
Croatia	18,944	1.9	Portugal	5,323	0.5
Switzerland	18,237	1.8	Turkey	5,220	0.5
Spain	17,847	1.8	Mexico	5,095	0.5
Somalia	17,389	1.8	South Korea	5,053	0.5
Macedonia	15,426	1.6	Belgium	4,820	0.5
Greece	14,821	1.5	Cape Verde	4,688	0.5
India	14,629	1.5	Libya	4,625	0.5
Ghana	12,550	1.3	Czech Republic	4,596	0.5
Argentina	10,494	1.1	Slovenia	4,107	0.4

Source: Holders of 'permits to stay'; Caritas di Roma (1996, p. 69).

One important dimension of this differentiation is the assymetric sex distribution of many of the immigrant nationalities, some of which are overwhelmingly male, whilst others have a large female majority (table 1.5). Overall there is a slight male majority (53.7 per cent as against 46.3 per cent females) but, as table 1.5 shows, most of the 24 largest nationalities have an excess of females. This paradox is partly explained by the fact that the gender assymetry is larger on the male side, where some of the largest communities have over 75 per cent males; on the female side most of the figures are in the range 55–70 per cent.

Table 1.5   Sex balance of Italy's 24 main immigrant nationalities, 31 December 1994

Excess of males		Excess of Females	
Nationality	% male	Nationality	% female
Morocco	81.5	USA	66.9
Ex-Yugoslavia	65.9	Philippines	69.7
Tunisia	84.9	Germany	58.0
Albania	72.7	GB	58.0
Senegal	95.7	France	61.2
Egypt	76.8	Switzerland	55.4
Sri Lanka	57.7	Spain	66.5
China	57.0	Brazil	72.2
Ghana	64.2	Poland	63.2
		India	53.3
		Romania	70.1
		Somalia	65.4
		Peru	71.7
		Austria	65.0
		Ethiopia	72.5

Source: Holders of 'permits to stay'; Caritas di Roma (1996, p. 87).

What are the distinguishing characteristics of countries with male as opposed to female majorities? It is clearly evident that the countries with the largest male majorities – Morocco, Tunisia, Egypt, Senegal – are all African Muslim states in which there is an established tradition of almost exclusively male emigration linked to 'male' occupations such as street-hawking, fishing, agricultural labour and construction work. Such migration is also often linked to cultural and economic factors which favour migration of young men prior to or immediately after marriage – as for example in the case of migration from Senegal where a tradition of long-distance migration of young men can be traced back over centuries (Condé and Diagne 1986).

Those countries with a female majority are more mixed and fall perhaps into three subgroups: developed countries (North America, Western Europe) whose residents in Italy are made up of 'mature' communities with an over-representation of middle-aged and elderly women; Catholic countries (the Philippines, Brazil, Peru, Poland) where women have found jobs in the domestic and care sectors; and former Italian colonies (Somalia, Ethiopia) where again female domestic employment in Italy is common.

Table 1.6   Immigrant nationalities in Italy: a regional breakdown, 1995

Region	1st	2nd	3rd
NORTH			
Valle d'Aosta	Morocco	France	Tunisia
Piedmont	Morocco	Albania	France
Lombardy	Morocco	Philippines	ex-Yugoslavia
Liguria	Morocco	Germany	France
Trentino-Alto Adige	Germany	Czech Republic	Morocco
Veneto	Morocco	ex-Yugoslavia	USA
Friuli-Venezia Giulia	ex-Yugoslavia	Croatia	USA
Emilia-Romagna	Morocco	Tunisia	Senegal
CENTRE			
Tuscany	USA	Morocco	Germany
Umbria	Morocco	Germany	Albania
Marche	Morocco	Albania	Macedonia
Lazio	Philippines	USA	ex-Yugoslavia
SOUTH			
Abruzzo	Macedonia	Albania	ex-Yugoslavia
Molise	Albania	Morocco	Poland
Campania	USA	Morocco	Tunisia
Puglia	Albania	USA	Morocco
Basilicata	Albania	Morocco	Tunisia
Calabria	Morocco	Philippines	Albania
ISLANDS			
Sicily	Tunisia	Morocco	USA
Sardinia	Senegal	Morocco	USA

Source: Holders of 'permits to stay'; Caritas di Roma (1996, pp. 325–31).

The variable regional distribution of different foreigner groups in Italy adds a further layer of complexity to the overall picture. Table 1.6 gives the three most important immigrant nationalities in each of Italy's 20 regions. Whilst Moroccans are the most numerous nationality in nine regions, mainly in the north and centre of Italy, Albanians are the largest group in three southern regions, with Americans the leading group in Tuscany and Campania. Geographical proximity partly explains the dominant role of Germans in Trentino-Alto Adige, citizens of the former Yugoslavia in Friuli-Venezia Giulia, and Tunisians in Sicily,

Macedonians in Abruzzo, and Albanians in Puglia.

Finally, some specific cases of ethnic, gender, occupational and regional specialisation can be mentioned. The mainly female Filipino community is concentrated in the major cities, especially Rome, where the main demand for domestic help is found amongst wealthy families. Tunisians, overwhelmingly males, are chiefly found in western Sicily where they have formed large colonies engaged in fishing and farm-work. The almost exclusively male Senegalese are chiefly engaged in street-vending and are widely distributed in urban and resort areas; only in Sardinia are they the dominant immigrant nationality (table 1.6). Moroccans are also involved in peddling goods on an itinerant basis but have also evolved to a range of other activities such as agricultural work, factory jobs and construction, especially in northern Italy.

Conclusion : the future of immigration in Southern Europe

Specifying the role played by economic conditions inside Southern Europe, rather than external 'push' factors, should not be taken to imply that the 'demand' for international migration comes solely from within Southern Europe, as the incident referred to at the start of this chapter indicates. However, an important purpose of this chapter, and the book, is to draw attention to the internal dynamic within Southern Europe which has played a major role in the turnaround of the region from an area of emigration to one of immigration. This internal dynamic is highly varied, as one would expect across four countries with different histories and varied economies that are proceeding in different ways and at different speeds towards development and integration in the new 'Fortress Europe' (Sapelli 1995). Nonetheless, common themes can be identified, which are drawn out in part in Chapter 7 by Apap (on Spain and Italy) and in Chapter 9 by Malheiros and Black (on Spain and Portugal), both of which explicitly adopt a comparative perspective.

This search for similarities is not simply an academic exercise. For whilst case studies of particular countries – such as those presented here – can tell us much about the detailed development of migration flows to Southern Europe, it is through transnational comparison that we can move to a clearer understanding of the forces that are generating these new immigrations, and the appropriateness of policy responses. This is made all the more important by the context of European integration, where the implementation of the Schengen agreement and the slow move towards harmonisation of border controls, if not immigration policy, is gradually edging the EU towards a pan-European response (Collinson 1993 and 1996).

In this context the observation, made by a number of contributors to this volume, that immigration to Southern Europe is closely linked to the nature of Southern European labour markets, is an important one. Not only does this mean that policy to impose ever-stricter border controls and policing of immigration may be inappropriate, but it also implies that any social agenda to combat the rise of exclusion of minority groups needs to take account of the important role played by this new generation of migrants in Southern Europe, as well as the more established migrant minorities in Northern Europe. To view international migrants in Southern Europe as 'desperate' or 'illegal' groups, who would be better off in their countries of origin, is to miss the essential economic rationale that has brought them to the region in the first place.

In this chapter we have presented a model of the 'migration turnaround' in Southern Europe which focuses on changing labour demand and highlights the dualistic nature of labour markets as a key element in facilitating mass 'unskilled' immigration. In this sense, our argument bears similarity to that of Sassen (1988) referred to earlier, who also focused on the structural causes of such immigration, in her case to 'world cities'. In turn, both perspectives potentially sit within a broader strand of theoretical literature which is concerned with the economic and social transformation of advanced societies – the so-called transition to 'flexible accumulation' (Sayer and Walker 1992). However, the argument advanced above, and the chapters which follow, are not suggesting that Southern European immigration can be explained as a by-product of this transition. Indeed, as Leontidou (1993) has argued, the process of transition to a more 'flexible' economy in Southern Europe has a number of specificities, rooted in the particular historical circumstances and social formations of the region and individual countries/regions/cities, which belie any attempt to impose an over-arching theoretical framework. Rome, Madrid, Athens and Lisbon are not 'world cities', nor do they act alone as poles of attraction for international migrants even within the context of the growth of international migration towards the four countries. As such, predictions of the future of international migration in the region also need to pay attention to the specific circumstances of economic development and social change in the region. Predictions based on Northern European or ideal-type 'Western advanced economy' models of migration change are likely to be no more accurate than the blithe assumption of a demographic or economic 'push' from the countries of the 'South'.

References

Barsotti, O. (1988) *La Presenza Straniera in Toscana.* Milan: Franco Angeli.

Barsotti, O. and Lecchini, L. (1994) Social and economic aspects of foreign immigration to Italy, in Fassmann, H. and Münz, R., eds. *European Migration in the Late Twentieth Century.* Aldershot: Edward Elgar, pp. 81–92.

Campani, G., Carchedi, F. and Tassinari, A., eds. (1994) *L'Immigrazione Silenziosa: Le Comunità Cinesi in Italia.* Turin: Edizioni della Fondazione Giovanni Agnelli.

Campani, G. and Maddii, L. (1992) Un monde à part: les Chinois en Toscane, *Revue Européenne des Migrations Internationales,* 8(3), pp. 51–72.

Caritas di Roma (1996) *Immigrazione Dossier Statistico '96.* Rome: Anterem.

Collinson, S. (1993) *Beyond Borders: West European Migration Policy towards the 21st Century.* London: Royal Institute of International Affairs and Wyndham Place Trust.

Collinson, S. (1996) *Shore to Shore: the Politics of Migration in Euro-Maghreb Relations.* London: Royal Institute of International Affairs.

Condé, J. and Diagne, P. (1986) *South-North International Migration. A Case Study of Malian, Mauritanian and Senegalese from the Senegal River Valley in France.* Paris: OECD Development Centre Papers.

Dell'Aringa, C. and Neri, F. (1987) Illegal immigrants and the informal economy in Italy, *Labour,* 1(2), pp. 107–26.

Guarrasi, V. (1983) Prime valutazioni sulla presenza di lavoratori stranieri in Sicilia, *Studi Emigrazione,* 71, pp. 356–62.

Hadjimichalis, C. (1987) *Uneven Development and Regionalism: State, Territory and Class in Southern Europe.* London: Croom Helm.

Herranz Gómez, Y. (1991) Un pequeño empresariado latinoamericano en Madrid, *Sociología del Trabajo,* 13, pp. 75–95.

Hudson, R. and Lewis, J. (1984) Capital accumulation: the industrialization of Southern Europe? in Williams, A. M., ed. *Southern Europe Transformed: Political and Economic Change in Greece, Italy, Portugal and Spain.* London: Harper and Row, pp. 179–207.

Hudson, R. and Lewis, J. (1985) Introduction: recent economic, social and political changes in Southern Europe, in Hudson, R. and Lewis, J., eds. *Uneven Development in Southern Europe: Studies of Accumulation, Class, Migration and the State.* London: Methuen, pp. 1–53.

Iosifides, T. and King, R. (1996) Recent immigration to Southern Europe: the socio-economic and labour market contexts, *Journal of Area Studies,* 9, pp. 70–94.

Kindleberger, C. P. (1967) *Europe's Postwar Growth: the Role of Labor Supply.* New York: Oxford University Press.

King, R. (1985) *The Industrial Geography of Italy.* London: Croom Helm.

King, R. (1993) Recent immigration to Italy: character, causes and consequences, *GeoJournal,* 30(3), pp. 283–92.

King, R. and Konjhodzic, I. (1995) *Labour, Employment and Migration in Southern Europe.* Brighton: University of Sussex Research Papers in Geography 19.

King, R. and Konjhodzic, I. (1996) Labour, employment and migration in

Southern Europe, in Van Oudenaren, J., ed. *Employment, Economic Development and Migration in Southern Europe and the Maghreb*. Santa Monica CA: RAND, pp. 7–106.

King, R. and Rybaczuk, K. (1993) Southern Europe and the international division of labour: from emigration to immigration, in King, R., ed. *The New Geography of European Migrations*. London: Belhaven Press, pp. 175–206.

Leontidou, L. (1993) Postmodernism and the city: Mediterranean versions, *Urban Studies*, 30(6), pp. 920–65.

Lewis, W. A. (1958) Economic development with unlimited supplies of labour, in Agarwal, A. N. and Singh, S. P., eds. *The Economics of Underdevelopment*. Oxford: Oxford University Press, pp. 400–49.

Mingione, E. (1995) Labour market segmentation and informal work in Southern Europe, *European Urban and Regional Studies*, 2(2), pp. 121–43.

Montanari, A. and Cortese, A. (1993) South to North migration in a Mediterranean perspective, in King, R., ed. *Mass Migrations in Europe: the Legacy and the Future*. London: Belhaven Press, pp. 212–33.

Pugliese, E. (1993) Restructuring of the labour market and the role of Third World migrations in Europe, *Society and Space*, 11(4), pp. 513–22.

Sapelli, G. (1995) *Southern Europe since 1945: Tradition and Modernity in Portugal, Spain, Italy, Greece and Turkey*. London: Longman.

Sassen, S. (1988) *The Mobility of Capital and Labour*. Cambridge: Cambridge University Press.

Sayer, A. and Walker, R. (1992) *The New Social Economy: Reworking the Division of Labour*. Oxford: Blackwell.

Simon, G. (1987) Migration in Southern Europe: an overview, in *The Future of Migration*. Paris: OECD, pp. 258–91.

Slater, M. (1984) Italy: surviving into the 1980s, in Williams, A. M., ed. *Southern Europe Transformed: Political and Economic Change in Greece, Italy, Portugal and Spain*. London: Harper and Row, pp. 61–83.

Venturini, A. (1988) An interpretation of Mediterranean migration, *Labour*, 2(1), pp. 125–54.

Watson, E. (1994) *The Changing Role of Women in Sardinia*. Brighton: University of Sussex, unpublished M.Phil. thesis.

Werth, M. and Körner, H. (1991) Immigration of citizens from third countries into the southern member states of the EEC, *Social Europe*, Supplement 1/91, pp. 1–134.

Williams, A. M., King, R. and Warnes, A. M. (1997) A place in the sun: international retirement migration from Northern to Southern Europe, *European Urban and Regional Studies*, 4(2), pp. 115–34.

2

Immigrants in the Athens Labour Market: A Comparative Survey of Albanians, Egyptians and Filipinos

Theodoros Iosifides

This chapter contains a comparative analysis and discussion of the findings of recent field research undertaken in the Athens conurbation concerning the labour market position, functions and conditions of three immigrant groups – Albanians, Egyptians and Filipinos.[1] Findings of the research are presented and discussed in a comparative perspective in order to highlight similarities and differences between the immigrant groups and to give a general picture of the Athenian labour market regarding relatively recent labour immigration. The chapter starts with a brief discussion of the methodological problems and approaches employed in the field. It continues with an overview of some of the most important elements that characterise the Greek socio-economic formation and labour market – in other words an outline of the context within which labour immigration takes place. Next the research findings relating to the immigrants' labour market position, functions and conditions are presented in some detail and the chapter concludes by summarising the most important of these findings in a comparative perspective. The rest of this introduction is dedicated to some brief remarks about the transformation of Greece from a traditional emigration country to one of immigration.

1 The fieldwork was undertaken in Athens from September 1995 until March 1996 and culminated in my D.Phil. thesis (Iosifides 1997).

For the most of the twentieth century Greece was a country of mass emigration towards various destinations world-wide. Greek emigration can be broadly divided into two sub-periods: before and after the Second World War. Between 1900 and 1924 an estimated 420,000 left the country for overseas destinations, mainly the United States.[2] After the Second World War, due to severe social and economic problems, emigration accelerated and the exodus was covertly supported by successive Greek governments as an additional aspect of their economic and development policies. Available data indicate a gross emigration of around 1.4 million Greeks during the period 1945–74 but this does not take into account unregistered emigration and return migration flows. During most of the post-war emigration period Germany was the destination of the majority of migrants. Other significant destinations were Belgium, Australia, the United States and Canada. The broad causes of post-war Greek emigration can be related to various factors ranging from political reasons, especially after the 1946–9 civil war, to high levels of open unemployment, poverty and hardship both in the countryside and in several towns and cities (Fakiolas and King 1996). However after 1970 emigration started to decline and return migration began to take place on a large scale. The most important contributing factors to this change were the relative deterioration of economic and labour market conditions in various destination countries, the difficulties of proper assimilation in host countries (especially in Germany), and the restoration of parliamentary democracy in Greece in 1974, after which there followed a period of economic development and low unemployment.

In the 1980s, foreign immigration replaced return migration as the key element in the positive migratory balance of the country. The immigrant population in Greece comprises three main categories. First there are ethnic-Greek immigrants from several republics of the former USSR, Albania and to a lesser extent from other eastern European countries. According to the National Foundation for the Reception and Settlement of Greek Return Migrants, between 1987 and 1993 47,436 ethnic-Greeks arrived and settled in the country, mainly from the former Soviet Union. In reality many more came. The second category is that of the legally employed foreigners. In 1992 there were 33,892 legally employed foreigners in the country, two-thirds of whom were from other EU or European countries (Katsoridas 1994). The third and in many respects most important category is constituted by nationals of several East European, African and Asian countries. Only estimations can be made about their approximate number because the vast majority are undocu-

---

2 During the same period (specifically after 1922) 1.5 million Greek refugees came to Greece from Asia Minor (Papademetriou 1979).

mented. Various estimates put the numbers of Albanians at between 150,000 and 200,000, Poles at around 100,000, Egyptians at about 55,000 and Filipinos at between 30,000 and 40,000 (see Fakiolas and King 1996). There are also smaller but nevertheless significant immigrant communities from Iraq, Pakistan, Bulgaria, former Yugoslavia and various African countries. Estimates based on numbers of deportations and on various empirical observations put the overall total number at between 300,000 and 450,000, that is between 8 and 11 per cent of a total labour force of 3.9 million. It seems that Greece has, in proportion to its population, more immigrants than any other Southern European country.

The most important reasons for the transformation of Greece into an immigration country are briefly as follows

- The first reason is mainly geographical and is related to the relative ease of entry into the country through its extended mountainous borders and the numerous islands of the Aegean Sea. Despite recent efforts made by the government, the control of the borders remains inadequate to prevent the inflows. Furthermore the heavy reliance of the country on shipping and tourism makes it more easily accessible by potential immigrants.
- The second reason is related to the imposing of stricter immigration controls by the traditional host countries of North-West Europe in combination with the relatively lax Greek immigration policy. Hence there is a 'diversion effect'.
- The third reason is the relative narrowing of the economic differential between Greece and other more advanced European countries in recent decades in combination with intense economic and demographic pressures in Third World countries and especially on the other side of the Mediterranean.
- Another strong push factor is political and economic change in the countries of Eastern Europe after 1989–90. The massive influx of Albanians into Greece after 1990 and the increasing numbers of entrants from countries such as the former Yugoslavia, Poland and Bulgaria can be attributed mainly to this factor.
- The last important reason is the demand for low-paid, unskilled migrant labour due to the specific socio-economic and labour market characteristics of the country. This point was explored in some detail in the opening chapter of the book. Here I will just point to three interrelated reasons which explain this demand in the Greek case. First is the persistence of a large informal economy in Greece and the fragmentation of the economy into numerous, in many cases family organised, small and very small firms. Second is the seasonality and labour intensity of many sectors of the Greek economy

such as agriculture, construction, tourism and other services. The third reason is the rejection of low-paid, low-status jobs by natives due to higher educational levels, higher socio-economic aspirations and delayed labour market entrance of the young.

Data and methodology

The most important component of my fieldwork research in the Athens conurbation was that of interviewing samples of immigrants residing and working in the area. The Athens area was selected because it concentrates the vast majority – around 80 per cent – of the immigrant population of Greece. Furthermore, the Athens-based immigrants tend to have permanent or semi-permanent characteristics in comparison with those in peripheral regions or in the islands, although there are exceptions (for example the Poles – as explained below). The targeted subsets of the whole immigrant population in Athens were originally the four major groups of immigrants: Albanians, Poles, Egyptians and Filipinos. Their selection was based on various official and previous research estimates, although their exact numbers are unknown. However the early stages of the fieldwork revealed that one group – the Poles – were problematic as a target population and had to be dropped. The main reasons for that decision were their dispersal and 'invisibility' in the city, their non-permanent residential character (one estimate given to me suggested that only 15 per cent are all-year-round residents), and the lack of a formal community structure.

The fieldwork research in Athens was conducted by a combination of methods, one of the most important of which was the 'snowball' approach through which the majority of the interviews were taken. The selection of a non-probability sampling method (among others) is justified for a series of reasons such as the lack of knowledge of the exact immigrant population in the city, and the impossibility of constructing a reliable sampling frame because the vast majority of the targeted population is characterised by illegality and residential instability. For many migration surveys, and especially for surveys about immigrant populations that include a majority of undocumented workers, non-probability or judgement samples have been the rule (Bilsborrow et al. 1984; Cornelius 1982). Furthermore the purpose of the study, which was the identification of underlying processes and practices in the labour market related to immigrant employment, increased the desirability of employing more qualitative approaches.

Interviews with individual immigrants in Athens were obtained through a semi-structured interview schedule. All the interviews were face-to-face, relatively short 'informational' interviews. Short interviews were preferred because of the nature of the research and the targeted population, because of the characteristics of the immigrants interviewed and the physical setting of many of the interviews, and because of the comparative nature of the research. As regards this last point, the comparative nature of the research tended to direct me to collect some systematic data (including some measurable data) as a basis for comparison. Reliable comparisons would have been more difficult to achieve relying only on qualitative information gleaned from fewer in-depth interviews. Nevertheless the lack of in-depth interviews was compensated, to a great extent, by including a participant observation dimension in the research. The interview schedule contained mainly open questions, the majority of which did not require long answers. The purpose of the interviews was to obtain basic information about the immigrants' employment arrangements in Athens, their position in the labour market and their working and living conditions in the city.

Apart from the snowball method used in order to take interviews, other methods were used as well. These were, briefly, participant observation in various immigrant areas, settings and residences, and interviewing employers and immigrants in their working environments. These additional methods were both necessary and desirable. They were necessary because many informants could not cooperate for a very long period of time or because their social networks were limited. So the snowball process sometimes reached its limits rather quickly. A multi-method approach was desirable because it enabled me to enrich the information obtained through interviews and to capture, to a great extent, the general picture of the employment situation of the three researched groups. The role of key informants proved to be extremely important for the completion of the research process. In many cases they acted as unofficial translators when the language problems were great. Total confidentiality and anonymity were always guaranteed and this was a necessary precondition for obtaining any information required, given the illegal status of the majority of interviewees. Through the whole fieldwork research process it became possible to take 141 interviews from individual immigrants (almost equally divided between the three immigrant groups but also including a small number of other nationalities such as Iraqis and Pakistanis), plus a relatively large and rich amount of information in the form of field notes from observation, participation and lengthy discussions with immigrant representatives, groups of immigrants, employers, policy makers and officials, and information from various secondary data and press reports.

Before presenting and discussing the findings of this fieldwork it is necessary to outline the socio-economic and labour market context within which labour immigration takes place. The next part of the chapter is dedicated to this task.

The socio-economic and labour market context

Three important and interrelated features of the Greek economy and labour market with direct implications for immigrant employment are labour market segmentation, the persistence of small firms and the existence and expansion of a large informal, unregulated sector. The Greek labour market is divided into segments of jobs with different requirements and characteristics . Although the actual situation is much more complex, it can be broadly divided into a primary and a secondary segment. For primary jobs, employers usually organise 'internal' labour markets involving both well defined career ladders for individuals and a series of motives and incentives. On the other hand in the secondary segments employers adopt an 'extensive' strategy, seeking to minimise their commitments 'relying on piecework systems, voluntary quits of the discontented and sacking of unsatisfactory workers to compensate for more perfunctory recruitment and personnel practices' (Gordon 1995, p. 140). Secondary labour markets are characterised by specific gender, age and nationality/ethnicity features, and by instability, temporality, lower remuneration and casuality. Evidence for the existence of secondary labour markets in Greece and their functions can be found in a series of empirical research findings published over recent years (Balourdos 1995; Pelagidis 1995; Vaiou and Hadjimichalis 1990). An important feature of this literature is that it shows that while education plays an important role in primary labour markets it does not play such a role in their secondary counterparts. Evidence for this finding can also be found in my own research, as we shall see in the next part of this chapter. Finally, evidence from the research quoted above and from the present study reveals the specific ways that ethnic minorities have been incorporated in the labour market; national or gender differentiations create characteristics on the base of which some segments of the labour force become marginalised while others remain in a privileged position.

The persistence of small firms in Greek industry, services and the economy in general is a phenomenon of great importance for this research, as small firms increase the demand for flexible, cheap and in many cases immigrant labour. Small firms in Greece are often seen as the driving force towards greater production and labour market flexibilisation. Labour process flexibility has led to an increase of polarisation between the well-paid, well-protected 'core' workers and, on the other hand, the insecure, casualised, unskilled peripheral workers. Hence it has reinforced the tendency towards labour market

segmentation. Moreover the structure of Greek small firms is also characterised by duality. On the one hand there are dynamic, expanding
firms, and on the other hand there are the more traditional, uncompet-
itive and slowly-adjusting firms. However both types of firm seek to
spread market risks by flexibilising labour and controlling labour costs.
This trend has led to further intensification of work, and, as a result,
subcontracting, casualisation, domestic outwork and informal working
practices have increased (Lyberaki 1988). The abundance of the migrant
labour force in Greece is ideal for employment in small firms, usually
informally and under bad working conditions, as we shall see presently.
Finally it is also important to realise that the expansion of small firms in
Greece is largely an urban phenomenon that is particularly concentrated in Athens. Leontidou (1990, p. 182) has pointed out the contrast
between the increase in size of industrial establishments in Greece as a
whole, and the trend towards smaller units in Athens, driven especially
by two waves of 'informalisation' which took place during 1958–69 and
1973–84 (and since).

The existence and expansion of a large informal sector in Greece is
one of the most important characteristics of the socio-economic and
labour market structure of the country. Informal sector activities are
unregulated by the institutions of society, existing in a legal and social
environment in which similar economic activities are regulated (Portes
et al. 1989). The size of the informal economy in Greece was estimated
to be about 27 per cent of the GDP in 1987 rising to 35 per cent in 1995
(Kanellopoulos et al. 1995). Widespread informal activity can be found
in industry and artisan firms; in health, education and recreation; in
services, trade, housing rentals and construction; and in transport and
communications. On the contrary, limited informal activities can be
found in sectors such as mines, agriculture and banking and insurance
services.

However, defining the informal sector is not a completely straightforward task because informal activities must be seen more as a
socio-economic process rather than an object. Rather than being a set of
survival tactics and practices or a euphemism for poverty, informal
activities are part of an income generation process. Also, informal
economic activities are not a totally distinct set of activities from the
regulated formal economy but are articulated with it by a series of inter-
relationships and interdependencies, so that informal activity can be
seen as an integral part of the whole economy and as a continuum with
the formal sector. Finally the informal economy is not homogeneous but
is highly hierarchical. A relatively clear distinction exists between, on
the one hand, organised black market work in which employees work
either for companies which operate wholly underground or for regular

companies which employ some staff on a black market basis and, on the other hand, individual black market work which ranges from the casual one-off cash-in-hand job to the concealment of a substantial part (if not all) of their earnings by the self-employed (Williams and Winderbank 1995). Both parts are relevant for immigrant employment in the Greek informal sector. In fact, the informal sector accounts for the employment of almost all of the undocumented immigrants in the country. Research findings presented in the next part of this chapter give support to this assertion and also show the development of socio-economic relations within the informal economy between 'organisers' of informal work and 'dependents', the latter being usually immigrant workers.

The labour market position and functions of immigrants in Athens

Before examining the labour market and employment characteristics of immigrants in the city it is useful to give, very briefly, some of the most important of their general characteristics in order to act as a background to the later discussion and analysis. As already mentioned above, the nationalities of the interviewee immigrants were Albanian, Egyptian and Filipino. Most of the Albanians and Egyptians were male. Since nearly all the Filipinos in my survey were female I shall henceforth denote them as Filipinas. The vast majority of all the immigrants I interviewed were young, between 20 and 35 years of age. The main emigration reasons were found to be unemployment, underemployment and poverty in their respective countries of origin, while the majority chose Greece as their destination because of relative ease of entry into the country and because of employment opportunities. Employment considerations attracted the vast majority of them to Athens. Most of the Albanians arrived in the country overland while the other two groups came by sea or air. The majority are recent entrants (in the last ten years) with a proportion of the Filipinas being in Greece longer. Migrants' links with their native country are mainly related to sending remittances to family members and relatives, although with varying degrees of sending frequency between individuals and immigrant groups. A significant proportion of immigrants have relatives in Greece or Athens, usually non-dependent family members. Finally, although the majority of interviewee immigrants want to stay in Greece and Athens for the foreseeable future, a high proportion of them want to return home eventually, whilst some want to move to another country.

Education and training

The educational background and experience of training of the interviewees is characterised by important differences between the three
immigrant groups, and by marked intra-group similarity, as shown in
table 2.1 Clear differences exist between the Albanians and Egyptians
on the one hand, and the Filipinas on the other. Very few Albanians and
Egyptians had post-secondary qualifications. There was a subtle difference between these two groups in that whilst almost 70 per cent of
Albanians had primary or secondary education, the Egyptians were
more heterogeneous, including a significant number with no formal
education, but also some respondents with technical or other training
(often as electricians and mechanics). Albanians with technical training
had followed agricultural courses. By contrast the Filipinas held much
better qualifications. Nearly a third had higher education qualifications,
i.e. they were university graduates or had teaching or nursing diplomas.
No Filipina respondents were without any formal education –
compared to 15 Egyptians and 8 Albanians.

Table 2.1   Education and training obtained in the country of origin

Qualification	Albanians	Egyptians	Filipinas	Others	Total
No formal education	8	15	–	3	26
Primary	21	11	13	1	46
Secondary	11	12	12	2	37
College/University	1	1	14	–	16
Technical/other	5	9	2	–	16
Total	46	48	41	6	141

Source: Author's survey, 1996.

These differences in respondents' educational levels reflected, to a large
extent, the educational systems of their respective countries. Albania
has a tradition of low educational standards and illiteracy (80 per cent
in 1944). Although the communist government reduced illiteracy
substantially, overall educational levels remained low because of the
socio–economic situation of the country (Hall 1994, pp. 74–7). Given the
size of the country, the educational problem of Egypt is much greater.
Lack of resources means that increases in student and pupil numbers
are accompanied by falling standards (Mabro 1974). On the other hand
the Philippines, despite being a poor country marked by wide disparities in terms of income distribution and geographical contrasts, has
relatively high educational standards, partly as a legacy of American
colonialism and the principles of free and universal public education.

English is widely spoken and is used in the educational system along-side local languages, and universities partly follow the American system (Vreeland et al. 1976).

Interestingly, the educational backgrounds and levels of the immigrants discussed above are not necessarily reflected in the jobs they do in Athens. With Filipinas both gender and education – and ability to speak English – are important. For the rest, individuals with different educational levels and skills were found doing the same kinds of jobs and under the same working conditions. This, it can be argued, is a further indication of the existence of labour market segmentation where the most important controls over employment type and labour market position are legal, nationality and gender characteristics rather than skills or qualifications or other aspects of investment in human capital. This diagnosis is confirmed by the fact that very few – only 6 per cent – of the interviewees had obtained any formal education or training in Greece. For the vast majority of respondents, work experience was minimal in terms of the acquisition of new skills. Further details on job types will be discussed shortly.

Employment, unemployment and underemployment

The general situation of immigrants was that of substantial unemployment in the countries of origin, followed by that of employment in Athens. This, of course, is hardly surprising, since most of the subjects of the interview survey could be considered as labour migrants migrating largely for employment and income reasons, as we saw earlier.

Overall, two-thirds of the interviewees were unemployed or predominantly underemployed in their country of origin. This proportion was higher for the Filipinas (gender being an important factor here) and lowest for the Albanians (where it was still nearly a half). The political and socio-economic conditions of the countries of origin explain the interviewees' history of unemployment. In Albania the dramatic political changes of 1989–90 and associated economic disruption of the early 1990s created a great deal of unemployment; even those who still held work felt the insecurity of the new era, and feared imminent joblessness. Most Egyptians and Filipinas interviewed also spoke about widespread unemployment in their home countries. Many of the Egyptians were doing menial, short-term jobs, whilst many Filipinas had been helping to look after their families and households. Several Egyptians and Filipinas referred to the financial help they had from relatives and friends in order to meet their basic migration costs.

The employment situation changed significantly in Athens where nearly three-quarters of the interviewees were in more or less full-time employment. I say 'more or less' because there is a continuum between full-time employment through part-time, temporary or seasonal work to more serious underemployment and unemployment.

Type of employment in Athens

Table 2.2 sets out some basic features of the interviewees' employment categories. For those respondents who were unemployed at the time of interview but had worked in Athens, the table incorporates their previous employment type. Almost half of the Albanians interviewed were working in construction, mainly as helpers doing hard manual work. There are two types of construction work where immigrants are involved. On the one hand there is house-building or repair work and on the other the much larger, mainly public works projects in progress in Athens. There are important differences between these two types of construction work (the 'household type' and the 'public works type') in terms of recruitment, stability and work satisfaction, as we shall see later on. One important difference worth mentioning here is the involvement of subcontractors in public works construction. Subcontractors usually undertake a limited part of the overall project and often they recruit immigrants in order to reduce the costs of the part in their responsibility. They make additional profits according to the differential between pre-planned budget costs and real costs.

Table 2.2 Type of employment in Athens

Employment type	Albanians	Egyptians	Filipinos	Others	Total
Construction	22	18	1	–	41
Cleaning	10	1	1	–	12
Small manufacturing firms	13	15	1	2	31
Street-vending	–	13	–	2	15
Shipping	–	1	2	–	3
Domestic work	–	–	28	–	28
Personal services	–	–	8	–	8
Never worked	1	–	–	2	3
Total	46	48	41	6	141

Source: Author's survey, 1996.

More than one fifth of the Albanian interviewees were found to work in cleaning. This type again can be divided between the 'household sector' (cleaning of households and other household spaces) and the cleaning of larger buildings, public or private. This latter type is mainly a 'task type' where work is completed in one or two days. In the 'household sector' regularity of work is higher, especially for those immigrants who try to keep contacts with the household for potential re-employment in the future. Finally some 28 per cent of Albanians worked in small businesses, mainly in hotels and restaurants as dish-washers and cleaners, and in transport and removal companies as helpers and manual workers.

While the number of Egyptian interviewees found to work in construction was relatively high (37.5 per cent), there were two points of differentiation between them and the Albanians regarding overall employment characteristics. Firstly, there were no significant cleaning activities for the Egyptians, and secondly over a quarter of the Egyptian interviewees were self-employed, undertaking street-vending activities. They sell goods such as clothing, cutlery, jewellery, lottery tickets etc., either in the organised open markets or more haphazardly in the streets, preferring usually the crowded central areas of the city. Egyptians tend to have a tradition of open-market trading in their countries of origin; hence they undertake 'entrepreneurial' activities more easily than the Albanians who come from a country with no tradition of a market economy. Finally a relatively high percentage of Egyptian immigrants (31 per cent) were employed in small firms – mainly in various small removal, paper, clothing and transport companies, and to a lesser extent in restaurants, take-aways and shops.

The Filipina case is strongly affected by the gender factor that differentiates it substantially from the other two immigrant groups. The vast majority of Filipina immigrants in Athens, almost 88 per cent, work in the 'household sector' offering services such as domestic work, baby-sitting, nursing the elderly, etc. Over two-thirds are domestic workers staying with their employers. About 20 per cent offer similar services on a mainly part-time basis. The combination of an ageing population in Greece, higher participation rates for women in the labour market and a traditionally weak welfare state has led to an increase in demand for the services mentioned above. Furthermore Filipinas are considered to be hard-working, loyal and honest; yet they are low-paid even when they are employed by wealthy households. Especially for middle-class households, the employment of a Filipina maid has become a 'status symbol' – a statement of success and upward social mobility.

Overall the greatest similarities regarding employment type can be found between Albanians and Egyptians where construction and small-firm employment account for 76 and 69 per cent respectively. Construction work accounts for about 29 per cent of all immigrants. The second most important sector is the small-firm sector which accounts for 22 per cent, and the third is domestic work, almost exclusively occupied by the Filipinas, which accounts for 20 per cent.

The question of labour market competition needs more detailed discussion. Our earlier account pointed to the existence of an effective dual labour market in Greece, and to the segmentation of employment into broadly non-competitive sectors and niches. Hence Greek unemployment should not be affected, unless the expansion of one sub-market staffed by immigrants is at the expense of another staffed by natives. Two specific observations from my fieldwork research support the notion that immigrant employment in Athens has limited effects on the employment (or unemployment) of natives. First, the employment of foreigners, especially by small firms, seems to be essential for economic survival by many owners and employers. Their inability to hire natives with the same wages drives them to seek immigrant labour. If that type of labour was not available they would either reduce their productive capacity or even close down their firms. Furthermore the employment of immigrants, with pay and working conditions that would be unacceptable by the natives, not only helps the survival of many of these companies, but also helps those natives formally employed in the firms to keep their jobs. A second observation is that many of the jobs that immigrants undertake are created precisely because of their presence and availability. To give just one example, often the only alternative for a household head who needs to have their house repaired, is to do the work directly or with the help of other family members. Such a person would be unwilling, and in many cases unable, to pay the much higher amount of money charged by Greek workmen for the job. Nevertheless the possibility of significant competition in some segments of the labour market should be examined by further empirical research.

Organisers and dependents: socio-economic relations within the informal sector

The formal/informal interplay and the distinction between the organisers of informal and black market work and dependent immigrant labourers were found to be present in almost all sectors which contain immigrant employment.

Regarding the 'household construction' sector, when the skill requirements of the task are low, immigrants are usually employed directly by the household head and informally. On the other hand when the skill requirements are relatively high, immigrants are used as helpers by native builders or other skilled workers whose relationship with the household leaders, at least on payments, is usually formal. In the former case household heads act as the organisers of informal work, whereas in the latter this role is played by the skilled builders. In both cases, organisers of informal work benefit from immigrants' employment by reducing the cost of unskilled manual work which constitutes a high proportion of the overall work in this sector. Regarding public works construction, subcontractors act as the organisers of informal work. In most of the cases they employ two categories of labour. The first is that of high or medium skilled workers and the second is that of low-skilled labourers. Almost all immigrants were found to be employed in the latter. While in the first category economic relations between subcontractors and employees are usually formal, in the second category immigrants' employment is informal and casual depending on the varying needs of the project.

The division of labour according to skill levels, employment stability and level of informal arrangements is even more evident in small firms which are dominant in the Greek economy and constitute one of the main driving forces towards informalisation and labour market segmentation in the country. A relatively clear distinction exists within the Greek small-firm sector between the central, primary workforce and the secondary. The former consists usually of family labour and special expertise workers and the latter of the more casual, unstable and low-skilled labour which, in most of the cases, is employed informally and under precarious, exploitative and hard working conditions. Employers in small firms, as organisers of informal work, benefit in two ways: firstly, they reduce their firms' labour costs, and secondly they increase the numerical flexibility of their firms, as demand for their products and services is, in many cases, characterised by substantial seasonal fluctuations.

The Filipinas, who work in the household service sector, are characterised by a distinct legal status, as we shall see in the next part of the chapter. For the purposes of the immediate discussion one can note that the Filipina immigrants in Athens are divided into two categories: those who hold a work permit and the undocumented. The latter work, in most cases, informally, with low payments, long hours of daily work, no social insurance and health benefits, restricted outings and hardship. But even the former do not escape exploitation because their employers use them in ways that infringe their legal status and entitlements.

Immigrants engaged in cleaning activities display similar characteristics to those employed in household and construction work. This employment is again a 'task' type, characterised by great casualness and instability. In many cases, however, immigrants work regularly (every one or two weeks and so on) for the same employer, accepting disadvantageous informal practices, pay and working conditions, in return for a slight reduction in job insecurity.

Only those Egyptian immigrants who work as street-vendors seem to be engaged actively in the informal economy, acting in most cases as the main organisers of their own informal work. Nevertheless their relations with the suppliers of goods represent, in many cases, ties of hidden dependency especially when the supplier keeps a proportion of the total earnings, a very rare practice in formal supplier-trader economic relationships. In this way suppliers not only assist the organisation of informal trade activities but also make additional profits. These extra profits accrue firstly because the activity is informal, and secondly because the vendor is an immigrant, weak in socio-economic and legal power and rich in vulnerability.

The evidence presented above challenges the view of the informal sector as simply a survival strategy of the poor, taking place in marginalised or peripheral localities. This latter view ignores the heterogeneity and social stratification within the informal economy and tends to see it as separate from formal regulated economic activities. My research reveals that the organisers of informal work in Athens are either small firm owners, subcontractors, skilled workers or household heads, almost all of middle-income and middle-class orientation and already employed. Their economic activities constitute a variable mix of formal and informal practices influenced by moves towards greater flexibility, labour cost considerations and different skill requirements. So viewing and analysing informal work from the dependents' side conceals the fact that its generation and organisation also reflect paid employment and formal sector practices and that it is an income generation system which mirrors and reinforces social stratification and inequalities.

Illegality, instability and how work is found

The key words to describe the nature of immigrants' employment in Athens – or least that of immigrants from countries like Albania, Egypt and the Philippines – are *insecure, unstable, marginal* and *low-status*. In order to avoid the risk of creating false semantics, it is necessary to make an initial distinction between *employment instability* (defined as the frequency of change of types of employment – e.g. from construction work to street vending) and *employment insecurity* (the length of each job held, the likelihood of being laid off etc.).

As regards employment instability, nearly half of the Albanians interviewed has had experience of two or three types of work (see table 2.3). The Egyptians have been moderately mobile between different types of work and the Filipinas the least mobile, despite their longer presence – this is due to their specialisation in the domestic work and care sectors. As regards employment insecurity, more than half of all immigrants interviewed held their current jobs for less than a year and a quarter of them for less than three months (see table 2.4).

Table 2.3 Number of employment types during working period in Athens

	Albanians	Egyptians	Filipinas	Total
Two	15	8	3	26
Three	7	2	–	9
Total	22	10	3	35

Source: Author's survey, 1996.

Table 2.4 Length of current job holding in Athens for post-1990 entrants

Approximate length	Albanians	Egyptians	Filipinas	Others	Total
1–3 months	20	11	2	–	33
3–6 months	8	4	2	–	14
6–12 months	9	10	2	2	23
1–2 years	5	9	7	2	23
2–4 years	–	10	7	–	17
over 4 years	–	–	2	–	2
Total	42	44	22	4	112

Source: Author's survey, 1996.

The significant differences that exist between the three immigrant groups as regards employment insecurity can be largely explained by the different employment profiles of the three nationalities. Immigrant jobs can be usefully divided, for the purpose of this analysis, into 'task' jobs, relatively stable jobs and stable jobs. Task jobs are usually held for a limited period of time from a few days to a few months and are mainly construction and cleaning jobs. The relatively stable jobs last from six months to one year, and are usually jobs with small firms, especially those operating in the hotel and restaurant sector, and removal firms. These jobs are also, in many cases, characterised by seasonality. Stable jobs are usually held for at least one year and are of three types: long-term positions in small firms; domestic service; and street-vending.

Albanians have the greatest degree of job insecurity as they are concentrated in construction, cleaning and tourism-related small firms. Egyptians are in the middle, since they are mainly employed as workers in small firms or self-employed as street-traders, although a significant minority is engaged in construction. The most 'secure' group are the

Filipinas where the majority have held the same job for at least a year.

The contrast noted above between the instability and insecurity of the employment situations of Albanians and Egyptians, on the one hand, and the greater stability of the working patterns of Filipinas on the other hand, has a good deal to do with the legal status of the three groups. Nearly all the Albanians and Egyptians interviewed were undocumented. Despite this similarity, the two groups differ as regard the legality of entering Greece – the vast majority of Albanians enter illegally whereas the Egyptians usually enter with tourist or student visas and then overstay. The majority of the Filipinas enter the country legally holding an employer-specific work permit. Those who change jobs and employers, and hence forfeit their original work permit, usually become undocumented immigrants.

Illegality, instability and insecurity are all related to another aspect of the 'immigrant story' in Athens: how work is found. The role of the informal social networks of immigrants (networks of friends and/or relatives) in the city is crucial in finding a job, especially for Albanians and Egyptians. Another popular way of finding a job is personal search, either directly or through the market-place practice. In this latter case, numerous immigrants, often of the same nationality, concentrate in specific places, usually certain squares, and at specific hours, mainly very early in the morning, and wait for potential employers to hire them. This practice, which is basically passive, was found to be very common in Athens, especially for Albanians and Egyptians. The Filipino case is quite different. Here the major role is played by recruitment agencies, both in the Philippines and in Athens. Recruitment agencies in the Philippines arrange to find work positions in foreign countries for Filipinas, usually in the domestic sector, and also take care of their legal documents such as work and stay permits. The charge is a commission of about 2,000 to 3,000 US dollars. This commission is in many cases converted to a debt which the immigrant has to pay back to the recruitment agency when she starts working in the foreign country. Furthermore recruitment agencies in Athens play an equally important role. They act as intermediaries between employers and immigrants, earning commissions from both of them, although in this case the commission which the immigrant pays is much lower. Usually undocumented Filipinas (who are not in possession of a renewed work permit because they left their first employer) use recruitment agencies in Athens in order to obtain another job.

Field research in the city revealed a high degree of dissatisfaction related to the recruitment agencies, especially those in the Philippines, for a series of reasons such as high commissions and debts, broken promises about wage levels and working conditions in the destination country, and the potential trap of the employer-specific work permit arrangement.

Hours of work, means of pay and incomes

Regarding hours of daily work, the vast majority of interviewee immigrants worked at least eight hours per day and a significant proportion – about 15 per cent – more than ten hours. Those who worked the longest were the Filipinas, although a few of them also worked less than eight hours (mainly those engaged in employment on a part-time basis). Most of the Filipinas live and work in a particular environment (employer's house) where, to a certain extent, work intermingles with leisure and free time. Other situations in which migrants worked long hours were those jobs which were 'task-related' with no specific daily rate of hours – for instanc   Albanians and Egyptians working in construction.

Means of pay vary, mainly according to the sector and employment type. First of all in construction a variety of ways of payment can be found, according to type of work. The 'task' jobs are characterised by irregular, daily, weekly or other payments, while jobs in the public works construction sector are usually paid monthly. The same patterns can be observed in small firms as well. Cleaning work is characterised by the 'task' pattern and is usually paid daily or weekly. On the other hand, domestic work, which is generally the most stable and durable, is paid monthly. Related services to domestic work are usually undertaken on a part-time basis and ways of payment vary according to the specific agreement between the employer and the provider of the service. Street-vending is paid directly by the customer (per-item payment).

Incomes generated by the immigrants interviewed in Athens will be discussed in two interrelated ways: firstly according to immigrant national groups and secondly according to work type and sector. In relation to both gross and net (gross minus rent payments) income the Albanians seem to earn less, as table 2.5 shows. This is because of type of work characteristics, as we shall see shortly. However, there may be another discriminatory factor involved: Lazaridis (1996, p. 344) found that the association of Albanians with various criminal activities meant that employers were less willing to hire them, and hence paid them less than other immigrant workers.

The Egyptians earn the highest gross income mainly because of relatively better pay in small firms and especially from street-vending activities. However the Filipinas seem to have a higher net income at their disposal because they 'enjoy' some benefits such as accommodation and food when they stay in their employers' houses.

Moving now to employment types, firstly construction is divided into better- and less-paid jobs. The former belong to the 'household' sector while the latter are public works or large project jobs. Almost two-thirds of small-firm jobs are paid above average and this proportion is even higher for street-vending activities. Generally all immigrant employment is underpaid, despite variations between immigrant groups and sectors. Immigrants are paid at best two-thirds and, in many cases, barely half of the minimum wage of an unskilled Greek worker.

Table 2.5 Approximate gross and net average monthly income in Athens (in US $)

	Albanians	Egyptians	Filipinas	Others	Total
Gross income	374	434	385	439	408
Net income	311	352	364	354	345

Source: Author's survey, 1996.

My research in Athens revealed an average immigrant monthly gross income of just over $400 and an average monthly net income of about $345. These incomes were cross-checked in various ways, through employers, government departments, etc. Finally my research also revealed an average monthly rent payment of $60 per person (here it must be taken into account that the majority of immigrant interviewees in Athens share accommodation with friends and / or relatives, usually of the same nationality).

Satisfaction, discrimination and harassment

Around 60 per cent of all the respondents reported themselves to be generally satisfied with their lives and working conditions in Athens. There were no marked differences between the three immigrant groups, with the exception that Egyptians appeared somewhat happier than the other groups. Street-vending and employment in small firms record higher levels of work satisfaction than construction and cleaning: some explanations for this comparison can be found earlier and are mainly related to job security and levels of earning. However the notion of 'life and work satisfaction' has always to be used with caution. Work satisfaction is historically and socially constructed and is characterised by relativity. For our case, immigrants' satisfaction is relative in comparison to their situation in the country of origin. As several of them said during interviews and in other meetings and discussions, they tolerate a relatively harsh working life in Athens as long as they hold a job which allows them to maintain themselves and either save something or send money back to their family and relatives in their country of origin.

One of the reasons why Albanians express somewhat lower levels of satisfaction than the other two groups is that they appear to experience higher levels of discrimination and harassment in their working environments and elsewhere in the city. Overall, 35 per cent of all respondents felt that they had been harassed or discriminated, the proportions being 48 per cent for the Albanians, 41 per cent for the Filipinas and 17 per cent for the Egyptians. The significant difference here is the low score for the Egyptians. There have traditionally been good relationships between Greece and Egypt, due to long-standing trading patterns and more recent flows of tourists (from Greece to Egypt) and students (from Egypt to Greece). The Filipinas and the Albanians tended to report different kinds of harassment according to their different work and living arrangements and their general relations with natives. But while harassment towards the Filipinas can be attributed mainly to their employment arrangements, harassment towards the Albanians can be attributed to both features mentioned above. Some of the reasons for the general anti-Albanian feeling in Greece can be found in the uneasy relations between Albania and Greece, in their massive and sudden presence in the country after 1990, and in their 'stigmatisation' through widely-publicised criminality amongst a minority of them, which has led to hostile attitudes towards the whole group (Lazaridis 1996).

Conclusions

The findings of this chapter can be summarised and integrated under two broad headings: the characteristics of the Greek labour market as a setting for immigration, and the employment experiences of the three nationalities interviewed.

First, there is now an entrenched and persistent demand within the Greek economy and society for foreign, low-paid labour. This demand is especially concentrated in the secondary and informal sections of the labour market, in sectors which are characterised by high labour intensity, seasonal demand fluctuations, low technology and limited competitiveness. Migrant labour is also used in more 'modern' sectors of the economy such as small firms and public works as a peripheral workforce to achieve greater flexibility and to reduce costs.

Second, and following from the above, there is a substantial degree of polarisation and segmentation in the Greek labour market which has fed off, but not necessarily been caused by, the supply of cheap and flexible immigrant labour. The chief contrast is between highly-paid and low-paid jobs, the latter undertaken by immigrant workers.

Third, the informal sector in Greece is characterised by heterogeneity and stratification. Immigrants are almost invariably cast in the role of 'dependents', reliant on the 'organisers' within the informal sector for access to work. Nevertheless there is a substantial complementarity between formal and informal sector economic activities and a high degree of interdependency too. In reality the informal and formal sectors are less 'sectors' as such than a series of 'processes' and 'practices', often engaged in simultaneously by the same firm or even the same person.

Finally, the specific characteristics of Greek society and its economy (dominated by small firms operating partly or wholly in the informal sector), together with a recent phase of economic crisis and consequent restructuring to achieve greater labour market flexibility, have led to an increased demand for migrant labour. Despite rising overall unemployment, this has not generated serious conflict in the labour market place.

The main findings of the research amongst immigrants in Athens are summarised in figure 2.1 and can be highlighted in six main conclusions.

First, there are significant differences between the educational levels of the Filipinas on the one hand, who are often highly educated, and the low educational standards of the other two groups. Nevertheless education and training appear to play a minor role in the employment taken on by, or available to, the immigrants. A combination of labour market segmentation according to nationality and gender is the main contributing factor. This having been said, it is also probably true that the educational experience of the Filipinas, plus the ability of many of them to speak English, is a factor in their appeal to middle and upper-class Greek households which employ them as maids and child-minders.

Second, much immigrant work is characterised by its precariousness and marginal status. With the exception again of the Filipina group, respondents' jobs were characterised by a high degree both of instability between sectors or types of employment, and of insecurity or short-term nature. Long hours, low pay and an almost total lack of social insurance were found to be other characteristics of immigrant labour. Immigrants' status as 'illegal' or undocumented workers (except for some of the Filipinas) makes them vulnerable to exploitation regarding pay and other conditions of work.

Characteristic	Albanians	Egyptians	Filipinos
Educational levels	mainly low (primary and secondary); some vocational training		above average, including many with higher education
Proportion unemployed before migration	48%	69%	85%
Employment type in Athens	construction, cleaning	construction, small firms, street-vending	domestic and related services
Employment stability	unstable	mixed	more stable
Employment security	low	medium/mixed	longer
Finding a job	friends and/or relatives, personal search		recruitment agencies, advertisements
Legal status	undocumented		legal and undocumented
Hours of daily work	9.8	9.0	10.1
Means of payment	monthly/daily/ weekly	monthly/weekly/ per item	monthly/other
Satisfaction	generally satisfied	higher satisfaction	generally satisfied
Discrimination	higher	lower	medium
Gross income	lower	higher	medium
Net income	lower	medium	higher

Figure 2.1   Employment characteristics of immigrants in Athens

Third, despite high levels of discrimination and harassment, most migrants appear relatively satisfied with their situation as immigrant workers in Athens. These levels of satisfaction must, however, be seen against the background of the situation in their countries of origin, where most originate from a setting of poverty, unemployment, lack of opportunity, and economic disruption. Levels of satisfaction are somewhat higher for the Egyptians and for particular types of work, notably employment in small firms and work as street-vendors and market-traders. Fourth, the difficult and trying social environment in which immigrants live and work must be appreciated. In particular, there is widespread discrimination and harassment coming from three sources: police and state authorities, employers and to a lesser extent from ordinary Greek citizens. Ethnic stereotyping has become widespread and particularly affects the Albanians: indeed Lazaridis (1996, p. 345) has remarked that Greek society is now characterised by 'Albanophobia' due to a combination of the complex antagonisms between Greece and Albania, the mass influx of Albanians in the early 1990s and their alleged criminality.

Fifth, immigrants' social networks and general social solidarity are important both in combating discrimination and social exclusion and in helping them to find work, housing and other forms of support, given their objective situation on the margins of the host society and within the 'shadow' economy.

Sixth, immigrants seem to satisfy both a real demand for certain kinds of labour in the labour market, and are adept at creating their own niches of work where none existed before. Although there is an interplay between the availability of migrant labour and the dynamism of the Greek informal sector, the roots of the informal economy and labour market are to be found in the historical and structural features of the evolution of the Greek social formation, and not simply in the recent presence of immigrants in the country. Arguments about the competition in the labour market between immigrant and Greek workers must remain partly unresolved due to the lack of empirical research, but the case for immigrants causing higher unemployment remains unconvincing. For instance one study (reported in *Elefthetotypia*, 27 February 1996) of Albanians estimated their contribution to Greek GDP at 2.3 per cent and that only 5.8 per cent of them had substituted Greeks from employment. This last low figure was due to the fact that Albanians pick up jobs rejected by Greeks and are willing to work for wages which are, in many cases, less than half the Greek level; however their productivity is 23 per cent lower. Furthermore their use of social infrastructure such as schools and health services is very limited because of their illegal status and the fact that family migration has not yet developed.

Finally one can speculate on the future contours of a Greek migration policy. Here there is likely to be a strong divergence between what is desirable on humanitarian, ethical and social policy grounds, and what is pragmatic on political and economic criteria. Regarding the former, a meeting of representatives of the various immigrant communities and organisations held at the National Technical University of Athens in March 1996 resulted in the following proposals and demands:

- Legalisation and regularisation of all foreigners in Greece, without preconditions.
- Granting of work permits to all immigrants in Greece without a condition of a link to an employer or to a specific employment position.
- Strict enforcement of labour laws for the protection of the rights of foreign immigrants in Greece.
- Free access of all immigrants to the full range of health services.
- Granting of equal civil rights to all economic immigrants and refugees in Greece.
- The right to family reunion.
- Autonomy of the rights of female immigrants.
- The right of education for the children of immigrants both in Greek and their native language, and the right of access to education of all levels.

However, as recent reviews of Greek migration policy have shown (Fakiolas and King 1996; Lazaridis 1996), Greek measures applied to migration have been reactive rather than strategic and have sought to control and repress new inflows rather than facilitate the proper management of the immigration that is taking place or work towards the integration of the foreigners living and working in Greece. The chief provisions of the 'Alien Immigrants and Refugees Law' of December 1991 are to bolster the guards and patrols along Greece's borders with Albania and Turkey, and to impose fines on immigration traffickers and those employing illegal immigrants. For the time being a policy of pragmatism and *laisser faire* holds sway. Hence some measures are introduced to satisfy Greece's obligations under the Schengen agreement and to appease some anti-immigrant sections of public opinion; but the failure either to completely control immigration or to legalise and integrate those already living in Greece reflects a desire to maximise economic benefit from cheap and flexible labour whilst holding off the perceived social costs of family reunion and permanent settlement. How long Greece can sustain this 'non-policy' remains to be seen.

References

Balourdos, D. (1995) Income and employment in Greece: designatory factors and empirical evidence, *Topos, Review of Urban and Regional Studies*, 10/95, pp. 43–78 (in Greek).

Bilsborrow, R., Oberai, A.S. and Standing, G., eds. (1984) *Migration Surveys in Low Income Countries: Guidelines for Survey and Questionnaire Design*. London: Croom Helm.

Cornelius, W. (1982) Interviewing undocumented immigrants: methodological reflections based on fieldwork in Mexico and the US, *International Migration Review*, 16(2) pp. 378–411.

Fakiolas, R. and King, R. (1996) Emigration, return, immigration: a review and evaluation of Greece's post war experience of international migration, *International Journal of Population Geography*, 2(2), pp. 171–90.

Gordon, I. (1995) Migration in a segmented labour market, *Transactions of the Institute of British Geographers*, 20(2), pp. 139–55.

Hall, D.R. (1994) *Albania and the Albanians.* London: Pinter.

Iosifides, T. (1997) *Recent Foreign Immigration and the Labour Market in Athens.* Brighton: University of Sussex, unpublished D.Phil. thesis.

Kanellopoulos, K., Kousoulakos, I. and Rapanos, B., eds. (1995) *Para-Economy and Tax Evasion: Estimations and Economic Impacts.* Athens: KEPE (in Greek).

Katsoridas, D. (1994) *Foreign Workers in Greece.* Athens: Iamos (in Greek).

Lazaridis, G. (1996) Immigration to Greece: a critical evaluation of Greek policy, *New Community*, 22(2), pp. 335–48.

Leontidou, L. (1990) *The Mediterranean City in Transition: Social Change and Urban Development.* Cambridge: Cambridge University Press.

Lyberaki, A. (1988) *Small Firms and Flexible Specialisation in the Greek Industry.* Brighton: University of Sussex, unpublished D.Phil. thesis.

Mabro, R. (1974) *The Egyptian Economy.* Oxford: Clarendon Press.

Papademetriou, D. (1979) Greece, in Krane, R.E., ed. *International Labor Migration in Europe.* New York: Preager, pp. 187–200.

Pelagidis, T. (1995) The dark side of labour flexibility: fieldwork in greater Thessaloniki, *Topos, Review of Urban and Regional Studies*, 9/95, pp. 95–119 (in Greek).

Portes, A., Castells, M. and Benton, L., eds. (1989) *The Informal Economy: Studies in Advanced and Less Developed Countries.* London: The Johns Hopkins University Press.

Vaiou, D. and Hadjimichalis, C. (1990) Local labour markets and uneven regional development in northern Greece, *Review of Social Research*, 77, pp. 15–61 (in Greek).

Vreeland, N., Hurwitz, G.B., Just, P., Moeller, P.W. and Shinn, R.S. (1976) *Area Handbook for the Philippines.* Washington DC: Foreign Area Studies of the American University.

Williams, C.C. and Winderbank, I. (1995) Black market work in the European Community: peripheral work for peripheral localities? *International Journal of Urban and Regional Research*, 19(1), pp. 23–39.

3

Foreign Labour Immigration in High-Unemployment Spain: The Role of African-Born Workers in the Girona Labour Market

Cristóbal Mendoza

Legally resident foreigners represent only a small percentage of the population in Spain. With a foreign population share of just 1.1 per cent in 1993, Spain's stock of foreigners stands well below that of many Central and Northern European countries. However, the number of foreigners in Spain rose sharply in the 1980s and 1990s. At the end of 1994, the total foreign population was 461,364 (Ministerio de Asuntos Sociales 1996), which was more than double the 1984 figure. These new inflows into Spain have occurred in a context of high unemployment (22.9 per cent of the labour force was unemployed in 1995, which was twice than the EU average of 11.2 per cent, and three times the OECD average of 7.6 per cent; OECD 1996). In fact, the unemployment rate steadily increased through the 1980s and 1990s, and as over half of those who were unemployed in 1995 had been so for more than one year[1], the increase in foreign inflows has occurred alongside substantial long-term unemployment.

It could be argued that this high level of unemployment has been caused by an increased employment participation rate. In particular, along with the incapacity of the Spanish economy to create new jobs

---

1 See recent issues of the quarterly *Encuesta de Poblacion Activa*, Madrid: INE. This is the main source for other employment data given in the Introduction.

(Fina 1993), a primary factor in rising unemployment might be thought
to be an increasing female participation rate in the labour force. The
female participation rate certainly has increased in the last few decades
(for instance, it rose from 28.5 per cent of the labour force in 1986 to 36.2
per cent in 1995). However, in Spain the female participation rate is still
low in comparison with other OECD countries (Fina 1993). Moreover,
the participation rate of the 16–64 year old population in the labour
market was lower in 1994 (48.8 per cent) than in 1964 (51.5 per cent).
Irrespective of the changing balance of the Spanish workforce, the
reality is that Spain has not created sufficient jobs for those who want
employment. In fact, many of the new jobs created in the 1980s and
1990s have been temporary. Spain now has the highest incidence of
temporary employment in its labour force in the OECD. In 1994 such
jobs comprised 33.7 per cent of employment (OECD 1996), which was
twice the 1987 figure. The incidence of temporary employment is higher
for the young (87.5 per cent for employees aged 16–19 years in 1994 and
70.6 per cent for those aged 20–24) and for women (37.9 per cent for
employed women compared with 31.4 per cent for men). This growth
in casualisation has occurred in parallel with the increase in the foreign
population.

This chapter focuses on the role that foreign workers play in the high-
unemployment context of an increasingly precarious Spanish labour
market. Macro-economic views on the role of foreign labour have
followed two main (and opposed) theoretical lines: those of neo-classical and structural approaches. Neo-classical theories of labour
markets emphasise that immigrant performance in the labour market
improves as they adapt to destination countries; through, for instance,
investing in human capital after emigration. For example, Chiswick
(1978), in his study of foreign-born men in the USA, and Long (1980), in
his research of foreign-born women in the same country, came to the
conclusion that the 'Americanization' of immigrants had a positive
effect on their earnings. Behind this lies the assumption that the performance of workers depends on pre-market differences among people
(their innate ability, their upbringing and their education) and is not an
outcome of the operation of labour markets.

In contrast to this neo-classical image which portrays foreigners as
entering a unified labour market, structural theories emphasise the
social context of the migration process and support the idea that immigrants tend to hold jobs that are distinct from those of the indigenous
work force. Among structural theories, dual labour market theorists
affirm that the explanation of wage dispersion lies in fundamental institutional differences between two dissimilar treatments of labour which
result in the presence of not one, but (at least) two quite different earn-

ing functions. As Morrison (1990, p. 493) argues, 'The labour market is segmented into two broad types with the essential difference being the way in which labour in the two segments is "priced". The rules and procedures for the operation of the "secondary" labour market differ from the rules which govern the pricing of labour in the "primary" market'.

Dual labour market literature implicitly assumes that foreign workers occupy jobs in the secondary sector. As Piore (1979, p. 17) argues, 'there is something in common among jobs held by migrants in widely diverse geographic areas and very different historical periods: the jobs tend to be unskilled, generally but not always low paying, and to carry or connote inferior social status'. This approach may reduce the process of integration of foreign labour to a unique outcome. However, foreigners are not the only group to be found in the secondary labour market (another example is young people). Furthermore, not all foreign workers are employees in the secondary labour market. Indeed, Bailey (1987, p. 7) found in the USA that 'almost all foreign-born groups are over-represented among small business owners, and the research in this area generally concludes that entrepreneurship has played an important role in the economic adjustment of many immigrants'.

The objective of this chapter is to analyse the processes of integration of foreign labour into the Spanish labour market. Specifically, the chapter focuses on the role that immigrants of African origin play in labour markets of the province of Girona (northern Catalonia). The key questions are:

- Do immigrants occupy marginal and unskilled jobs in the secondary labour market in Spain in general, and Girona in particular, as the dual labour market theory suggests? If so, does this hold true across all economic sectors?
- Is there a lack of competition between immigrants and natives in the labour market, as the dual labour market theory assumes?
- Alternatively, are the pre-market characteristics of these workers important in permitting integration and competition with local workers for some groups, but limiting opportunities for others?

To achieve these aims, the chapter is divided into two main sections. In the first, a general description of the foreign population and of recent inflows into Spain is presented, drawing on data from the 1991 legalisation process to cast light on the shadow areas of the Spanish labour market. Then, in the second section, the results of a survey of African immigrants in the province of Girona are presented, including an examination of the economic sectors in which Africans are employed, the 'needs' of different economic sectors for foreign labour, and the human capital of African workers. In synthesis, I argue that whilst certain aspects of dual labour market theory are supported by the experience of African workers in Spain in general, and Girona in particular, notably the marginalisation of foreign workers into certain unskilled jobs, there are some aspects of this experience that do not fit with expectations.

Spain: a new immigration country?

As we saw in chapter 1, the literature on Southern Europe has recently focused on the change in international migration trends, with the region having moved from being a zone of out-migration to one of immigration. From the analysis of official statistics, this section identifies what lies behind this change, who these new immigrants are, what kind of jobs they do and where they live. Although it is clear that a high share of the new immigrants are from Third World countries, official statistics only partially reflect the number and characteristics of the foreign labour force.

Labour inflows and the increase of foreign residents in the 1980s and 1990s

The large increase in the number of foreigners in Spain in the 1980s and 1990s was not unique in the recent immigration history of Spain. In 1970, for example, the number of foreigners (148,400) was 129 per cent above the 1960 figure (INE 1962 and 1972). Yet the increase in numbers in the 1960s was largely composed of immigrants from northern and central Europe (Solana and Pascual de Sans 1994). In contrast, Figure 3.1 highlights the changing balance in foreign residents after 1980. EU residents still make up an important share of new arrivals, and their total numbers have grown steadily over the last fifteen years.[2] In fact, almost one in two foreign residents (47.8 per cent) in Spain in 1994 came from within the EU. However, more substantial increases were recorded for Africans. Their numbers rose from 4,067 residents in 1980 to 82,607 in 1994. Furthermore, the largest African group, the Moroccans, constituted 63,939 immigrants in 1994, making them the largest nationality overall in official statistics (Ministerio de Asuntos Sociales 1996) .

This growth in numbers of foreign residents has been accompanied by an increase in the number of foreign workers in the 1980s and 1990s. The stock of foreign workers rose from 70,566 at the end of 1989 (Ministerio de Trabajo y Seguridad Social 1991) to 119,321 in 1994

2   The decrease in numbers in 1989 is due to a data file review which especially affected the numbers of EU nationals listed. Until 1989 the number of residence permits at the end of each year was calculated by adding permits issued during the year to existing permits, without discounting expired permits.

(Ministerio de Asuntos Sociales 1996). This represents an increase of 69.1 per cent over the 1989 figure[3] and implies a higher ratio of workers to population (47.5 per cent) than is found for the whole Spanish population (38.6 per cent in 1995).[4] This provides one indication of the importance of labour flows in immigration amongst non-EU nationals.

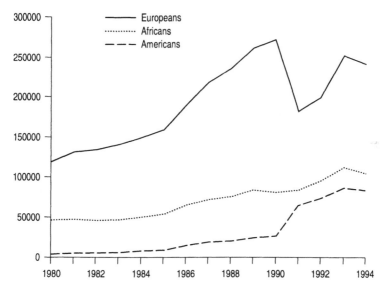

Figure 3.1   Evolution of legal foreign residents in Spain, by continent of origin, 1980–94
Source: Ministerio de Asuntos Sociales (1996).

The Spanish government has undertaken two legalisation processes in 1985/86 and 1991 to bring illegal foreign workers and their families already living in the country into legality (see Apap, Chapter 7). In the first, a total of 34,832 residence permits were issued (Izquierdo 1992), whilst the 1991 legalisation process doubled the number of foreign

3   This increase occurred despite the fact that these statistics do not provide complete coverage of non-Spanish EU workers. The stock of foreigners holding a work permit was not published until 1989. The EU nationals who are self-employed have been excluded from a work permit since the entry of Spain into the EU (specifically, since the enforcement of the Real Decreto 1099/1986). From 1 January 1992 (1 January 1993 for those from Luxembourg), non-Spanish EU citizens have not needed a work permit to obtain (legal) employment in Spain. At the end of December 1991, the number of EU nationals holding a work permit in Spain was 46,479 (27.2 per cent of the total), according to the *Estadística de Permisos de Trabajo a Extranjeros*, issued by the Ministerio de Trabajo y Seguridad Social (1993).
4   See *Boletín Mensual de Estadística*, Madrid: INE; data for late 1996.

workers, with the stock of legal foreign workers passing from 85,372 at
the end of 1990 to 171,033 by the end of 1991 (table 3.1). The growth in
African numbers was 297 per cent over this period, so Africans constituted 30 per cent of the legal foreign labour force in 1991 (excluding the
self-employed from the EU). By economic sector, agriculture and
construction experienced considerable relative increases (reaching 345
per cent in the case of agriculture), suggesting that these sectors had
employed larger numbers of illegal workers prior to 1991.

Focusing on the legalisation process data, the *regularización* gave legal
residence status to 109,135 foreign workers and to 5,889 relatives of
these workers who were already living in Spain (Aragón and Chozas
1993). Apart from the overwhelming number of Moroccans (44.6 per
cent of the total), other important African nationalities in the legalisation process were Algerians (3,074), Senegalese (2,186) and Gambians
(2,054). In total, Africans obtained 56.9 per cent of the permits issued
during the legalisation process.

Table 3.1 Work permits issued by nationality and sector of activity (1990 and
1991)

	1990		1991		Growth 1990/91
	no	%	no	%	%
Nationality					
Moroccans	8,844	10.4	41,095	24.0	364.7
Total Africans	12,884	15.1	51,155	29.9	297.0
Total permits	85,372	100.0	171,033	100.0	100.3
Economic sector					
Agriculture	3,437	4.0	15,289	8.9	344.8
Manufacturing	12,830	15.0	20,984	12.3	63.6
Construction	6,054	7.1	18,218	10.7	200.9
Services	62,476	73.2	114,888	67.2	83.9
Non classified	575	0.7	1,654	1.0	187.7
Total permits	**85,372**	**100.0**	**171,033**	**100.0**	**100.3**

Source: Ministerio de Trabajo y Seguridad Social (1991).

In the *regularización* process, four occupations were dominant:
domestic sector employees (21,694), agricultural labourers (16,736),
construction workers (14,228) and waiters, kitchen assistants and other
unskilled jobs in hotels and restaurants (11,182: Aragón and Chozas
1993). In 1993, after the legalisation process, the Spanish Government
decided to enforce a quota system to fill labour shortages, estimated
from unemployment figures, and channel new inflows into deficient

employment niches. However, rather than channelling inflows, the quota system is used to legalise existing illegal foreign workers.[5] Reflecting the tighter new immigration regulations, statistics show low foreign labour inflows into Spain in the following two years, with 19,044 new work permits being issued in 1993 (i.e. excluding re-issued permits) and 21,543 in 1994.

From official statistics, two main dynamics may be observed regarding foreign inflows into Spain. First, the EU is the place of origin of almost half of all foreigners residing in Spain. In 1991, 29.4 per cent of these EU residents were employees.[6] As the self-employed population is not included in this percentage, the participation rate of EU nationals may be closer to the Spanish rate (38.6 per cent in 1995). Secondly, non-EU nationals, especially Moroccans, have seen an important growth in numbers in the last decade. As the legalisation process data suggests, non-EU inflows are mainly workers who occupy low-skilled jobs in the Spanish labour market.

Spain: from leisure to work?

The number of foreigners is not equally spread across Spain, with Madrid and Barcelona having high concentrations, and accounting for just over a third of the total number of legally resident foreigners whose province of residence was known in 1994 (Ministerio de Asuntos Sociales 1996). The first five provinces by number of resident foreigners had more than a half of the national total (56.8 per cent), while the first ten accounted for 73.7 per cent in 1994 (table 3.2). The Mediterranean coast from Málaga to Girona, Madrid and the Canary Islands are the top resident destinations for foreigners.

As table 3.2 (overleaf) shows, there are different location patterns for EU and non-EU citizens. Tourist provinces are clearly attracting EU nationalities (in Alicante, 74.8 per cent of foreigners are from the EU; in the Balearics, 68.8 per cent; in Santa Cruz de Tenerife, 68.5 per cent), whereas the smallest percentages of EU residents among the total number of foreign population are found in Madrid and Barcelona. However, rather than the total size of the foreign labour force, the

5   The 1993 quota was 20,600 for the whole of Spain (10,000 for agricultural labourers, 1,100 for construction workers, 6,000 for domestic sector employees and 3,500 for non-qualified jobs in the service industries). Just 25.2 per cent of these were taken up (5,200 permits). In 1994, 37,277 people applied for a work permit within the 20,600 quota established by the Government (Ministerio de Asuntos Sociales 1996). In 1995, 17,000 permits, out of the 25,000 quota, were issued in response to previous applications which fullfilled the prerequisites.
6   Calculated from the number of work permits and residence permits on 31 December 1991.

importance of foreign workers in provincial economies should be seen in relative terms. Figure 3.2 maps the percentage of work permit holders in relation to the labour force at a provincial level. Apart from the African cities of Ceuta and Melilla, Girona is the province with the highest percentage of non-EU legal workers in its labour force (2.1 per cent), followed by Madrid (2.0 per cent). The percentages range from 1 per cent to 1.5 per cent for the other three Catalan provinces (Barcelona, Tarragona and Lleida), as well as for the Balearic Islands, Almería and Las Palmas in the Canary Islands. No other provinces have more than 1 per cent of their workers as non-EU immigrants.

Table 3.2   Legal foreign residents and legal EU residents in Spain in selected provinces (1994)

Province (by rank order of % foreign residents)	Foreign residents		EU nationals		EU/total
	No	%	No	%	%
1. Madrid	93,606	20.9	27,427	13.0	29.3
2. Barcelona	65,080	14.5	20,462	9.7	31.4
3. Alicante	38,787	8.6	29,029	13.8	74.8
4. Málaga	31,634	7.0	19,420	9.2	61.4
5. Balears	25,891	5.8	17,821	8.5	68.8
6. Sta.Cruz Tenerife	24,643	5.5	16,882	8.0	68.5
7. Las Palmas	22,787	5.1	10,716	5.1	47.0
8. Valencia	12,982	2.9	5,537	2.6	42.7
9. Tarragona	7,865	1.8	3,288	1.6	41.8
10. Girona	7,734	1.7	3,359	1.6	43.4
Spain	**448,869**	**100.0**	**210,221**	**100.0**	**46.8**

Source: Comisión Interministerial de Extranjería (1995).

Moving from foreign residents to foreign workers, table 3.3 compares the occupations of non-EU workers with that of the Spanish labour force in the nine provinces with the highest percentages of foreign workers.[7] These provinces can be classified in three main groups according to their labour market structure: agricultural provinces (Lleida and Almería) whose agricultural labour force is far larger than the Spanish average; service sector provinces (Ceuta and Melilla, Las Palmas, the Balearic Islands and Madrid); and the other three Catalan provinces (Barcelona, Tarragona and Girona), which have a well-diver-

7   Calculated as number of work permits held by foreigners at the end of 1994 as a percentage of the total working and short-term unemployed population recorded in the last quarter of 1994.

sified economy and an important manufacturing base (for example the province of Barcelona has 32.1 per cent of its population in manufacturing, compared to the Spanish average of 21.0 per cent).

In comparative terms, migrants work more in the primary sector than the local labour force in all the provinces, except the Canaries province of Las Palmas (table 3.3). Extreme divergences are found in Tarragona where 31.1 per cent of non-EU workers are in agriculture, compared with 10.7 per cent of the total labour force, in Lleida (29.9 per cent as opposed to 15.5 per cent) and especially in Almería. In this last province, a quarter of the working population is in the primary sector, but 73.8 per cent of the foreigner work permits were issued for primary sector activities. It seems that non-EU immigrants are working in highly competitive agricultural zones, such as the horticulture industry in Almería, whose competitive position may have been boosted by the Spain's entry into the EU (García-Ramon 1985).

Table 3.3 Local labour force and non-EU legal workers by sector of activity in selected provinces in 1994 (%)

Province (by rank order of % foreign workers)	Agriculture		Manufacturing		Construction		Services	
	Spanish	Foreign	Spanish	Foreign	Spanish	Foreign	Spanish	Foreign
1. Ceuta & Melilla	1.9	3.0	5.7	4.1	11.1	22.9	81.4	70.0
2. Girona	6.5	17.5	23.3	16.2	11.9	20.7	58.2	45.6
3. Madrid	0.8	1.5	18.8	6.0	9.4	11.3	71.0	81.2
4. Las Palmas	5.5	2.1	7.6	4.6	9.4	2.9	77.5	90.4
5. Barcelona	1.2	8.7	32.1	14.5	7.2	12.9	59.6	64.0
6. Balears	2.6	8.5	14.0	4.4	11.8	13.2	71.6	73.9
7. Lleida	15.5	29.9	15.4	21.4	13.1	17.3	55.9	31.4
8. Almería	25.5	73.8	8.3	3.0	9.5	1.8	56.7	21.4
9. Tarragona	10.7	31.1	21.7	9.5	11.8	18.2	55.8	41.2
Spain	**9.6**	**11.5**	**21.0**	**8.7**	**10.4**	**10.4**	**59.1**	**69.5**

Source: Ministerio de Asuntos Sociales (1996).

However, nationally the agricultural sector has been sharply losing workers over the last few decades, with its percentage share of the labour force falling from 21.4 per cent 1975 to just 9.3 per cent in 1995. Recent growth in the demand for Mediterranean products as a consequence of entry into the EU may be one of the reasons for the need for foreign labour in a sector which had lost many workers, although employers may have other reasons (e.g. keeping salaries low) for hiring non-EU nationals rather than Spanish workers.

Cristóbal Mendoza

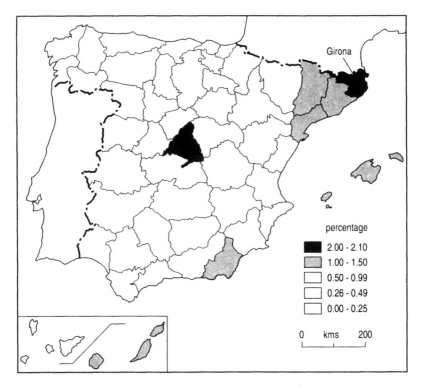

Figure 3.2 Foreign holders of work permits as a proportion of the active population, provinces of Spain, December 1994

Apart from Almería, it was the service sectors that attracted the majority of migrants in the rest of the major immigrant provinces. There are two different kinds of province in which foreigners in service industries outnumber the local labour force. First of all, there are service-oriented provinces (Las Palmas, Madrid and the Balearic Islands) with an overwhelming majority of non-EU workers in services. Then there are provinces with more diversified economies, which have a more balanced pattern of foreign labour force participation (the Catalan provinces). The manufacturing sector provides employment for relatively few non-EU workers. Only in Catalonia does their employment share stand in a roughly equal position to that of the local labour force.

By province, Madrid has 81.2 per cent of its work permits issued for service activities. This is because of the importance of the domestic sector in this province. In the legalisation process, 11,733 work permits were issued for domestic activities in Madrid, which was half of the total

Spanish number (Ministerio de Trabajo y Seguridad Social 1993). In short, non-EU foreigners work in the economic sectors that are more important in the provinces where they live (Almería, agriculture; the Balearics or Las Palmas, services, etc.). Nevertheless, across the country as a whole, non-EU workers are over-represented, in comparative terms, in agriculture and construction and under-represented in industry.

African workers in northern Catalonia

As noted above, Girona has the highest percentage share of non-EU workers of any province in Spain. This section focuses on the position of African immigrants in local labour markets in Girona, in order to address two main questions: (i) locally, does migrant integration in the labour market follow the pattern of local workers? (ii) sectorally, what kind of jobs (skilled versus unskilled, temporary versus permanent, contract versus non contract) are migrants doing in the different economic sectors? The final section then examines whether language and literacy skills, and previous experience in the labour market of immigrants' countries of origin, are valued in the current jobs of these workers in Girona.

The province of Girona: a booming and well-diversified economy

Situated in the north-east of the Iberian Peninsula, the Catalan province of Girona is one of the richest areas in Spain. It has passed from being the seventh province in terms of per capita income in 1973 to first in the ranking of the 50 Spanish provinces in 1991 and from eighth in 1971 to first in 1991 in terms of production per capita (Banco Bilbao Vizcaya 1995). According to Valenzuela (1991), tourism is directly responsible for the Balearics and Girona occupying the first two places in the per capita income table. However, although tourism is important, the province has one of the more diversified economies of the Spanish provinces (table 3.3).

Girona has had one of the fastest growing populations of any province in Spain: it rose from 177,539 inhabitants in 1960 to 509,628 in 1991, a growth of 187 per cent. This growth was partly a result of immigration from the rest of Spain. Valenzuela (1991) argued that rural Andalusia (Jaén and Granada especially) provided the least-qualified labour working in hotels and catering on the Costa Brava. Legal foreign residents in the province represented 1.5 per cent of the population in 1991, which was three times the 1981 figure. As a tourist area, Girona has always been a place of residence for a non-working, non-Spanish

population, mainly from Northern Europe. However the weight of
Europeans within the number of foreigners has constantly dropped as
a result of the increasing immigration of African workers.

Girona presents a balanced distribution of foreign workers across all
the economic sectors, reflecting the well-diversified economic base of
the region. Given that African workers are found in the dominant
economic sectors of each province of Spain, investigating a diversified
economy like Girona should give insights into economic integration
patterns elsewhere. Thus, the demand for seasonal (and non-seasonal)
labourers in Girona's agriculture may be representative of other agricultural regions of the Mediterranean area, such as Almería, Murcia or
Lleida. The demand for foreign workers in construction and tourist-
related activities in Girona should not be different from other
tourist-dominated areas, like the Balearic Islands, Málaga or Alicante.
Finally, the manufacturing base of the province may be helpful in
drawing conclusions about integration of the foreign labour force in
other industrial areas, such as Barcelona or Madrid.

As Gozálvez et al. (1995) point out, Girona is likely to be one of the
areas where foreign workers will increase in numbers most easily. The
province has a large tourism-oriented coast, with a transient population;
a strong economic diversification; an increasing percentage of elderly
residents in many inland towns and high incomes per capita (in the
Spanish context), which makes it difficult to pay low wages to local
workers, even though some activities might not survive without such
low wages.

Methodology

A total of 151 interviews with African immigrants (87 Moroccan
nationals and 64 from Western African countries, mainly from Gambia
38 and Senegal 23) were carried out in the coastal area of the province
in Girona, in the *comarques* of Alt Empordà, Baix Empordà and La Selva.
In this area, four kinds of localities were defined, based on the characteristics of the local labour market (as identified through 1991 Census
data by municipality which was provided by the Catalan Institute of
Statistics):

(a) Small localities (the largest municipality is Sant Pere Pescador,
with 1,199 inhabitants) in which an important share of their labour force
works in the *primary sector*. La Pera, with 381 inhabitants, has the lowest
percentage of workers in primary sector (23.8 per cent) in the sample.
Primary activities accounted for 6.6 per cent of the labour force of the
province of Girona and 3.7 per cent in the whole of Catalonia.

(b) Medium-sized localities (Figueres, with 34,573 inhabitants and

Blanes, with 25,663) which have *more diversified service-oriented local economies*. The bulk of jobs are located in the service sector in these towns (62.0 per cent in the case of Figueres), but manufacturing employs about a quarter of their working population. The primary sector has insignificant weight.

(c) Localities heavily reliant on *tourism*. The tertiary sector here accounted for more than 50 per cent of the workforce. Construction occupies more workers in these localities than the average for either Catalonia (8.2 per cent) or Girona (12.4 per cent).

(d) *Manufacturing-based localities*, where the proportion of the workforce in this sector is well above the provincial or the Catalan average. The range of values recorded for this sector in the study areas is lowest in Santa Coloma de Farners (42.6 per cent) and highest in Breda (62.3 per cent).

Africans in the Girona labour market

Before analysing the kind of jobs and the sectors of activity in which immigrants are employed, it is interesting to note the levels of unemployment and economic inactivity of the interviewed population, which were surprisingly low. The unemployment rate was 13.2 per cent, with unemployed workers spread across the surveyed localities, whilst a mere 2.7 per cent of those surveyed were economically inactive. However, it is worth noting that occasional workers, such as gardeners or people who collect pine cones in the forest have been included in the category of the working population. This goes some way to explain the discrepancy with figures produced by Gozálvez et al. (1995), who considered occasional workers in the primary sector and in service industries to be unemployed, and as a result calculated an unemployment rate of 40 per cent among Moroccans and 15 per cent among Senegalese. Overall, the unemployment rate found amongst the sample population is close to the average of 13.0 per cent for Girona province in 1995.

As the fieldwork was phased over two periods (July–August 1995 and October–December 1995), it was also possible to note that none of the sample population was unemployed during the summer period. A similar seasonal trend is observed in the province as a whole: the unemployment rate fell to 10.6 per cent in the summer of 1995 compared with a figure of 13.2 per cent for the second quarter of the year.[8]

A second element of employment status concerned the importance of self-employment. At the time they were interviewed, just three out of

8 Data from *Boletín Mensual de Estadística*, Madrid: INE, for 1996.

151 African workers surveyed were self-employed. Nevertheless, a larger number, about 20 of those interviewed, had been self-employed at some stage during their time in Spain. This self-employed population generally undertook service activities within their communities of origin (such as 'ethnic' shops, halal butchery, and renting houses to new immigrants). This is not to say that all self-employed Africans have businesses directed at their own communities, although there may be a relationship between the growing African population and a rising demand for African products which increases opportunities for self-employment. As work permit statistics for Spain as a whole show, there is a higher percentage of self-employment among the African working population than the number found in the Girona survey (15.1 per cent of all African work permits in Spain by the end of 1994 were for self-employment). This may reflect a concentration of African business activity in larger cities, where there is a greater demand African products because of the presence of a larger African community or more heterogeneous consumption practices among Spanish residents.

Table 3.4 shows the distribution of current or most recent jobs by economic sector of those interviewed in each locality type. This table shows some correlation between the sector of employment and the type of locality in which individuals live. Specifically, 19 out of 34 of those interviewed who lived in a locality dominated by primary sector activities worked in the primary sector, just as 34 of the 58 who lived in service-based localities worked in the tertiary sector. Perhaps the most remarkable data in the table is that more than half of those interviewed in manufacturing localities also worked in this sector. This is noteworthy since the Government's quota system does not allow non-EU foreigners to take jobs in the manufacturing sector. Equally noticeable is the number of employees in the primary sector (10 out of 30) in the two small cities with a diversified employment structure, although in both cases, the immigrants concerned worked in rural localities nearby, to which these cities were historically linked. These data suggest that the sample population 'fits' the local employment structure, and is not restricted to certain sectors in all localities, in spite of legal restrictions.

The construction sector also shows an interesting pattern. Somewhat surprisingly, the lowest percentage of employment in this sector was found in tourist-dominated service centres. However, a representative of the construction employers' association (Unió d'Empresaris de la Construcció de la Província de Girona) did point out that few new accommodation facilities are being built in Girona, as a result of a crisis of confidence over growth in this sector. New buildings for the tourist sector are predominantly for second homes in quiet, inland towns, far from the busy coastal axis.

Table 3.4   Current sector of economic activity of sample population by locality type (no. individuals)

Locality type	Primary	Manufacturing	Services	Construction	Total
Primary	19	2	7	6	34
Manufacturing	5	14	6	4	29
Services	13	6	34	5	58
Diversified	10	2	12	6	30
Total	47	24	59	21	151

Source: Author's survey, 1995.

In general, it seems that the sample population is working in the same economic sectors as the local labour force, suggesting that the barriers normally associated with a secondary labour market may not operate in this case. However, the same conclusion cannot be drawn if one examines the first jobs obtained by immigrants on arrival, where there are some economic sectors more open to initial employment than others. Table 3.5 shows the economic sectors in which those interviewed had found their first job in Spain. It is clear from this table that the primary sector played a leading role in introducing the sample population into the Spanish labour market, as almost half of those interviewed had their first job in this sector. Moreover, despite differences in later employment described above, this sector was the dominant place of initial employment for workers across all locality types, with the exception of those currently living in service-dominated localities, where the majority of those interviewed had entered the Spanish labour market through the tertiary sector. This suggests some progression within the labour market amongst the sample population, for example from the primary to the manufacturing sector. In this regard, it is worth noting that work permits in manufacturing are not granted to newly-arriving immigrant workers, only becoming available in certain cases after some years in Spain. Thus for example, the majority of the Senegalese workers interviewed in the inland localities of La Selva *comarca* who are now in manufacturing, were previously agricultural labourers in the neighbouring province of Barcelona.

Regarding the type of jobs held by the sample, data presented in table 3.6 also show that the majority are employed in non-skilled jobs in all economic sectors, again an indicator of some labour market segmentation. Demand for unskilled work seems to be higher in construction and in the primary sector than in manufacturing and services. Specifically, 90 per cent of interviewees in these two sectors were in unskilled jobs, whereas in manufacturing, qualified workers made up 21 per cent of the survey respondents.

Table 3.5 Sector of first job in Spain of sample population by present locality type (no. individuals)

Locality type	Primary	Manufacturing	Services	Construction	Total
Primary	23	0	6	5	34
Manufacturing	13	3	9	4	29
Services	21	2	27	8	58
Diversified	17	1	7	5	30
Total	74	6	49	22	151

Source: Author's survey, 1995.

Table 3.6 Skills level of sample population by current economic sector (no. individuals)

Skills level	Primary	Manufacturing	Services	Construction	Total
Skilled	5	5	12	1	23
Unskilled	42	19	47	20	128
Total	47	24	59	21	151

Source: Author's survey, 1995.

Whether the skilled workers interviewed had obtained their training in Spain or in their countries of origin was also addressed in the survey, since this sheds some light on the pattern of recruitment of foreign labour into the local labour market. In total, half of the skilled workers interviewed reported that they had learned the job in Spain (notably agricultural foremen and skilled industrial workers), whereas the remainder had learned their professions in their countries of origin (including blacksmiths, tailors, skilled agricultural workers, and carpenters). The pattern for the first group points to the possibility that promotion inside the Spanish labour market is possible, but is nonetheless limited to a few categories of workers, and driven by the needs of the labour market. However, the presence of the second group suggests that there is a shortage of certain categories of skilled worker within Spain.

It is also interesting to note the relative precariousness of the jobs held by the immigrant workers surveyed, with a large majority holding either temporary jobs, or having no contract of employment at all (table 3.7). In the primary sector, for example, 17 out 47 employees interviewed had no contract. Within this sector, there are a number of marginal forestry activities, such as work picking up pine cones or brushing forests, which are characterised by non-contract piece-rate payments. Another source of informality comes from seasonal work in agriculture. Seasonal migration has long played a crucial role for certain crops such as fruit and vegetables in Mediterranean Europe (Berlan 1986), and this is now largely composed of foreign workers. As Valderrama (1994, p. 222) puts it, 'Mediterranean agriculture increasingly needs a cheap labour force which is not found in the European countries. In Europe, the agricultural sector of Mediterranean regions has the highest proportion of foreign workers, either legal or illegal'.

Table 3.7 Contractual status of sample population by current economic sector (no. individuals)

Contractual	Primary	Manufacturing	Services	Construction	Total
No employment contract	17	2	12	3	34
Temporary contract	24	18	35	14	91
Permanent contract	6	4	9	4	23
Self-employed	–	–	3	–	3
Total	47	24	59	21	151

Source: Author's survey, 1995.

Manufacturing again presents the exception to the rule, as just two of the 24 interviewees in this sector had no contract. This helps to confirm the hypothesis that the manufacturing sector is a final-stop sector, with lower rates of informality. However, many of the jobs undertaken, for example in small ceramics or marble-transforming firms, medium-sized metal industries, agricultural processing industries and timber yards, are also attractive to local workers. This raises the question of why employers prefer immigrant workers. Regarding the particular case of industries in southern Girona, Gozálvez et al. (1995) suggest that low wages paid to foreigners in the agricultural sector have triggered an imitation process among employers in other economic sectors. Manufacturing employers have thus lowered salaries to agricultural level by hiring immigrants.

The pattern of using immigrants when employment returns and security are not high is further seen in the construction sector. Compared to other countries, the construction sector in Spain has few large companies: for example, the largest construction firm (Dragados y Construcciones, with 11,692 employees in 1988) is only of medium-size by world standards (Salmon 1991). Consistent with this, two thirds of construction workers interviewed (14 out of 21) were employed in firms with less than 10 employees. Although further research on employers is required to substantiate this point, it appears that small, vulnerable construction firms rely on the flexibility of immigrants to adjust to business cycles in the sector.

Finally, immigrants work in a range of service activities in the province of Girona. Every subsector has its own dynamics regarding hiring policy, but in general the jobs immigrants obtain are again of low standing. This can be illustrated through an analysis of three subsectors. In each of these, a different process appears to be operating. Thus in garbage collection, there is some substitution of the local labour force with foreign workers in low-skilled jobs; in the accommodation sector, there is a clear labour segmentation between the jobs done by locals and foreigners; whilst in retail activities, there is an incipient creation of employment niches.

Garbage collection provides an interesting example of substitution of local labour with African workers. Companies collecting garbage in Girona largely employ Moroccans, who represent half of the labour force in these firms in some localities. Furthermore, an important percentage of these workers have permanent contracts. This reflects the dominance of one firm in the garbage collection and street cleaning service in northern Girona, which uses decentralised administration and relies strongly on its local foremen. The foremen, who are Moroccans, recruit employees from within their own community. However, despite their permanent contracts, workers described a number of abusive practices by Moroccan foremen towards employees, saying that they were sometimes forced to do unpaid work (such as cleaning up a public space after a concert), or to accept working hours that Spaniards refused. This pattern has been observed in other sectors, such as agriculture, where companies rely on immigrant foremen.

In contrast, even in tourist-dominated localities, accommodation services offer relatively few jobs for immigrant workers from the Third World. These jobs are more attractive for locals, as well as for Spanish or other European immigrants. A significant part of this sector is run by families who hire the same workers every season. Furthermore, no work permit is issued to non-EU workers for tourist-related activities, except for guarding, cleaning or gardening. The local administration argues that there are many unemployed Spanish workers who are willing to take up tourism-related jobs. In fact, temporary internal Spanish migration to coastal areas has been a traditional response to the peak summer demand of tourism (Lever 1987). Thus Moroccans (just one Western African was found in these jobs) occupy only the margins of employment in the sector, working for example as gardeners and watchmen on campsites, and kitchen assistants and cleaners in hotels. In this case, there is little direct competition between Spanish and non-EU workers as they occupy different segments of the labour market. These segments are clearly delimited by employers and the government[9].

The retail sector demonstrates a third feature of the service sector – the incipient creation of employment niches. Thus immigrants were found in jobs with a strong craft component in businesses such as bakeries, carpenters' workshops and in furniture-making. To a certain extent, tourism and its search for 'authenticity' has preserved these activities in a traditional form, and yet the necessary skilled workers are in short supply locally. Thus in some areas of skilled work (carpenters, cabinet-makers) or even semi-skilled work (bakery assistants), African workers have been able to move easily between different jobs within a highly narrow employment niche. However, this incipient market niche presents a quite different picture from the mainstream trends observed in Girona labour market, where demand for African workers is over-whelming for unskilled labour.

The data presented above suggest that different dynamics are at work in the diverse economic sectors (and even for particular occupa-tions) in the province of Girona. However, in general, it can be concluded that the number of permanently contracted workers is low, and work is generally of an unskilled nature. This makes the bargaining position of immigrants weak, as well as subjecting them to cyclical changes in the economy. Moreover, the lack of employment contract means that these workers face tough labour and living conditions, low salaries and, based on interviewees' reports, regular impositions of abusive practices by employers.

Africans in Girona: a low-qualified labour force?

As to whether the labour market trends outlined above represent de-skilling, or indeed a learning of new skills by immigrants on arrival in Spain, the evidence is less clear. In order to assess the level of qualifica-tions of the African labour force in Girona, two basic indicators were chosen from the survey:

- the immigrants' language skills, and in particular, their literacy and their knowledge of Spanish and Catalan; and
- their labour trajectory in their countries of origin.

Regarding the first point, data presented in table 3.8 shows that there was a clear difference between Moroccans and West Africans: the

9 However, it is worth noting that two Moroccans interviewed had changed their employment category in order to be accepted by the Girona office of the Ministry of Labour and Social Security. Indeed, the reality is that immigrants work where employers wish, no matter what category is defined on their work permit. However, the category does establish their salary. This practice is not restricted to the accommodation sector.

majority of Moroccans declared they could write and read whereas the
bulk of West Africans interviewed were not literate. Meanwhile, whilst
Spanish was spoken by the vast majority of respondents (138 out of 151),
Catalan was spoken by only 11.9 per cent of the interviewees, although
half could understand the language. To a certain extent, the low knowledge of Catalan is surprising in a area where Catalan is the normal
language of communication, and this may suggest a limited level of
social integration for African workers, perhaps as a result of high
migrant mobility patterns, short lengths of residence in Catalonia or lack
of social relations between Africans and locals. On the other hand, it
reflects the fact that African workers generally do not occupy jobs which
require particular language skills (e.g. clerical jobs).

Table 3.8 Literacy level of sample population by nationality (no. individuals)

Can you write and read your first language?	Moroccans	West Africans	Total
Yes	60	16	76
Yes, but with difficulties	15	14	29
No	12	34	46
Total	87	64	151

Source: Author's survey, 1995.

However, in determining the relationship between literacy levels and
labour integration, a number of problems arose. First, the small number
of skilled employees (19 out of 148) in the sample makes it difficult to
come to firm conclusions about whether literacy leads to skilled
employment; and although the majority of skilled workers, whether
Moroccans or West Africans, did have writing skills, the majority of
Moroccans in unskilled employment (67.6 per cent) also reported that
they knew how to write and read in Arabic. The lower proportion of
West Africans in unskilled employment who could read and write (21.8
per cent) suggests however that there may be some relationship
between place of origin, writing skills and integration in local labour
markets.

Differences were also found between Moroccan and West African
respondents in terms of their occupational background in their countries of origin, suggesting different labour market trajectories for the two
groups. Data presented in table 3.9 shows the relative importance of
non-family employees among Moroccans compared with the West
African group, suggesting a more market-oriented economy in
Morocco, and probably a more urban background for these migrants.

As the Colectivo IOE (1994) mention, the economic crisis in the late 1980s and 1990s pushed many middle-class members of Moroccan society, and especially young students from urban backgrounds, towards the idea of emigration. Indeed, Moroccans interviewed in this research came both from rural parts of the Rif (Northern Morocco), and from cities such as Nador, Tetuan or Tanger.

Table 3.9 Main occupation in the country of origin of sample population, by nationality (no. individuals)

Occupation	Moroccans	West Africans	Total
Employed on family land or in family business	27	49	76
Self-employed	12	3	15
Non-family employee	23	9	32
Unemployed or only occasional employment	25	3	28
Total	**87**	**64**	**151**

Source: Author's survey, 1995.

Table 3.9 does not show the kind of job (skilled or non-skilled), but the relationship to production (employee or employer; family or non-family; self-employment), and as such, it is not possible to affirm that there is a de-skilling process as a consequence of the migratory process. Nonetheless, the table displays a great diversity of situations in the country of origin for Moroccans, whereas the West Africans' immigration patterns fit more into conventional ideas of labour immigration from poor countries, as migrants have come mainly from a poorly-developed agricultural sector.

Conclusions

This chapter has attempted to cast some light on a relatively little-studied phenomenon, namely the increase of African immigration into the Spanish labour market. From being almost non-existent in official statistics, one African nationality (the Moroccans) is now the main legally resident foreign population in Spain. However, the total number of non-EU residents in Spain is still far lower than in central or northern Europe and new labour inflows have experienced a remarkable decline since 1992.

Quite differently from the inflows of immigrants into central and western Europe in the 1960s, labour immigration into Spain occurs in a high-unemployment context; the highest in the OECD. However, official statistics suggest that immigrants are employed in a range of activities across all the economic sectors of the Mediterranean provinces, with the same pattern being recorded for the Canary Islands and Madrid. Some economic sectors are more porous to the entry of foreign labour than others; namely, agriculture, construction and the domestic sector. Within these sectors, immigrants are not necessarily occupied in declining firms, as is witnessed by the employment of immigrants in the highly-productive agricultural sector of Almería. Meanwhile, data presented here from a survey of African workers in Girona confirms the general Spanish picture of immigrant workers fitting into local employment structures. Economic sector thus is not seen as crucial for the differentiation of labour inflows.

Regarding the kind of jobs that these workers do, the Girona survey points to the African labour force mainly doing unskilled jobs in secondary labour markets. This occurs across all economic sectors. Although every sector has its own particular dynamics, immigrants are found in the most unstable and seasonal parts of the labour market. In other words, even though employers may have different reasons for hiring foreign workers in manufacturing and agriculture, the outcome is similar. Linked to this, only a few of the jobs are permanent. This should be understood in the context of greater casualisation of the Spanish labour market as a whole. The casualisation of the labour market definitely smoothes the path of integration of unskilled foreign workers into secondary labour markets. This is not to say that casualisation just affects immigrants, for other groups, especially women and the young, suffer from it as well. Yet non-EU foreigners are probably the group that is most overtly at risk. Finally, the kind of jobs that Africans do in Girona is unaffected by their previous education or work experience.

This account confirms the thesis advanced by Piore (1979) in the sense that African workers fill unskilled jobs in the secondary labour market. Self-employment has not been developed to a great extent and access to skilled jobs for African workers is largely restricted to those sectors that are in short supply in local labour markets, although other groups of foreign workers, such as EU nationals, may have a more diversified pattern of integration. Meanwhile, in all this, it seems clear that the state is vital not just in the process of casualisation which is taking place in Spain, but also in limiting possibilities for foreign workers in the labour market depending on the worker's nationality.

Finally, however, while the dual labour market theory posits that the competition between native and foreign workers is minimal, the array of jobs that African workers occupy in Girona, and high unemployment and casualisation in the Spanish labour market, cast a doubt on this point. There are jobs created by African immigrants (e.g. ethnic businesses), jobs clearly rejected by locals (e.g. brushing forests), but for some other occupations (e.g. industrial workers) competition between foreigners and non-foreigners is clearly present. In addition, the dual labour market theory does not give an explanation of the concentration of foreigners in certain unskilled jobs, while other unskilled jobs are undertaken by natives. In this sense, it seems clear that any framework for the study of labour immigration in Spain needs to combine macro, structural approaches (with clear recognition of the importance of the dual labour market theory) with micro-scale analysis (e.g. the role that immigrants' networks play in channelling information about jobs), in order to reach a more complete understanding of the process of labour market change.

Acknowledgements

This research was funded by the 'Human Capital and Mobility' Programme of the Commission of the European Communities (Proposal no. ERB4001GT931634). The author would like to thank Dr Keith Hoggart (King's College London) and Dra. Angels Pascual de Sans (Universitat Autònoma de Barcelona) for their useful help and comments.

References

Aragón, R. and Chozas, J. (1993) *La Regularización de Inmigrantes durante 1991–1992*. Madrid: Ministerio de Trabajo y Seguridad Social (Collection "Informes y Estudios", 4).

Bailey, T. R. (1987) *Immigrant and Native Workers. Contrasts and Competition*. Boulder: Westview Press.

Banco Bilbao Vizcaya (1995) *Renta Nacional de España 91. Distribución Provincial. Avance 1992/1993*. Bilbao: Banco Bilbao Vizcaya.

Berlan, J. P. (1986) Agriculture et migrations, *Revue Européenne des Migrations Internationales*, 2(3), pp. 9–33.

Chiswick, B. R. (1978) The effect of Americanization on the earnings of foreign-born men, *Journal of Political Economy*, 86 (5), pp. 897–922.

Colectivo IOE (1994) *Marroquins a Catalunya*. Barcelona: Institut Català d'Estudis Mediterranis.

Comisión Interministerial de Extranjería (1995) *Anuario Estadístico de Extranjería 1994*. Madrid: Ministerio del Interior

Fina, L. (1993) The labour market: recent trends and prospects, in Montanari, A., ed. *Labour Market Structure and Development in Portugal, Spain, Italy, Greece and Turkey*. Naples: Edizioni Scientifiche Italiane (Collection IREM, 2), pp. 83–101.

García-Ramon, D. (1985) Old and new in Spanish farming, *Geographical Magazine*, 57 (3), pp. 128–33.

Gozálvez, V. et al. (1995) *Inmigrantes Marroquíes y Senegales en la España Mediterránea*. Valencia: Generalitat Valenciana.

INE (1962 and 1972) *España. Anuario Estadístico.* Madrid: Instituto Nacional de Estadística.

Izquierdo, A. (1992) *La Inmigración en España 1980–1990.* Madrid: Ministerio de Trabajo y Seguridad Social (Collection "Informes Serie General", 17)

Lever, A. (1987) Spanish tourism migrants. The case of Lloret de Mar, *Annals of Tourism Research*, 14 (4), pp. 449–70.

Long, J. E. (1980) The effect of Americanization on earnings: some evidence for women, *Journal of Political Economy*, 88 (3), pp. 620–9.

Ministerio de Asuntos Sociales (1996) *Anuario de Migraciones.* Madrid: Dirección General de Migraciones.

Ministerio de Trabajo y Seguridad Social (1991) *Estadística de Permisos de Trabajo a Extranjeros.* Madrid: Ministerio de Trabajo y Seguridad Social.

Ministerio de Trabajo y Seguridad Social (1993) *Contingente para 1993.* Madrid: Dirección General de Migraciones.

Morrison, P.S. (1990) Segmentation theory applied to local, regional and spatial labour markets, *Progress in Human Geography*, 14 (4), pp. 488–528.

OECD (1996) *Employment Outlook.* Paris: Organisation for Economic Cooperation and Development.

Piore, M. J. (1979) *Birds of Passage. Migrant Labor and Industrial Societies.* Cambridge: Cambridge University Press.

Salmon, K.G. (1991) *The Modern Spanish Economy. Transformation and Integration into Europe.* London: Pinter.

Solana, A.M. and Pascual de Sans, A. (1994) Els residents estrangers a Espanya, *Documents d'Analisi Geografica*, 24, pp. 169–80

Valderrama , G. (1994) *El Fenómeno Migratorio en los Países del Sur de la Unión Europea como Factor de Cambio Social: El Caso del Sector Agrícola.* Madrid: Universidad Complutense de Madrid, unpublished Ph.D. thesis.

Valenzuela, M. (1991) Spain: the phenomenon of mass tourism, in Williams, A.M. and Shaw, G., eds., *Tourism and Economic Development: Western European Experiences.* London: Belhaven Press, pp. 40–60.

4

Gender-Selective Migration: Somalian and Filipina Women in Rome

Victoria Chell

———

Within the past 20–30 years, Italy has changed from being a country of net emigration to one of net immigration. As pointed out in Chapter 1, three distinct trends contributed to the 'migration turnaround': a rapid decline in Italian emigration; the return of Italian nationals from abroad; and, most important of all, a significant immigration from various countries of the 'South'. Initially, this immigration to Italy was fairly limited: mainly women from Cape Verde, the Philippines and Eritrea who were employed as domestics; and an agricultural labour force made up of men from North Africa, particularly Morocco and Tunisia. These migration flows started to become significant in the early 1970s, but since the early 1980s the number of immigrants entering Italy has increased sharply and has involved a greater range of nationalities, including recent refugees from Somalia.

At the heart of this chapter are the implications of international migration for female migrants of different origins and with different expectations, who have arrived in Italy at a tumultuous and unprecedented period in Italian migration history. This chapter can be seen as a specific and detailed response to the important remark made in Chapter 1 about the marked gender and work selectivities of the various national migration streams which have entered Southern Europe in the last 20 years. My analysis can also be seen as a vindication of the powerful argument of Morokvasic (amongst others) who has pointed out the falsity of the gender-blind and reductionist stances of much writing about migration where it is implied that most 'active' migrants are male and that females migrate only as wives and dependents (Morokvasic 1983). My findings challenge this superficial and mistaken conception of migrant women and of the female migrant condition. Although it is difficult to make sweeping generalisations because of the diversity of experience uncovered, my research in Rome shows that women often play active, independent and protagonistic roles in contemporary migration to Italy. This recognition leads to the conclusive acknowledgement that women who migrate need to be considered as economic and social actors in their own right.

Key questions and research methodology

In response to the general need for a better understanding of the role of women in international migration, and also to investigate in more detail Italy as a country of immigration, this contribution focuses on the immigration of women from Somalia and the Philippines in Rome. Refugees from Somalia are relatively recent arrivals; the Filipinos are a longer-established migrant community in the city.

The following 'essential questions' have been encapsulated within this study, each forming a section of the chapter:

- First, how has the phenomenon of female migration to Italy arisen? There have been some attempts to consider female migration in relation to general transformations of the world economy (notably by Sassen 1988), but these ideas need to be addressed in the specific context of Italy.
- Second, who are these women, and what are their reasons for migrating? Here it will be shown that the female respondents of this study appear as protagonists in a migration process which has ceased to be exclusively a 'male thing'.
- The third question relates to female migrants' experience: how they have developed mechanisms for migration; maintained support networks; planned new migrations; formed strategies for adaptation and insertion into the labour force; and laid schemes for return or perhaps sponsoring further migration from their place of origin. Such developments alter power and status relationships between the sexes and across generations. However, my data suggest that migrant women working in Italy do not experience an increase in power and status commensurate with their roles as primary earners; instead they tend to remain in social isolation with limited integration into the host society.
- Finally, as the analysis of the Filipino and Somalian migration process unfolds, the evidence available allows me to propose a

number of hypotheses concerning the behaviour of migrant women with respect to both their economic and non-economic activities. These are presented in the final section of the chapter.

The information in this chapter is drawn from my recently-completed doctoral thesis (Chell 1995).[1] The data comes from three main sources: national statistical data; self-completion questionnaires filled out by 100 Filipinas [2] and 60 Somalian women; and in-depth interviews with 14 Filipinas and 10 Somalians. These information sources were supplemented by interviews with Italian government officials and representatives of the Philippines and Somalia; interviews with officials from the NGOs concerned with the two groups; and information drawn from diaries kept for this study by chosen individuals.

Italy and female labour

Female migration to Italy from the Philippines and Somalia (and from other countries of female migration such as Cape Verde and the Dominican Republic) is closely related to the evolving participation of Italian women in the national economy and to the consequent creation of demand for female immigration to perform domestic and related work. Bettio (1988) explains that, until the 1970s, confinement of Italian women to the family and household (both as daughters and as wives and mothers) led to the relatively limited participation of women in the labour market. Another relevant factor was the withdrawal of female labour into areas uncovered by official statistics, such as seasonal work and domestic production or outwork.

By contrast, a new set of factors operated since the 1970s to encourage, or push, Italian women into paid work. These included changing fertility patterns, the decreasing value (and increased cost) of offspring as contributors to the family income, the need for a dual income to combat the recession of the early 1980s, and an improvement in the national welfare, health and social security systems. Perhaps the key factor, however, was the tertiarisation of the Italian economy, and the growing feminisation of the service sector, partly driven by the rapidly rising educational standards of women born in the post-war decades.

1   The research was supported by an ESRC postgraduate studentship and by a grant from the Dudley Stamp Memorial Fund. Approximately 12 months was spent in Rome: a preliminary visit during 1992, and a longer spell during 1993 and early 1994. My results are testimony to the graciousness of time afforded by the women involved with this study – working women who had barely time to themselves.
2   I use the term Filipino to refer to the community as a collective, Filipina (plural Filipinas) to refer to women from the Philippines.

With the liberation of Italian women from the home, there then existed the demand for a working population to substitute this lost domestic labour. Female migrants filled this demand, the mechanics and complexities of which were well understood by the migrant women themselves. As one Somalian respondent said to me:

> Letting us enter Italy is a very clever move on the part of the Italians because they are freeing their workforce so that they can be more productive some- where else. If we went away Italy would collapse, there would be no-one to turn the cogs of the country, and all those Italians who are freed to be working somewhere else more productively in society would be constrained through having to do the more menial tasks that we perform.

With time, demand has grown beyond mere household chores of cleaning and cooking and has moved increasingly towards the supple- mentation of expensive and scarce 'social provisions' such as childcare and looking after elderly people. I would suggest that the over-repre- sentation of migrant women in the domestic and care sectors of the labour force is an object of real concern; foreign women are specifically recruited to these marginalised occupational niches because of sexist (and racist) stereotypes. Moreover, this is not just an Italian phenom- enon. Global presumptions about men's and women's work are obvious within the dominant flows of migrant workers from labour-exporting to labour-importing countries. Such conjectures not only affect the gender-specific recruitment of people within a country, but they also mean the narrow selection of countries such as the Philippines for 'domestic' work over other labour-exploiting nations. Indeed 'Filipina' and 'domestic servant' seem to have become synonymous in employers' minds in Italy, Greece and Spain (see Lega Italo-Filippina Filippini Emigrati 1991; Weinart 1991).

Filipina and Somalian women in Italy

This section concentrates on two themes relating to the group and indi- vidual characteristics of women from Somalia and the Philippines who are living and working in Rome: first, some general profile characteris- tics of the two immigrant groups; and second an account of why they migrated.

Profile data of the two respondent groups

Filipino migration to Italy accelerated during the late 1970s and throughout the 1980s. By 1981 there were already an estimated 15,000

Filipinos in Italy, 8,000 of whom were concentrated in Rome. In addition to the pull factor of labour demand described in the previous section, the post-1974 Philippine government promulgated a policy of labour deployment overseas designed as part of the national economic policy to decrease unemployment at home (Abella 1979; Chant and McIlwaine 1995).

According to the Commission for Philippine Migrants in Europe, there are about 500,000 Filipinos in Europe; 80% of them are concentrated in four countries, in descending order Italy, Spain, Greece and the United Kingdom. Italian government statistics are usually based on numbers of foreigners in possession of a *permesso di soggiorno* or 'permit to stay' and are issued by the Interior Ministry (see Chapter 1 for more details). By 1990 the number of Filipinos with permits to stay in Italy had risen to over 35,000 and throughout the first half of the 1990s the numbers oscillated between 41,000 and 46,000 (Caritas di Roma 1995, p. 90).

Filipinos are the fourth largest immigrant community in Italy after Moroccans, citizens of the United States and citizens of the former Yugoslavia. At the end of 1995, Ministry of Interior figures show that 40.9 per cent of Filipinos were residing in Lazio (the overwhelming majority of these were in Rome itself) and that 69.7 per cent of the national total of Filipino immigrants were female (Caritas di Roma 1996, pp. 87, 98). Compared to most other immigrant nationalities in Italy, Filipinos are disproportionately concentrated in Rome and Lazio where they are, in fact, the biggest migrant group (17,752, of whom 12,292 were women, in 1995).

This concentration is largely explained by the parallel concentration in Rome of wealthy and middle-class families who act as their chief employers, and by the abundance of office employment for Italian women in the nation's bureaucratic capital, heightening the demand for 'replacement' domestic labour.

The Somalian community in Italy and Rome has both similarities and differences to the Filipino one. It too is predominantly female (65.4 per cent) and is over-represented in Rome and Lazio (6,619 in Lazio in 1995, out of a national total of 17,389, i.e. 38.1 per cent). However, its pattern of growth is more recent, swollen by refugee flows which have been added to the much smaller and longer-established communities of diplomats and students (Somalia was at one time an Italian colony). In fact, the size of the Somalian community in Italy has doubled since 1990 (for the detailed figures see Caritas di Roma 1995, p. 90; 1996, pp. 69, 87, 329).

However, it should be stressed that the figures given in the previous two paragraphs are for legal immigrants and exclude those who are undocumented. Estimates made by leaders of the Somalian Community in Italy place the total (documented and undocumented) at around 50,000, the major concentrations being in Rome and Naples; whilst research completed by Korsieporn (1989) for the Gramsci Institute gives a figure of 160,000 Filipinos in Italy, including undocumented workers.

I now move on to present some background data on the two groups of respondents, drawn from both the questionnaires and the depth interviews. The length of residence in Italy differed greatly between two groups. The majority of Filipina respondents had worked in Rome for more than two years (67 per cent), and 14 per cent had been in Rome for more than ten years. By contrast, 60 per cent of the Somalian women had been in Rome only since 1990 or after (the questionnaires, it should be noted, were administered in 1993), and none of them had been resident in Italy for as long as the longest-staying Filipinas. This difference closely reflects the reason for the timing of the Somalian migrations, which occurred after civil unrest developed in 1989.

It also seems that there was a greater propensity for mobility amongst many Somalian migrants, both prior to moving to Italy and within Italy, and a certain proportion intended to move on to other countries such as the United Kingdom and Canada in search of better incomes and prospects. Within the Filipina group there had been little internal mobility in Italy, probably because their migrations were more pre-planned and because of their position of greater stability and better remuneration within the labour market (more details on this are given below). In reality, for both groups it was clear they they are less mobile than studies of migrants in general have supposed. This can be readily understood if it is considered that being mobile means every time finding accommodation, new friends, a peer group which helps and protects, and a circle of acquaintances which offers a sense of security.

Although I do not include a lengthy discussion of Italian immigration legislation in this chapter, it is necessary to note that alterations in Italian immigration legislation during the late 1980s and early 1990s had a profound bearing on the timing and nature of the flows of both groups. The Italian government's use of regularisations as an integral component of immigration 'policy' enhanced the attractiveness of Italy for new migrants who came in the hope of a further regularisation. From the questionnaires and interviews there was corroboratory evidence of a direct link between Italian policy initiatives and the entry date of the women. Significant proportions of the Filipina respondents either entered Italy on a tourist visa (37 per cent) before the end of the 1980s, whilst those who arrived later in expectation of a regularisation similar to the two passed in 1986 and 1989–90 had no visa (34 per cent). A smaller percentage (14 per cent) had taken advantage of the bilateral agreement between the Philippines and Italy which allows 'direct hiring' by an Italian employer who may recruit a domestic or care worker from the Philippines on a two-yearly renewable contract. The immigration of Somalian women not only coincided with the onset of heightened civil disturbances in the home country, but also took advantage of regularisation opportunities offered by the Martelli Law of early 1990.

Although there are some differences in economic activity between the two groups, the majority were employed in the domestic work sector. Yet, there was a distinct duality in their income levels, which requires some explanation. The figures are striking. The modal income for Somalian respondents was 400,000–800,000 lire per month, and no Somalian woman earnt more than 1.2 million lire per month. The Filipinas' incomes were much higher: 800,000–1.2 million on average, with the highest reaching over 2 million[3].

These incomes, and their range, depend on the precise type of work, the hours worked, and whether the woman lived in the employer's home. Those who lived with their employer tended not to have another job. Live-out workers could earn more money through working for one employer in the morning, another in the afternoon and perhaps a third at the weekend. Such a multiple pattern would increase overall earnings by perhaps a third or even a half, but some of this would be lost on providing their own accommodation. For instance, a typical live-out worker might earn 900,000 lire per month for the morning job, plus another 600,000 for the afternoon; typically, 400,000–500,000 lire would then be spent on shared accommodation. The highest domestic wages, however, were earnt by *'assistensas'* who are qualified nurses employed by private households to administer medicines and nursing care and who receive 2–2.5 million.[4]

The aggregation of several factors explains the wage differential between Filipinas and Somalians. Part of the income gap is explained by the greater experience and qualifications of the Filipinas many of whom are highly educated, with university degrees and a good knowledge of English. These same features were noted by Iosifides (chapter 2) for the Filipinas working as domestics in Athens. Somalian women lack experience of the domestic service market and hence the best opportunities are denied to them. Thus the market for domestics has become highly segmented, Somalian women falling at the lower end

3   The present exchange rate (December 1996) is about 2,500 lire to the British pound and 1,500 lire to the US dollar.
4   The term 'assistensa' is used by migrants themselves to describe this more highly qualified variant of the domestic service sector. It is not a standard Italian term.

Name	Age	Nationality	Place of birth	Marital status	Children	Year of arrival	Mode of entry	Legal status	Original profession	Employment in Rome	Living arrangements
Alice	41	Filipina	Manila	Married	1	1990	Contracted	Documented	Nurse	Full-time assistensa	Private flat with family
Ayasia	23	Filipina	Luzon	Single	-	1992	Fiumicino Airport	Undocumented	Midwife	Full-time domestic to several employers	Lives with mother
Chicillea	38	Filipina	Samar	Married	7	1984	Fiumicino Airport	Documented	High-school leaver	Part-time domestic; bank worker	Flat with husband
Cora	29	Filipina	Manila	Single	-	1982	Tourist visa; Fiumicino	Documented	Student	Full-time domestic	Live-in
Dorean	36	Filipina	Mindanao	Single	-	1986	Fiumicino Airport	Documented	Doctor	Full-time assistensa	Private flat with friends
Febe	48	Filipina	Samar	Married	4	1985	Agency; border entry	Documented	Teacher	Full-time domestic	Live-in
Fulgenia	38	Filipina	Manila	Married	1	1990	Contract	Documented	Nurse	Full-time assistensa	Private flat with family
Gherada	58	Filipina	Luzon	Widowed	5	1985	Border entry	Documented	Teacher	Part-time domestic	Private flat with friends
Gina	25	Filipina	Mindanao	Single	-	1987	Agency; Fiumicino	Documented	Graduate in commerce	Full-time domestic	Live-in
Irma	41	Filipina	Manila	Single	1	1981	Direct hire; Fiumicino	Documented	Teacher	Part-time domestic	Private flat with family
Jessica	21	Filipina	Mindanao	Single	-	1993	Tourist visa; Fiumicino	Undocumented	Graduate in computing	Part-time domestic	Lives with mother
Josie	42	Filipina	Mindanao	Married	2	1985	Agency; border entry	Documented	Teacher	Full-time domestic	Live-in
Mercedes	33	Filipina	Quezon City	Married	3	1984	Fiumicino Airport	Documented	Graduate in Science	Part-time domestic	Private flat with friends
Molonay	26	Filipina	Samar	Single	-	1991	Switzerland; border entry	Undocumented	Graduate in commerce	Full-time domestic	Live-in
Amas	16	Somalian	Mogadishu	Single	-	1993	Mogadishu-Fiumicino	Undocumented	Student	Part-time domestic	Lives with mother
Betula	23	Somalian	Mogadishu	Single	-	1992	Nairobi-Fiumicino	Undocumented	Bank teller	Full-time domestic	Live-in
Ester	22	Somalian	Mogadishu	Single	-	1992	Mogadishu-Fiumicino	Undocumented	Accountant	Full-time domestic	Live-in
Fatima	25	Somalian	Mogadishu	Single	-	1991	Mogadishu-Fiumicino	Undocumented	Air hostess	Full-time domestic	Live-in

Figure 4.1 Migration biographies of Filipina and Somalian women in Rome

and Filipinas monopolising the upper end. However, employer prejudice may also be a factor. As one Italian woman told me:

> Despite the disparity in the level of wages between those other groups and the Filipinas, the Filipinas are preferred because they are clean, efficient, honest and above all trustworthy with the children who can be left with them without the worry of the employer. They also learn Italian very quickly, and so when it comes to paying them there is less regret because they double up as a domestic, child-minder and part-time English teacher.

Figure 4.1 is an attempt to chart some biographical summaries of typical life-histories gained from the research. These summary biographies are selected from my in-depth interviews. The chart clearly attests to the later arrival of Somalian women in Italy and also sets out other variables which will underlie my subsequent discussion. The names are fictitious.

The journey – why migrate?

Whether women are independent decision-makers or simply the followers of men (or some combination of these two), the migratory process almost always involves other individuals too. Usually, the family in the country of origin plays a role in selecting who will migrate, as we also saw in Iosifides's account of Filipino migration to Greece (see chapter 2). For Filipino migration to Italy (and the rest of Southern Europe), young female adults are usually chosen: a strategy determined both by the extreme shortage of employment opportunities for women in the Philippines, and by the gender-selective nature of the labour market in Italy. If the migrants are married with children, the remaining extended family takes care of the children and husband: hence the family sacrifices its unity for the sake of migration. Such 'commodification' of migrant women appears to be ongoing, as I shall demonstrate presently.

The Filipinas' answers to questions about migration motivation reflect the dominant theme of the individual migration project: economic gain. When asked to state their main reason for emigration, nearly all Filipina respondents (92 per cent) maintained that economic survival and/or the economic improvement of the family unit was the major cause. Among the specific economic reasons given for working overseas, the following were frequently cited: to supplement a husband's wage in the Philippines; to send children to school; to save for the future; or to build a house. In addition to these factors, 30 per cent mentioned the chance to become legally established through a future regularisation, 25 per cent stated that ease of entry was a significant reason for choosing Italy, 18 per cent were joining family members already living in Italy, and 8 per cent came to Italy for study purposes. With their close association with the domestic sphere, migration for the Filipinas was a direct result of women's imposed moral obligation of supporting their household back home. The choice of domestic work abroad was considered wholly appropriate to women's assigned role in Filipino society.

When the Somalian women were asked to state their main reason for emigrating, the unanimous answer was to escape the fear and disturbances caused by the civil war. Yet when asked why they entered Italy after their initial flight from Somalia, a large proportion (62 per cent) stated that it was to earn money to meet their basic needs and remit savings to their family members still in Somalia. By no means all Somalians had come straight to Rome. For instance, the stated migration of Betula (see figure 4.1) as Mogadishu-Rome belies the complexity of her actual migration path. Betula told of her flight to Addis Ababa and then to Nairobi to join her brother, where it was decided after a family consultation that she should be sent to Rome to try to support the family at this point in time. On further enquiry it was revealed that friends and other family members in Rome had suggested that Betula joined them there.

Hence for Somalians, Italy (and especially Rome) became the chosen destination as their period of exile lengthened and the assets with which they had fled Somalia dwindled away. Facing substantial economic hardship, many refugees decided to use their exile more productively and, with the encouragement of their family members, entered domestic service in Italy. Their eventual location in Rome was not based wholly on market forces; also important was proximity to Italian government institutions from which they could draw some help, including possible assistance to move on to another destination such as North America or Australia.

For both groups, migration was seen not only as a means to short-term financial gain for the migrant and, above all, her family, but also as a long-term fulfilment of goals and dreams. That the migrant women would have to endure hardships and considerable sacrifice was seen as an unavoidable, but worthwhile, price to pay. Amongst both groups residing in Rome, future *economic* aspirations were *prevalent* but *not exclusive*: migration is understood and experienced both in relation to economic settlement and in relation to personal and family achievement, and for some this included a cautious movement towards self-determination and autonomy.

The consequences of migration

The consequences of migration are, of course, manifold. Not all can be explored here. Certainly my research revealed numerous indications of the relative social isolation of these two groups of women working in Italy; yet female immigrants in Rome are more than just isolated women. They have their own personal networks, and they can count on the assistance of church and voluntary agencies. They also have to learn to try to fit into Italian society, or at least cope with its demands. In this respect migrant women share many of the problems faced by women in Italy in general. As Palomba and Righi write (1992, p. 26): 'Their problems (the migrant women) – a house, a school for the children if they are with them, sexuality, fertility control – are magnified by the fact that the battles fought by Italian women in terms of social services have already been lost'. Migrant women are even less well equipped (or perhaps are not willing) to fight these battles than Italian women; and in addition the migrant woman has to confront daily the extra problems of social isolation, gender (and racial) stereotyping, and male domination.

The fact that working migrant women are earning a wage and supporting themselves leads to a pervasive assumption that just being a migrant woman worker involves a challenge to traditional gender roles. Yet, paradoxically, most of these women are in economic sectors which perpetuate and exaggerate the image of the woman as mother/carer/homemaker. And little independence is gained, because of the financial obligation to remit as much as possible to support family members in the home country. Furthermore, not only are the notions of achieving personal and economic independence through migration largely mythical, but the migrants also endure great personal costs of dislocation from home and family, including being separated from their own children.

Changing family relationships

Migration has presented many problems for Filipina and Somalian women. Families are often divided and recomposed according to the demands and structure of the labour markets in Italy, whilst women who migrate alone leave a distorted family unit behind in their countries of origin. Even when couples migrate they may be forced to live separately because of the nature of the woman's work as a live-in domestic. Separation from family in the Philippines or Somalia is a product of physical, financial, legal and political impediments which the individual migrant has little or no control over: living on the other side of the world, unable to afford the fare home for regular visits, or perhaps not able to leave Italy for fear of not being able to enter again. This long-term separation obviously affects traditional marital roles: marriages may be delayed (or never take place), fertility is reduced, extra-marital relationships may develop, and family structures are altered.

The moral obligation to provide financial support to the household back home is strongly rooted, especially amongst the Filipinas. For those who are mothers and have migrated leaving behind their children in the Philippines (53 per cent of the respondent sample from the Philippines were mothers, but only a tiny majority of these had children with them in Rome), the children are generally looked after by female relatives: typically an aunt (often the migrant's sister) or a grandmother. If the children were living in the same house as the father, he was not usually entrusted with sole responsibility for the children – his care duties were part-time at most. This pattern leaves a strong feeling of indebtedness on the part of the migrant towards those left behind looking after children. Single women who had migrated were also indebted, since their parents had usually provided the funding for the migration.

This obligation of support does not necessarily end with the first migration. The networks established by earlier generations of migrants are not only being used as conduits of information for new migrants, but a 'substitution migration' is occurring which is facilitating the retirement of older female migrants and their replacement by their daughters. Given the higher ages and longer history of migration from the Philippines, this replacement phenomenon is confined to the Filipina group. The reciprocity of the situation means that the mother returns to the Philippines to care for the family (and perhaps her daughter's family), whilst the daughter emigrates to take the mother's place, supporting the latter's retirement with her own remittances, and gaining a measure of financial independence and adventure.

This cross-generational migration has been accelerated by the falling average age of Filipinas migrating to Italy. During the 1970s, when the first large wave of Filipina women arrived in Rome, many migrants were in their 30s and 40s. Since about 1985, unemployment and economic deterioration in the Philippines seem to have pushed younger women, including those graduating from college and high school, directly into migrating. It used to be that it was the mother who migrated as she left her children at home, where she would support their education. Now the newly-grown-up children in the Philippines convince their mother to return to manage the family, whilst the daughters migrate to Italy. This turn-around in roles has meant that unlike previously where the woman had her children before she migrated, and subsequently migrated to support them, the daughter is now migrating early in her reproductive life and so is delaying her family. It is important to note the significance of this development for future generations of Filipinas, as the migration could be indefinitely repeated across the generations.

On the other hand, it may seem illogical to migrate only in the knowledge that it will trigger further migrations, further separation of families, and further emotional hardship. When asked why women migrate to Italy to pay for the children's upbringing and education when there is a distinct chance that the children will also migrate, the explanation of Sister Guadelupe, a Filipina nun I interviewed, ran compellingly as follows:

> If they do not spend the money on education and if they do not at least try to better themselves in the hope of improving their futures then there is no real hope for them. At least when they have education, there is the opportunity for the future if they need it, and the constant hope that the situation will improve in the Philippines. It is also some kind of status symbol, to have this education. When you go through some places in the Philippines you will see displayed in the windows of the houses the degree certificate for all the village to see. It is a thing that the Filipinas are immensely proud of.

So, Filipina women migrate and are indebted to their family members who look after relatives at home. This indebtedness is repaid by remittances and payments for children's education; the daughters are, in turn, indebted to their mothers and often emigrate to replace their mothers. This is because, despite education, financial rewards and security are greater in domestic service abroad than in professional employment at home.

Economic relationships

For large numbers of Filipina and Somalian women in Italy, migration has meant a practical commitment to supporting not only themselves but also, and pre-eminently, their households and extended families. Such financial and moral commitments are sustained through poorly-paid and relatively unskilled work in the domestic service sector. This sector seems to be relatively well insulated from the vagaries of the Italian economy, and so rates of unemployment amongst foreign domestic and care workers are rather low compared to other sectors of the economy and the labour force. Compared to other sectors of migrant employment, domestic service is also relatively secure, with regular work and longer-term contracts.

Although the wages earnt by Filipina and Somalian domestic

workers are low by Italian income standards, when they are compared to the wage levels of male members of the same migrant groups – whether in Italy or in the home country – they are higher. This disparity in income status between women and men seems likely to widen further, mainly because of the continued demand for domestic service generated by increasing rates of participation of Italian women in the labour force. This discrepancy in earning power between immigrant women and their menfolk questions fundamentally whether the labour force participation of migrant women necessarily translates into an improvement in their status. Although often inactive or earning signif-icantly lower wages, the men exert a critical influence on the distribution and use of the women's earnings. Emancipation is as much dependent upon the continued existence of, or liberation from, strong family bonds or obligations in the country of origin as it is on the increased income of the women. These issues are raised in the following conversation between two immigrant women (A is a female Somalian aged 27, B is a female Somalian aged 25, and C is A's 29 year-old brother).

A: 'All of my money has gone into supporting the family in Mogadishu. It's the women who are supporting the families now.'
B: 'But we women have always done this. It's only the war which has made the families realise just how important women are for the family; maybe now we will get some of the respect we deserve as the country sees that it is the women who are keeping the men.'
A: 'C could get a job if he wanted to, but he won't, it's too menial; but I have to and B has to otherwise we wouldn't survive. They could get jobs, they could work with their hands and be demoralised like us but they won't, they have too much dignity. We do, we have to get dirty, but we think of our families first and then ourselves. The men are too egoistic: it's them first, then maybe the family, but even then maybe not.'
B: 'We have always worked, it's not just recently, even though the Koran says that women should not work and that they should play a second role to men. Through the women's role in the household, women have always been strong.'
A: 'But that isn't where the real power is. We've been denied it through our religion.'
B: 'It'll change now. Now that the war has come people have to see what women do.'
A: 'It'll take more than the war to change Somalian culture. Even though it is us who are earning the money, relations between us and the men haven't changed, have they? The men still think they are

the head of the household in all respects. It hasn't altered the power because the power is through money and we are giving it to them, to the men and to the family.'

Although men may be the minority in the Filipino and Somalian communities in Italy, they are the dominant and vocal minority. The role they play in the lives of the women has an undeniable influence on the latter's economic and social independence – or lack of it.

The pressures which are formed in some male-female relationships through the stress of the migration process seem to be exacerbated by the lack of jobs available for male migrants. It is not easy for them to find work in the saturated service sector of Rome, and the domestic service market is largely closed to them. As a result many Filipino men, especially, have returned to their home country. Others form new relationships, which are used to provide them with an economic safety-net. As Sister Gloria, a Filipina nun, told me:

> There are still Filipino men coming into the country, but it is a risk because there are many here who do not have jobs, they work maybe one or two hours a day, two or three times a week, and for the rest of the time they rely on the women. One man may have three or four women, and he hops from bed to bed, they support him. The women are soft-hearted, they are lonely, that is their problem, they are the homey type.

However, another process is also occurring. The success of the Filipina women in managing the domestic service sector and in achieving some upward mobility within it provides an entry route for a proportion of the Filipino men. Josie, a Filipina domestic worker, described this new economic trend:

> Many of the men who come here have a technique of getting of a job. They have to find a girlfriend to get a job; this is why so many marriages are in trouble in the Philipinnes. If a man spends some time with his girlfriend whilst she is doing her job the employers get to trust him, and then after a while the girlfriend leaves for another job. He will then take over the job. This is a way of getting around the reluctance of the Italians to employ men in the domestic sphere.

This is also further evidence of a stratification developing within the domestic and care sector. Legally resident, longer-established and better-qualified Filipinas move up into the *assistensa* category, creating space at the lower end of the domestic sector for other groups – undocumented and recently-arrived Filipinas, some Filipino men, and recent

arrivals from a variety of countries including Somalia, East European
and South American countries.

Conclusion

The aim of this study has been to identify and explore the role of female
migrants in international migration in Italy, concentrating on the work
and allied experiences of Filipinas and Somalians. These roles and experiences are now summed-up. Given the nature of my data, these
concluding points are presented as a set of descriptive hypotheses rather
than as firm conclusions, for which further research on what is undoubtedly a highly fluid situation would be required.

First, the economic setting. During the 1970s and the 1980s, the
expansion of the service sector in Italy generated a wealth of white-
collar office jobs which were largely filled by Italian women who, with
a heightened feminist consciousness and enhanced career ambitions,
preferred them to traditional domestic roles. Migrant women have,
therefore, satisfied a labour demand that did not originate in the
productive sector of the economy, but, rather, answered the domestic
needs of middle-class households. Indeed, it can be suggested that the
growing demand for domestic service workers came to be at the root of
a growing female migration to Italy, given that Italian nationals are no
longer willing to fill this demand. Meanwhile, structural mass unemployment in countries such as the Philippines has created a population
surplus which emigrates in order to achieve a better standard of living.
Of course, such economic determinism does not explain the specific
migratory link between the Philippines and Italy. Auxiliary data from
my research suggests that 'facilitating factors' such as the intermediary
role of the Catholic Church and the existence and reinforcement of
strong personal networks have a key role to play. Hence a culture of
migration to Italy has arisen in the Philippines, especially amongst
female migration networks. In Somalia, on the other hand, the causal
mechanism was clearly related to the civil war and prior colonial ties
with Italy.

Despite this marked difference in the origins of emigration from
Somalia and the Philippines, subsequent migration behaviour becomes
similar: a common involvement in the domestic work sector, and a
shared motivation to earn, save, and support family members. Even
after long periods spent in Italy, the migrant woman continues to
perceive her role as part of the family strategy designed to benefit the
family as a whole, not the individual. The physical separation of the
woman from her family, which is the inevitable product of this type of
semi-independent female migration, does not reduce family ties; in fact

it further cements the bond as the 'success' of the migrant becomes ever more closely tied to the 'success' of the family. For this reason (and for others), 'independent' female migration is not an emancipation for these women.

In gender-specific migration from the Philippines and Somalia to Italy, households undergo essential structural changes which are adapted above all to the needs and possibilities in the host country. Families divide, separate and reunite, and then perhaps split again, according to the opportunities of work and types of accommodation available. It was found that even if the women had been joined by their husbands in Rome, after a short time the selective demands of the Italian labour market and the inability of the couple to live as a unit would often mean a local separation or a return for the husband to the home country.

For the women, too, return migration has become an important aspect of their migration biographies. Not always, however, did it represent the final stage of the migration process and the attainment of the migration goal (cf. King 1986). However, it emerged that a migrant's return is not necessarily the end of the cycle, either for herself or her household. Evidence gathered from the Filipina respondents clearly demonstrated that the nature of Filipino migration is changing. Besides the process of family reunification by which males follow females to Italy, what I term 'inter-generational sequential migration' is occurring. This new pattern derives from several processes and factors: lack of desire to unite the family in Italy, an Italian immigration policy which discourages family reunion in Italy, and a high degree of importance placed on remittances and the welfare and continuity of the family in the country of origin. Hence there is a process of cross-generational replacement of female migrants by their daughters.

In conclusion, it is worth making the comment that, whilst the reconceptualisation of Italy as a country of immigration has been made in academic terms, the Italian government has largely failed to match this changed migration status by formulating an appropriate set of legislative, policy and welfare measures for the 'new immigrants'. This is an issue which is taken up by Apap in chapter 7.

References

Abella, P. (1979) *Export of Filipino Manpower*. Manilla: Ministry of Labour, Institute of Labour and Manpower Studies.

Bettio, F. (1988) Women, the State and the family in Italy: problems of female participation in historical perspective. In Rubery, J. ed., *Women and the Recession*. London: Routledge.

Caritas di Roma (1995) *Immigrazione Dossier Statistico*. Rome: Anterem.

Caritas di Roma (1996) *Immigrazione Dossier Statistico*. Rome: Anterem.

Chant, S. and McIlwaine, C. (1995) *Women of a Lesser Cost: Female Labour, Foreign Exchange and Philippine Development*. London: Pluto.

Chell, V.E. (1995) *The Arrival and Adaptation of New Migrants in Italy: A Study of Women from the Philippines and Somalia in Rome*. London: Queen Mary and Westfield College, University of London, Ph.D. thesis.

King, R. (1986) Return migration and regional economic development: an overview, in King, R., ed. *Return Migration and Regional Economic Problems*. London: Croom Helm, pp. 1–37.

Korsieporn, A. (1989) Female migrant labour: a case study of Filipino and Thai domestic workers in Rome, Italy, *Asian Review*, 3, pp. 54–68.

Lega Italo-Filippina Filippini Emigrati (1991) *Filipino Migrant Women in Domestic Work in Italy*. Geneva: International Labour Office, World Employment Programme, International Migration for Employment, Working Paper 53.

Morokvasic, M. (1993) Women in migration: beyond the reductionist outlook, in Phizacklea, A., ed. *One Way Ticket: Migration and Female Labour*. London: Routledge and Kegan Paul.

Palomba, R. and Righi, A. (1992) *Migrant Women in Italy: Foreign Workers and 'Migrant Wives'*. Rome: Istituto di Ricerca sulla Popolazione, Working Paper.

Sassen, S. (1988) *The Mobility of Capital and Labour*. Cambridge: Cambridge University Press.

Weinart, P. (1991) *Foreign Female Domestic Workers: Help Wanted!* Geneva: International Labour Office, World Employment Programme, International Migration for Employment, Working Paper 50.

5

Indians in Lisbon: Ethnic Entrepreneurship and the Migration Process

Jorge Malheiros

————————

Throughout the last twenty years there has been an increasing amount of research about the constitution of an entrepreneurial class among immigrants and ethnic minorities, especially in the hotel, restaurant and retail trade. This increase in scientific literature about the subject, especially in France, the United Kingdom and other countries of Northern Europe is associated both with the real increase in the number of shops owned by immigrants, and with the growing visibility of this 'ethnic commerce' in cities such as Paris (Ma Mung and Simon 1990), Brussels (Vanhoren and Bracke 1992) and Amsterdam (Boissevan 1992), as well as more widely across the UK and USA (Barrett et al. 1996). From an initial pattern of geographical concentration of community oriented businesses in certain urban areas, especially the inner city, there has also been some sectorial diversification and spatial spreading, although this remains limited.

Despite the emergence of this rich literature, the main questions raised for debate, as well as the theoretical approaches that have been formulated, are almost all based on the experiences of ethnic entrepreneurs settled in North American or British towns. As far as Southern European countries are concerned, with the exception of France, and the work of Knights (this volume, Chapter 6) on Bangladeshis in Rome and Herranz Gómez (1991) on Latin American shopkeepers in Madrid, scientific attention devoted to this issue remains meagre. As a result, the construction of a conceptual body of literature that incorporates the findings of the empirical research developed in Southern Europe is still in its infancy. The main reason for this lies in the relative youth of the process of immigration in these countries (Portugal, Spain, Italy and Greece). Thus, until very recently, research has tended to adopt a more comprehensive approach, focusing on the framework of immigration, or features of the labour market in general, rather than the experience of particular groups such as ethnic entrepreneurs.

Nonetheless, such broad studies point to a number of interesting questions concerning the presence of immigrants in the tertiary sector, which are important in understanding the nature of ethnic business in Southern European countries. First, unlike the previous immigration to Northern European countries, the tertiary sector concentrates a large percentage (more than 40 per cent in Italy; more than 50 per cent in Spain and Portugal) of the legal active population coming from non-European countries. Besides the structural changes of the economies of Southern European countries, which point to a natural growth of the service sector associated with the process of expansion and diversification of individual consumption, a number of researchers stress the links between the growth of a foreign presence in commerce, and the expansion of parallel markets, clearly visible in activities such as hawking (Barsotti and Lecchini 1989; Gozálvez Pérez 1996; King and Konjhodzic 1995; Malheiros 1996). This situation contributes to the growth of small businesses and the number of isolated workers, which is naturally reinforced by strategies of family work among certain immigrant groups, and also by the fragmentation of the tertiary labour market.

Focusing on the situation of a minority group over-represented in certain sections of wholesale and retail trade in Lisbon (the communities of Indian origin), this chapter seeks to address three main questions:

- How does this community fit in the global pattern of immigration experienced by Portugal?
- What are the characteristics of the entrepreneurialism developed by the members of this community, and especially what are its spatial characteristics?
- And finally, do these characteristics reproduce patterns normally associated with immigrant business, or do they show a different pattern?

Approaches to ethnic entrepreneurialism – a summary

Within existing literature on ethnic entrepreneurialism (Barrett et al. 1996; Vanhoren and Bracke 1992; Waldinger 1989), it is possible to identify four basic approaches (with some variants) to the development of business strategies among minority groups (figure 5.1). The *cultural*

	Cultural approach	Economic opportunities approach		Reactive approach	Interactionist approach
		Based on characteristics of the ethnic group	Based on characteristics of the host society		
Explanation for ethnic entrepreneurialism	Previous experience in commerce Availability of capital Cultural importance of discipline and orientations towards economic risk Strong kinship and family ties	Exploitation of advantage based on good knowledge of market for ethnic goods within community	Acquisition of capital, skills and knowledge of local market niches after initial period as employee	Unemployment, lack of alternative opportunities and labour market discrimination leads to entrepreneurialism as escape	Combines elements of other approaches
Basic criticisms of approach	Some migrant groups involved in business do not have a cultural background oriented to entrepreneurship Endogenous propensity for business still requires favourable local context	Limited by size of ethnic minority demand, which is often insufficient	Difficult to distinguish from reactive strategy	May be limited by protectionism which makes access to market niches difficult for foreign entrepreneurs Reactive strategy still requires finance and a suitable market	Despite its broader view, this approach can be over-inclusive, and fail to specify most salient factor

Figure 5.1 Approaches to ethnic entrepreneurialism: basic explanations and criticisms

approach stresses the importance of factors endogenous to the immigrant communities in the process of establishing ethnic businesses. This model restates, in a scientific way, traditional arguments justifying the over-representation of some ethnic groups (such as Jews, Lebanese, Indians, etc.) in some branches of commerce. For example, it suggests that the cultural heritage of some immigrant groups incorporates values of working discipline and economic risk which lead them towards entrepreneurial initiatives. Moreover, the strong sense of identity among these communities enables the mobilisation of kinship and family networks with the purpose of intensifying work (working long hours), reducing labour costs and finding financial support when needed. Additionally, some authors mention the importance of entrepreneurial experience in the countries of origin of some groups of immigrants (Ma Mung and Simon 1990; Vanhoren and Bracke 1992).

Despite the relevance of the arguments presented in this approach, its limitations become evident: firstly because some minority groups who have developed entrepreneurial strategies were pushed towards these strategies by the limitations posed by host authorities to the development of other economic activities. Thus legal restrictions on land ownership imposed on Indians in colonial East Africa and on Jews in several European countries during the Middle Ages provide examples of this situation. Secondly, a number of migrant groups in which entrepreneurialism is now important hardly possess a cultural heritage directed to business (for example, Cape Verdians in Lisbon or Portuguese in France). Finally, it can be argued that propensity for business among minorities will only be realised if the market conditions of the host country present niches where immigrant businesses can survive.

This latter remark leads to a second general approach, based on the _economic opportunities_ offered by the host country. The first variant of this approach derives from research that suggests an association between the proportion of ethnic entrepreneurs in an area and the proportion of residents belonging to that particular ethnic group (Ma Mung and Simon 1990; Waldinger 1989). Also, studies about the evolution of ethnic businesses, once again mostly based in the experiences of the Anglo-Saxon world, suggest that the first and dominant forms of ethnic entrepreneurialism that develop in host countries are directed to the local ethnic market (Barrett et al. 1996; Salt 1993; Vanhoren and Bracke 1992). This implies that a preferential location for such business activity is in quarters with a dominance of foreign residents. Ethnic entrepreneurs have some initial advantages in satisfying the needs of their compatriots due to their better knowledge of the specific consumption practices of the community and to the relations of trust that often exist between the members of a minority group in a strange society. However, commercial success in such cases clearly depends in part on the size and purchasing power of the ethnic community.

Within this approach there is also a second variant that tries to explain why certain members of foreign communities move to businesses directed to satisfy the needs of non-ethnic markets. After a period of development of skills and material accumulation as employees, some members of ethnic minorities start their own businesses in the sector where they have previously worked. The desire for more independence associated with segmentation and externalisation processes in a number of large firms may lead former employees to small business, especially in industry or industrial services. This is the case of several members of the Cape Verdian minority in Lisbon who run subcontracting companies in the construction sector.

The third kind of model (*reactive approach*) in certain respects complements the second variant presented. According to this perspective, the development of entrepreneurial strategies by immigrants is mainly a response to a situation of disadvantage and discrimination in the labour market. The evolution of the labour market situation of immigrants after the late 1970s has given stronger weight to this approach. Thus the important growth of unemployment among immigrants since the late 1970s (Castles et al. 1987; Tripier 1990), again associated with processes of segmentation and externalisation within medium and large firms, has also contributed to the development of entrepreneurial strategies among ethnic minorities. The main goal of these strategies was to ensure survival in a new economic context. Associated with this reactive perspective is, in many cases, the image of immigrants who are pushed into business without enough capital and knowledge to develop the activity. This may lead to situations of market saturation, business failure and minimal profit rates (Barrett et al. 1996).

Finally, the *interactionist approach* has the virtue of offering a more comprehensive approach to the phenomenon of ethnic entrepreneurialism. By combining the internal features associated with ethnic entrepreneurs and the structural features of the host society (employment situation, consumption trends, unexplored commercial niches, legal framework) this approach is more complete and offers a broader conceptual framework for research on ethnic entrepreneurialism. However, the diverse genesis and forms of organisation of ethnic entrepreneurs settled in different countries obliges researchers to select carefully their conceptual model, or the combination of elements that help to explain each particular case-study.

Meanwhile, it is important to stress that ethnic businesses are not randomly distributed among the different commerce and service sectors. Despite some evolution, most researchers stress concentration in low-order retail trades, restaurants and fast-food shops, street-hawking and small hotels. All these are mainly directed to a low/middle class demand, both ethnic and non-ethnic, and have in common a flexibility in opening hours, the possibility of intensifying the use of family labour, and the need for a relatively low initial investment. However, not only is an evolution to more competitive and demanding sectors occurring, but also some communities have become involved in businesses outside the above-mentioned sectors. The case study of Indian entrepreneurs in Lisbon which follows will touch on this question.

Indian Communities in Lisbon – migratory process and main features

Historical background

The contemporary presence of Indian communities in Lisbon is a process that must be understood within the framework of the evolution of the Portuguese colonial empire, including its dissolution. When the Portuguese established themselves in parts of India, notably Goa, and at several points along the coast of Mozambique during the 16th century, they allowed Hindu merchants from the West Coast of India and Muslim sailors to maintain and even to develop their commercial exchanges in the Indian Ocean. In practice, the maritime trade developed by Indians fitted well in the mercantile logic of the Portuguese Empire and, in some cases, Hindu traders were able to help the Portuguese in their fight against Muslims by their control of the Ocean.

When the nature of the Portuguese Empire changed and Mozambique became a potentially productive colony and not simply a stop-off point for the slave trade and for support of the Indian sea route, the role of Indian merchants underwent important changes. Efforts to colonise Mozambique in the second half of the 19th century created the conditions for the settlement of, and new commercial development by, Indian traders.

This process, which also occurred in British East African colonies, was the result of the penetration of the capitalist economy in Africa which brought the monetary exchange system to local populations and created new consumption habits. Profiting from their previous experience in trade, and from the absence of business competition (Europeans were too far away and it took some time before their attention was drawn to retail trade in Africa), Hindu, Muslim and Ismailian merchants coming from the West Coast of India started to become established all along the East Coast of Africa, including Mozambique.

In addition, Catholics from Goa found their way to Mozambique in this period. Although this group did not specialise in trade, their presence was notable in colonial public services (administration, health, justice) and in the Catholic church. This resulted from their 'noble' origins and high qualifications, but especially from their cultural proximity to the colonial rulers. This connection between Goanese and public services in Mozambique intensified in the last quarter of the 19th century, due to the development of the administrative structure of the territory.

Until the early 1960s, relations between the Indian communities established in Mozambique and the remaining Portuguese colonies in India (Goa, Damão and Diu) were kept under the logic of the Oriental Empire. Migratory networks as well as contract work were by then established, ensuring flows between the two areas. Then, in 1961, the loss of the Portuguese territories in India and their subsequent integration into India had natural effects on the Indian communities of Mozambique. On the one hand, the Salazar government expelled some Indian citizens from Mozambique as a retaliation measure. On the other hand, relations between India and Portugal were cut and the old migratory links suffered major interruptions. However, the Indian communities established in Mozambique kept their high level of organisation, as well as their importance in commerce.

Contemporary flows

Despite a few arrivals of individuals of Indian origin coming mainly from Goa and Mozambique in the 1950s and 1960s with the purpose of completing their college studies or professional training, the presence of Indian communities in Portugal only really became visible after 1974. This growth in the number of ethnic Indians in Portugal had its origins in the troubled political process that led to the independence of the Portuguese colonies in Africa, including Mozambique, in 1974/75. Strongly involved in economic activities, with a particular emphasis on retail and wholesale shops, many members of Indian communities found it impossible to continue living in a country moving towards a socialist regime, where nationalisation of businesses was one of the initial economic goals. Moreover, the 1973 experience of Uganda, where an Africanisation process led to the expulsion of Indian communities, was still present in the minds of many ethnic Indians in Mozambique. As political power was transferred to African leaders, many members of these minorities felt that some kind of retaliation could be developed against them and their families, and took the option of leaving the country. Meanwhile, as far as the Catholic Goanese community was concerned, their strong link to the Portuguese colonial administration, as well as a higher level of intermarriage, were additional factors contributing to their departure from Mozambique.

It is important to note that the Portuguese legislation (Decreto Lei 308/A of 1975) concerning the attribution of Portuguese nationality to those coming from ex-colonies was particularly favourable to ethnic Indians born in Africa or in Portuguese India, allowing them to opt for Portuguese nationality. Therefore, most of the members of Indian communities arriving in Portugal after 1974 had Portuguese nationality, a situation that was shared by some ethnic Indians who remained in Mozambique. Meanwhile, the migratory flow that became established in 1974/75 was prolonged for more than ten years due to the Mozambican civil war that prevented all attempts to reach political and economic stability in one of the poorest countries of the world. At the same time, the settlement of the Indian communities in Portugal created the necessary solidarity networks to support a migratory chain between Mozambique and Portugal.

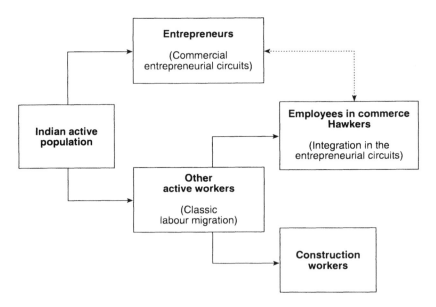

Figure 5.2 Simplified typology of Indian active population arriving in Lisbon

In the late 1980s the process of peace and democratisation in Mozambique, which led to the 1994 election, contributed to a significant decrease in the number of arrivals of ethnic Indians coming from this ex-colony. In contrast, however, the flow of immigrants arriving directly from India continued to rise throughout this period, such that after 1989, new arrivals amongst the Hindu community – who made up the bulk of new arrivals in recent years – had their main source in Diu, India.

Such new arrivals to the Indian communities in Lisbon follow, essentially, two basic patterns (figure 5.2): firstly, persons who arrive via the commercial circuits established by Indian communities, either as entrepreneurs or employees and street-hawkers; and secondly, workers who come into the secondary labour market, principally in the construction sector. Concerning the first type of flow, it is important to stress some diversification from initial origins, with source areas now including other countries of the East Coast of Africa as well as people coming directly from India (i.e. Diu, Goa and Gujarat), Pakistan and, more recently, Bangladesh. In the latter case, the presence of some ethnic Indian entrepreneurs in the construction sector supports networks that sustain this migration flow. Furthermore, the strong labour demand generated by several mega-projects of construction (such as the new Tagus bridge, the 1998 International Expo precinct, the new Ford-Volkswagen factory and the Columbus shopping centre) is also contributing to stimulate the arrival of new workers, mainly from Africa, but also from other origins, such as Diu.

General characteristics of the Indian communities in Lisbon

As a result of the migration processes described above, there are four Indian communities established in the Lisbon Metropolitan Area in the last 20 years: Hindus, Muslims, Ismailians[1] and Catholics from Goa. Besides their cultural and religious differences, also demographic, economic and geographical variables show the distinctive features of each community, although all but the Goanese identify themselves with the Indian ethnic group. The self-identification of the Goanese as Indo-European is supported by the long miscegenation process that occurred in Goa, which gave birth to a specific culture where the Catholic religion and Portuguese cultural practices (food, language, etc.) played determinant roles. This process of socio-cultural mixing was reinforced by the recruitment of Catholics from Goa to the clergy and into public

1 Although Ismailians are a group with origins in the Shi'a sect of Islam, their specific religious and socio-cultural organisation justifies separate classification from the broader Muslim group. Besides the specific nature of socio-cultural practices and holy places recognised by Ismailians, they also show distinct characteristics in both the business and residential realms.

service, not only in Goa but also in other places of the Portuguese Empire, including Mozambique.

The information which follows is based on in-depth interviews with community leaders and a questionnaire administered to 501 ethnic Indian families living in the Lisbon Metropolitan Area, corresponding to 2128 individuals, or approximately 8 per cent of the estimated population of Indian origin resident in Greater Lisbon. These questionnaires were distributed proportionally to the population of each of the different Indian communities of Lisbon[2] with the purpose of ensuring their representation in the sample. In addition, a separate survey of Indian shops in Lisbon was also conducted. This survey covered 55 establishments (46 per cent of the total number of ethnic Indian businesses of the area) concentrated in the part of inner city and its major access routes where such shops are over-represented, namely the Avenida Almirante Reis and the Martim Moniz area. The data collected enabled identification of commercial strategies, employment practices, financial support, product supplies and spatial distribution of businesses owned by ethnic Indian entrepreneurs. In addition to these data collection techniques, participant observation was also carried out in 1992, with follow-ups in 1995 and 1996.[3]

Table 5.1   Population of Indian origin by community, 1992

	Lisbon Metropolitan Area (LMA)		Other regions		Portugal		Concentration in LMA (%)
	No	%	No	%	No	%	
Hindus	8,000	30.5	800	11.3	8,800	26.4	90.9
Muslims	7,600	29.0	300	4.2	7,900	23.7	96.2
Ismailians	4,600	17.6	1,000	14.1	5,600	16.8	82.1
Goanese	6,000	22.9	5,000	70.4	11,000	33.0	54.6
TOTAL	26,200	100.0	7,100	100.0	33,300	100.0	78.7

Source: Recenseamento Geral da População, 1981; Author's questionnaire, 1992.

Taking all the communities together, the number of individuals living in Portugal is estimated at around 35,000, with a very high degree of concentration in Lisbon, except for the Goanese (table 5.1). As noted above, the Goanese differentiate themselves clearly from the other communities: there is an over-representation of white-collar profes-

2 The only exception is the Goanese community. Due to its geographical dispersion, the sample only included about 5 per cent of the estimated population of this group.
3 A more detailed account of much of this work is published in Portuguese in Malheiros (1996).

sionals and administrative workers (table 5.2), a very high level of education (almost 25 per cent of adults possess a college degree, compared to 10 per cent recorded for the Portuguese population as a whole in the 1991 census) and an older age structure (figure 5.3). All these features reflect the old link between Goanese and public service (administration, justice, medicine) as well as similar patterns of cultural behaviour of Portuguese and Goanese (for example in terms of similar fertility patterns, the high percentage of inter-marriage, etc.).

Table 5.2 Active population of Indian communities by economic activity, 1992

	Hindus		Muslims		Ismailians		Goanese	
	N°	%	N°	%	N°	%	N°	%
Professional and technical	1	0.3	8	3.4	12	5.2	60	36.6
Clerical	5	1.6	8	3.4	6	2.6	64	39.0
Commerce	147	46.2	151	63.7	149	65.1	6	3.7
Street traders	37	11.6	3	1.3	8	3.5	0	0.0
Hotel sector	6	1.9	22	9.3	19	8.3	3	1.8
Personal and domestic services	5	1.6	9	3.8	11	4.8	0	0.0
Business services	13	4.1	23	9.7	18	7.9	27	16.5
Industry	9	2.8	6	2.5	3	1.3	1	0.6
Construction	92	28.9	7	3.0	1	0.4	1	0.6
Transport/ Communications	3	0.9	0	0.0	2	0.9	2	1.2
TOTAL	318	100.0	237	100.0	229	100.0	164	100.0

Source: Author's questionnaire, 1992.

The other three communities, which account for the bulk of ethnic Indian entrepreneurs, present younger age structures, particularly the Hindus (figure 5.3), and a strong specialisation in commerce (table 5.2). Differences between the occupations of Hindus and the two groups of Muslims can however be identified, and point to their specific migration histories. Thus a higher level of social diversity was found in the Hindu community, with a large number of lower caste groups. This situation is sustained by labour migration directed to street-hawking, construction and commerce, mainly in the employment of richer Indians from across the different communities. The younger age structure and an over-representation of men in the 20–34 age-group are features normally associated with recently established immigrant groups.

In contrast, Muslims and Ismailians are predominantly involved in

Jorge Malheiros

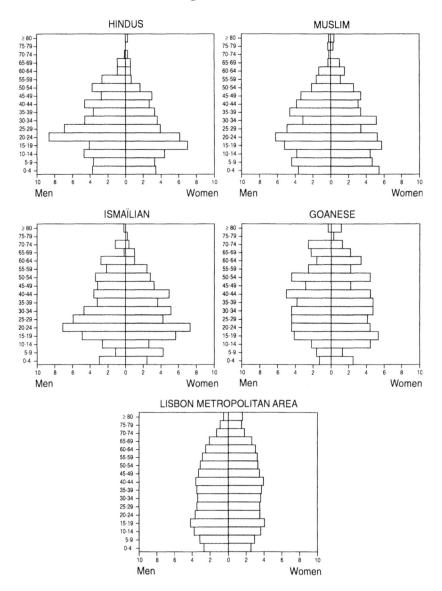

Figure 5.3   Age structure of the Indian communities and of the total population in the Lisbon Metropolitan Area

business and commerce, a specialisation which is particularly evident when the proportion of active Muslims and Ismailians working in commerce (more than 65 per cent) is compared with the average for the population of Greater Lisbon as a whole (around 15 per cent, according to the 1991 Census). Nonetheless, there is an apparent progress towards diversification in the service sector, as shown by the quite high proportion of hoteliers and providers of business services (such as car rental and accountancy).

Indian traders in Lisbon

Specialisation, geographical features and commercial strategies

Indian traders are not distributed randomly through the various sectors of commercial activity. In the case of Lisbon, there are two main commercial systems: the retail trade of furniture dominated by Ismailians and the commercial chain of products imported from the Far East (such as toys and electronic goods) controlled by Muslim and Hindu entrepreneurs (table 5.3). This chain starts with import/wholesale shops (bazaars) situated in a specific area of the inner city (figure 5.4), basically two streets and a new shopping centre in a run-down square near the centre of Lisbon (Martim Moniz). There is some vertical expansion of this chain through tobacconists, stationery and other small retail shops in the area. In addition, the chain also extends through Lisbon's markets and periodic fairs. However, although Indian traders and hawkers are well represented in all these commercial sectors, most retail sales of the products imported and distributed by the Indian wholesale shops are completed by Portuguese traders.

Table 5.3 Distribution of shops owned by Indians in the city of Lisbon, by sector, 1992

	Total shops	Indian-owned	% Indian-owned
WHOLESALE	1,449	98	6.8
RETAIL	11,639	196	1.7
of which			
Food	2,897	25	0.9
Chemists	779	15	1.9
Shoes/Clothing	2,380	34	1.4
Furniture	807	66	8.2
Misc. goods	265	13	4.9
Jewellers	743	10	1.3
Stationery/Tobacconists	288	21	7.3
Others	3,480	12	0.3

Sources: Compiled from Lista Telefónica Nacional - Páginas Amarelas 1992/93; Lista do Código Postal/Giro de Compras 1992; Lista da Comunidade Hindú; Author's survey of Indian shops in Lisbon; Recenseamento do Comércio 1991, CML, DMAC.

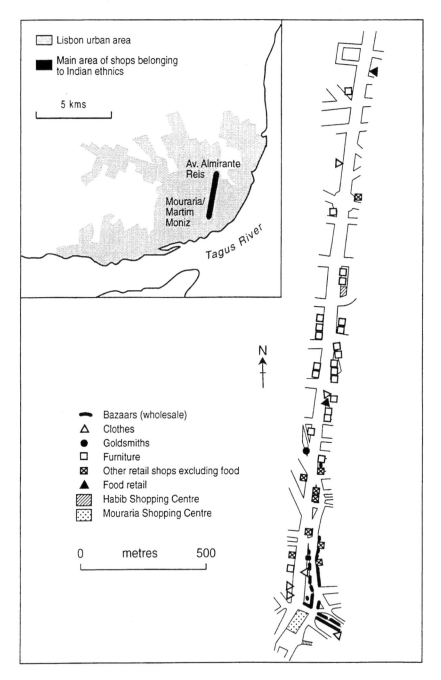

Figure 5.4 Indian ethnic businesses along the Avenida Almirante Reis and in the Martim Moniz area

The furniture shops represent a strategy of horizontal expansion and a concentration in retail activities. The furniture supplies of these shops are either imported, or bought from national factories owned by the Portuguese-born population. The location of these shops on a route connecting the suburbs with the secondary centre of Martim Moniz (figure 5.4) demonstrates a good knowledge of commercial strategy by Indian entrepreneurs. Whereas the wholesale shops (bazaars) occupy narrow secondary streets well-known by specific customers (such as hawkers), the furniture shops are placed in central streets where commercial spaces are large and well-lit.

Table 5.4 Population interviewed working in commerce according to professional status

Ethnic group	Population interviewed working in commerce	Employers and self-employed	
		No.	%
Hindus	184	123	66.7
Muslims	154	108	70.1
Ismailians	157	106	67.5
Total	495	337	68.0
Total for Lisbon and Tagus valley region	221,410	72,088	32.6

Source: Author's questionnaire, 1992.

The over-representation in commerce of members of the Hindu, Muslim and Ismailian communities points to their specific role in Portuguese society. Meanwhile, in analysing the geographical trajectories of Indian entrepreneurs it is possible to identify a continuation of commercial activities and, frequently, a specialisation in certain sectors of trade. For example, half of the wholesale traders who responded to the questionnaire carried out the same activity in Mozambique. Many of the remainder had transferred from clothes shops, which was an important sector of specialisation of Indian entrepreneurs in Mozambique (Mendes 1979), to the new activity of import and distribution of goods from the Far East. The furniture trade appears to be a unique specialisation of Indian entrepreneurs in Lisbon. Examples of such specialisation have not been found either in East Africa nor in other European countries, such as the United Kingdom. Overall, though, the durability of trade practices along the migratory path suggest a learning process in business and entrepreneurial strategies that has given these merchants the ability to adapt their commercial options to the conditions of new local environments. It is worth noting that two of the castes (Vania and Lohana) which are heavily represented in the Hindu community in Lisbon have long-standing associations with commerce, with the Vania involved in maritime trade in the Indian Ocean before the arrival of the Portuguese.

Although some features of Indian commerce in Lisbon are also shared by Portuguese merchants in the city, other characteristics reveal some unique elements. Firstly, the proportion of self-employed and employers amongst the Indian population in the commercial sector is much higher than for the Lisbon population as a whole in this sector (table 5.4). This shows a high degree of materialisation of aspirations to personal economic independence which are shared by many who work in commerce. In turn, this tendency towards economic autonomy in commerce is sustained by a close relationship between domestic, community and commercial strategies. Not only are firms frequently set up through the association of members of the same family, but also the capital necessary to start the business is generally found within the family or, in some cases, with community support, with these two situations accounting for 70 per cent of the businesses interviewed. Associations between white and Indian partners are rare, as is the use of bank loans. Regarding employment, endogenous practices are also privileged, with ethnic employees clearly over-represented, despite the use of Portuguese workers in some larger shops.

Economically, these businesses enjoy a reduction in costs due to the possibility of profiting from family work. This reduces the expenses associated with employing outside workers, and creates the conditions for flexible management and extended working hours, if necessary. The reduction of costs resulting from these strategies allows traders to work with small but competitive profit margins. Relationships between traders of the same community as well as between employers and employees of the same ethnic group are, at least outwardly, based on principles of confidence. Therefore the establishment of new shops is frequently supported, with advice and eventually capital, by the existing businessmen, who are frequently members of the extended family of the young entrepreneur.

The geographical concentration of shops also plays a role in the commercial system. To Indian traders, being together represents a situation of potential competition, but more normally of effective co-operation. Because most are small or medium entrepreneurs, geographical proximity allows the adoption of common strategies in the supply of products, especially if they are imported. In the system based on the import of goods from South-East Asia, the concentration of wholesale shops is also beneficial to customers because they are able to find what they need in a small area. As a whole, good management of the geographical concentration of shops helps create economies of scale. It is also important to note that the entrepreneurial systems controlled by Indian traders are not based on local ethnic markets, but rather sales are clearly dominated by non-Indian customers, who normally account for more than 75 per cent of sales. Indeed, in the inner city area where Indian businesses are concentrated, the number of residents of Indian origin is very low.

Table 5.5 presents the basic features of the two commercial circuits that have been discussed. Besides the differences found in the commercial strategies associated with each kind of business, another distinctive element is that of expansion and diversification of activities by Ismailians. Not only do they tend to employ more Portuguese workers, but they also show clearer strategies of sectoral diversification (especially to services) and geographical dispersion, indicated by the '+ −' notation on the table.

Table 5.5 Features of the two main commercial sectors of Indian entrepreneurs in Lisbon

	Import and distribution of goods from the Far East (mostly Hindus and Muslims)	Furniture retail trade (Ismailians)
Employment		
Self-employment	+	+
Employment of ethnic workers	+	+ −
Employment of family workers	+	+ −
Management and finance		
Family-run businesses	+	+
Family-financed businesses	+	+
Commercial strategies		
Horizontal integration	−	+
Vertical integration (import-wholesale-retail)	+	−
External supply	+	−
Aimed at non-ethnic customers	+	+
Trend to diversification	−	+ −
Geographical features		
Geographical concentration	+	+ −
Location in areas with significant Indian population	−	−
Presence in inner city	+	+ −

Effect of local conditions on settlement/expansion of ethnic commerce

National and local conditions have played an important role in the process of generating opportunities for ethnic Indian entrepreneurialism in Lisbon. However, the geographical and socio-economic environment offers possibilities that may or may not be used by the ethnic entrepreneurs. Regarding the geographical environment where the shops studied are located, two potential advantageous features may be found. On the one hand, this area of the inner city already had a traditional specialisation in wholesaling. Since the early 1970s, for example, Portuguese entrepreneurs were established in this area, and had developed commercial relations with street-hawkers and other small retailers. Meanwhile, in Almirante Reis, the main avenue where most of the retail furniture shops belonging to ethnic Indians are located, the establishment of furniture retailing predated the arrival of Indian entrepreneurs. However, the physical decay of the area and its reduced prestige had also contributed to a reduction in the cost of commercial space. Linked to this, the reduced economic capacity of small Indian entrepreneurs limited their access to areas of Lisbon with higher land values.

As far as the socio-economic context is concerned, two issues deserve highlighting. First, the high proportion of the Portuguese population with low incomes creates an important market for the cheap and low quality products imported from the Far East by Indian entrepreneurs. Moreover, the expansion of domestic consumption that occurred in Portugal in the late 1980s and in the early 1990s also contributed to enlarge this potential market. However, in recent years, the expansion of hypermarkets in the Lisbon Metropolitan Area has changed conditions in what is an increasingly competitive commercial sector, causing major problems for small businesses, including those belonging to ethnic Indians. Some Indian entrepreneurs are now altering their strategies to adapt to the presence of these large commercial outlets. Interestingly, it is now possible to find some of these retail traders buying large amounts of goods in hypermarkets for resale at fairs, street markets or even small shops. A second point to note is that when the first entrepreneurs became established in Lisbon, around 1976, they were able to benefit from some specific features of Portuguese society in the period of return from the ex-colonies. This movement involved the return of more than half a million individuals, of whom 60 per cent settled in the Lisbon Metropolitan Area. These new residents needed to buy houses, household equipment and furniture, and this increased opportunities for investment in furniture retailing. It is significant that some of the first furniture shops belonging to ethnic Indians were established in the suburbs to the south of Lisbon, an area of very significant residential expansion, especially during the 1970s. Finally, the absence of large commercial chains in the furniture sector reduces competition and allows more scope for Indian shops in this sector to survive, especially those which adopt strategies of family association.

Conclusion

This chapter has described the development of Indian ethnic entrepreneurialism in Lisbon, a phenomenon that started in the middle 1970s following the arrival of ethnic Indians from Mozambique after independence. Indian shops concentrated in a particular part of the inner city and its access routes, and became integrated in two main commercial sectors: the import and distribution of goods from the Far East, dominated by Hindus and Muslims; and furniture retailing, associated with Ismailians. Within these sectors, they have been remarkably resilient, providing employment not only for family members, but also for new Indian arrivals, and in some cases for non-Indians.

In comparing this experience with the theoretical approaches presented in first part of the chapter, many features of the interactive approach are evident, although with important nuances. For example, existing cultural traditions associated with commercial practices were present among several sections of the Indian community now settled in the Lisbon Metropolitan Area, with the important exception of the Goanese.

Nevertheless, the migratory process which brought these groups to Portugal passed through various stages, and original skills have been refined and adapted throughout this process. As King and Knights (1994) stress for Bangladeshi immigrants in Rome, those who move with a long migration history behind them have advantages over those who are migrating for the first time. If this is relevant for labour migrants, it is probably more important for migrant entrepreneurs who experience higher economic risks associated with their own initiatives.

Finally, although evolution of the cultural background of Indian entrepreneurs through their migration history is important in understanding the current pattern of ethnic business, the expansion of these businesses can only be fully understood with reference to the significance of ethnic networks, and the 'demonstration effect' associated with the expansion of all successful small businesses. In turn, this occurred in a national and local framework of relatively favourable conditions, including location within traditional shopping areas, and an almost unprecedented expansion of domestic consumption. It is the fortunate combination of these factors, rather than a simple (or simplistic) expla-

nation, which accounts for the apparent success of Indian entrepreneurialism in Lisbon today.

References

Barsotti, O. and Lecchini, L. (1989) L'immigration des pays du Tiers-Monde en
Italie, *Revue Européenne des Migrations Internationales*, 5(3), pp. 41–63.

Barrett, G.A., Jones, T.P. and McEvoy, D. (1996) Ethnic minority business: theoretical discourse in Britain and North America, *Urban Studies*, 33(4–5), pp.
783–809.

Boissevain, J. (1992) Les entreprises ethniques au Pays Bas, *Revue Européenne des
Migrations Internationales*, 8(2), pp. 97–106.

Castles, S., Booth, H. and Wallace, T. (1987) *Here for Good. Western Europe's New
Ethnic Minorities*. London: Pluto.

Herranz Gómez, Y. (1991) Un pequeño empresariado latinoamericano en
Madrid, *Sociologia del Trabajo*, 13, pp. 75–95.

Gozálvez Perez, V. (1996) L'immigration étrangère en Espagne (1985–1994),
Revue Européenne des Migrations Internationales, 12(1), pp. 11–33.

King, R. and Knights, M. (1994) Bangladeshis in Rome: a case of migratory
opportunism, in Gould W.T.S. and Findlay A.M., eds. *Population Migration
and the Changing World Order*. Chichester: Wiley, pp. 127–43.

King, R. and Konjhodzic, I. (1995) *Labour, Employment and Migration in Southern
Europe*. Brighton: University of Sussex Research Papers in Geography, 19.

Ma Mung, E. and Simon, G. (1990) *Commerçants Maghrébins et Asiatiques en
France. Agglomération Parisienne et Villes de L'Est*. Paris: Masson.

Malheiros, J.M. (1996) *Imigrantes na Região de Lisboa: os Anos da Mudança.
Imigração e Processo de Integração das Comunidades de Origem Indiana*. Lisbon:
Colibri.

Mendes, M.C. (1979) *Maputo antes da Independência: Geografia de uma Cidade
Colonial*. Lisbon: Centro de Estudos Geográficos, Faculdade de Letras,
Universidade de Lisboa.

Salt, J. (1993) The geographical impact of migration in Europe: lessons for
Europe from the new world, in King, R., ed., *The New Geography of European
Migrations*. London: Belhaven, pp. 246–59.

Tripier, M. (1990) *L'Immigration dans la Classe Ouvrière en France*. Paris:
L'Harmattan.

Vanhoren, I. and Bracke, S. (1992) *Entrepreneuriat Ethnique dans la Region
Bruxelles-Capitale*. Leuven: HIVA, Katholieke Universiteit Leuven.

Waldinger, R. (1989) Structural opportunity or ethnic advantage? Immigrant
business development in New York, *International Migration Review*, 23(1), pp.
48–72.

6

Migrants as Networkers: The Economics of Bangladeshi Migration to Rome

Melanie Knights

Since the late 1980s the Bangladeshi community in Rome has grown rapidly to become the largest in Europe outside the United Kingdom. The vast majority of the 12,000 or so Bangladeshis who are currently present in the city arrived clandestinely but they quickly proved remarkably adept at acquiring legal status in Italy. By contrast their penetration of Italy's formal labour market has been weak and, as this chapter will show, their economic activities have been largely confined to the parallel economy.

Official statistics and derivative accounts of migration to Italy have revealed little about the nature and dynamics of Bangladeshi migration to Rome. This is largely because of the clandestine nature of the community's formation and the informal nature of its economic functioning; the same may be said of numerous other lesser-known ethnic communities fast becoming established in the city.

The Bangladeshi community in Rome is typical of many recent immigrant groups establishing themselves in Southern Europe and it provides a good example of how we must change our preconceptions about studying international migrations if we are to understand the pressures causing them and the mechanisms guiding them. Below I describe how my attention shifted from Bangladeshi economic activity in Rome to the economic functioning of the Bangladeshi migratory network as I tried to justify, in economic terms, community settlement in the city. The Bangladeshi migrants will be seen to be an economically marginal but far-from-passive element in the overwhelmingly tertiary economy of Rome, continuously re-inventing themselves in order to survive and to keep pace with the growth in their numbers driven by the migratory network.

The account given in this chapter is part of a wider research project which aimed at exploring the origins of Bangladeshis in the city, the process of their migration to Rome and the various stages of community development.[1] I employed a variety of methodologies including a questionnaire, interviews, participant observation and analysis of archival material. The majority of the account below, however, is derived from two periods of participant observation from January 1992 to September 1993 and from March 1994 to April 1995. It will be preceded by some background to Bangladeshi migration and the functioning of the Bangladeshi migratory network. The second section of the chapter ponders why, with so few real opportunities for economic advancement in Rome, there is such a major concentration of Bangladeshis in the city. In fact, over 90 per cent of the Bangladeshis in Italy live in Rome, the highest degree of concentration in the capital of any sizeable immigrant group in Italy. The third part of the chapter seeks to answer this question through an analysis of what I call covert economic activity, while the fourth section links these findings to others relating to the origins and settlement patterns of the community. Having established the 'networking' impetus behind the community's growth, I then briefly consider the economic mechanisms behind the increasing marginalisation and economic decline of the community.

Bangladeshis in Rome: an extension of the global network

On the face of it there is little reason for Bangladeshis to migrate to Italy. There are no historical ties between Italy and Bangladesh, the two countries share no cultural affinity, no common language and there are no obvious religious or geographical links between them. Rome might also be considered as an unlikely choice for Bangladeshi settlement, given that the predominant demand in the Roman labour market is for female domestic workers (see Chell, Chapter 4) and the Bangladeshi community is over 90 per cent male with different employment aspirations.

However, if we look at the evolution of emigration from Bangladesh,

1 This research project culminated in my D.Phil. thesis (Knights 1996a). Other parts of this research which have been published already and which are therefore complementary to the present chapter include findings about immigration methods and routes (King and Knights 1994), the economic and social organisation of the community (Knights 1996b), and its micro-political structures (Knights 1996c). My doctoral research started at Trinity College Dublin and was completed at the University of Sussex. Financially it was assisted by studentships from these two universities and a Leverhulme Study Abroad Scholarship for 1994/5.

we can see that Rome is merely an extension of an expanding global migration network able to adapt to prevailing economic and political conditions worldwide. The first emigrants left a few selected villages in the northeastern district of Sylhet in the 1950s to work in Britain's industrial economy (Gardner 1992). In the 1970s the labour catchment area widened to include other districts in response to the growing labour demand in the Middle East (Osmani 1986). Other migrants left for Europe, largely to the countries operating asylum schemes. Some took advantage of settlement programmes in the United States, Canada and Australia. By the end of the 1980s, high earnings in the expanding economies of the Far East lured Bangladeshis eastwards even without assured employment prospects, while the collapse of communism in the former Soviet Union presented even riskier opportunities in the world's fledgling capitalist states (Knights 1996c).

A series of measures to discourage illegal immigrants in North European countries combined with a dearth of controls, periodical amnesties for illegal immigrants and flourishing parallel economies in Southern Europe are some of the factors put forward to explain 'new' migrations to the South of the continent (King and Rybaczuk 1993, and see also Chapter 1 of the present volume).

Rather like a barometer of opportunity, the Bangladeshi migratory network has expanded and grown in response to opportunities as they have arisen in various parts of the world. Wherever it surfaces, however, the network is characterised by its cohesiveness. The strength of kinship and family ties is illustrated by the fact that the majority of Bangladeshis in the UK still trace their origins to Sylhet (Gardner 1992). Cultural ties are also very strong among Bangladeshis abroad. The unifying force of language and culinary traditions cannot be underestimated when seeking to explain the Bangladeshi tendency to live in close proximity to one another.

The Bangladeshi liberation movement was based on the Bengali language movement and Bengali food takes on almost spiritual qualities among migrants (Gardner 1993). Finally, a tradition of brokers has facilitated the migratory process for countless Bangladeshis, smoothing travel arrangements, overcoming bureaucratic hurdles and exploiting employment opportunities. The existence of brokers explains why so many Bangladeshis in the UK come from Sylhet (Mahmood 1990) and how so many Bangladeshis were able to obtain 'no objection certificates' enabling them to work in the Middle East (Osmani 1986). Below we will see how important the role of brokers has been to community establishment in Rome.

The Bangladeshi community established itself in Rome from a few hundred individuals in 1989 to over 4,000 by the end of June 1990. The majority of the group entered the country clandestinely but acquired legal status in the amnesty provided by Italy's 1990 Martelli Law. The community distinguished itself by its rapid assembly in Rome, its capacity for organisation and its solidarity. It soon became conspicuous because of its residential concentration, predominance of men and large numbers of street-hawkers. As the community continued to grow throughout the period of my fieldwork, so these tendencies became more marked.

Observation of the Bangladeshi migratory network in Rome revealed distinct regional chains which, although integral to the overall network, displayed different characteristics. Each chain displayed different settlement patterns, cultural practices and migratory histories (Knights 1996c).

The chains were also linked to the political hierarchy of the community and to different types of economic activity. As we will see below, these links between regional origin, political hierarchy and economic activities proved a key to understanding the economic rationale behind Bangladeshi migration to Rome which was not immediately apparent from initial observation of Bangladeshi insertion into the Roman labour market.

Types of economic activity in Rome

In 1990 Bangladeshis made a striking entrance into the Roman labour market, and their economic activities have made a significant contribution to the transformation of Rome's 'streetscape'. They may be roughly divided into three types: employees, street-hawkers and entrepreneurs.

Employment

The Roman employment market is characterised by a structural labour surplus and a severe mismatch between labour supply and demand (Caritas di Roma 1992, pp. 191–3). This is confirmed by my observations of the participation of Bangladeshis in the Roman labour market. Bangladeshis form part of a predominantly male workforce seeking unskilled industrial work in a labour market where the chief demand for migrant labour in the formal economy is for female domestic workers.

The participation of Bangladeshis in the formal economy has so far been limited to a small minority who were among the first to arrive in Italy; perhaps had some skill to offer; or who took advantage of training schemes funded by the Lazio Region.[2] The Caritas dossier shows that in 1993, only 306 Bangladeshis had found work through official channels and only 20 appeared to be registered at the employment office by the end of that year (Caritas di Roma 1994, pp. 280, 282). Compared with over 4,000 documented Bangladeshis in the city at that time and at least as many undocumented compatriots, these are small figures indeed. Thus, whether legally present or undocumented, Bangladeshis tend to work in diverse sectors of the secondary labour market and submerged economy, and are largely confined to unskilled, precarious, seasonal and low-paid work. On the whole this is neither commensurate with their qualifications nor with their experience and it certainly does not match their expectations.

I encountered Bangladeshis working as employees in six main areas of the Roman economy: agriculture, the hotel and restaurant trade, domestic service, construction, services and commerce. Work in agriculture varied from one Bangladeshi living and working full-time on a small-holding quite close to the city, to those travelling further afield to do seasonal piecework at harvest time. The rates of pay varied between 35,000 lire a day for work on a tobacco farm to the slightly higher rate of 6,000 lire an hour for picking tomatoes.[3] The full-time employee working on the small-holding lived rent-free in a separate dwelling on the property and was paid 1.3 million lire per month in the informal economy. Although his employer wanted to employ him legally, it was almost impossible under the regulations in place during the time of my fieldwork.[4]

Work in the hotel and restaurant trades varied between specialised and unskilled jobs. Some Bangladeshis were employed as cooks in Italian restaurants while others became specialised pizza cooks or *pizzettari*. By Roman standards, the pay for this work was quite good: about 2 million lire a month for the cook and up to 3 million for a good *pizzettaro*. Other work in hotels and restaurants was paid less: barwork, 1.2 million per month; assistant cook, about the same; kitchen work, 1.3 million; waiting, 50,000 lire per session; and washing up, 1 million per month. Generally these rates of pay were lower than for Italian workers doing the same work. In one restaurant the owner had allegedly replaced an Italian cook earning 3 million lire per month with another

2   These schemes included training to be electricians, plumbers, mechanics etc. Other privately funded schemes included one course funded by AGIP (the state petroleum agency) training immigrants to become petrol pump attendants.
3   During my fieldwork the lira's value fell from approximately 2,200 to the British pound in 1992 to around 2,700 in 1995. At the time of writing (December 1996) the rate is about 2,500, or 1,500 to the US dollar.
4   A subsequent amnesty in 1996 would have made this possible. However, at the time of my fieldwork, the Bangladeshi would have had to return to Dhaka to register at the Italian consulate. His employer could then have applied for him to work as a domestic worker. Clearly few Bangladeshis were prepared to adopt this risky strategy.

Italian earning 2.5 million who was in turn replaced by a Bangladeshi cook earning 2 million lire per month. A kitchen worker told me that although he was theoretically paid the same as Italians, the Italians all received an extra 800,000 lire bonus in cash every month.

Domestic work ranged from live-in domestics to an official, full-time job with a public cleaning contractor paying between 1 and 1.3 million per month. It was extremely rare to find a Bangladeshi doing live-in domestic work.

Work in the construction industry was more common, ranging from brick-laying and painting and decorating to more specialised work like welding or glass cutting. The pay for this kind of work ranged from 1.1 to 1.8 million per month, but was often on a casual basis paying 50,000–60,000 lire per day. Italian casual workers were reportedly paid more.

Bangladeshis were also employed in service jobs, often as an assistant to the owner or to an Italian worker. They worked as petrol pump attendants, car wash attendants, car valets, electricians', plumbers' and mechanics' mates and in courier delivery companies and newspaper distribution. Earnings were modest: 1.2–1.4 million per month (sometimes plus tips) or between 30,000 and 60,000 lire per day.

Commercial activities in the city also employed Bangladeshis, although in a very menial capacity. One particular marketing enterprise specialising in household items and ornaments had a single retail outlet by the Trevi Fountain, but numerous shop windows dotted around the city centre. Bangladeshis were posted at each display window to accompany interested customers to the shop. Bangladeshis were also commonly employed by small market traders or licence holders of itinerant refreshment bars in the city. Pay varied from 30,000 to as much as 80,000 lire per day and the conditions of employment also varied greatly. Market stall assistants tended to start very early, finishing at lunch time, while the conditions of some Bangladeshis working on refreshment stalls verged on slavery. One well-known family of traders in Rome, owning several refreshment, fruit stalls and chestnut-selling licences at major tourist sites, hired many Bangladeshi assistants. They were all housed together in dormitories outside town and worked every single day of the month from very early in the morning until very late at night for no more than 30,000 lire per day.

Bangladeshis tend to avoid very heavy physical work but were often employed as assistants. They gained a reputation for hard work and not challenging their employer. On several occasions Bangladeshis complained to me about employers who refused to pay them. In November 1992, one undocumented Bangladeshi reportedly shot his employer, having suffered maltreatment and non-payment for several months. Undocumented immigrants clearly have no redress against this kind of exploitation. Finally, most Bangladeshis I met had had several jobs in Rome. Most had experienced periods of unemployment and many juggled two part-time jobs simultaneously. Only one of the Bangladeshis known to me, working as a contract cleaner in a bank, remained in the same job throughout the entire period of my fieldwork. However he too had several other more precarious evening jobs which lasted for a few months at a time.

Street-hawking

Bangladeshi street-hawkers very quickly became a prominent feature of Roman street life in the early 1990s. Their involvement in hawking flourished during the period of my fieldwork. Activity ranged from the sale of a few items at cross-roads and in the street to a diverse range of goods sold at several unlicensed 'outlets'. Initially Bangladeshis followed the example of the Polish and Moroccan *lavavetri* who cleaned windscreens at the cross-roads. On major intersections, as one Bangladeshi cleaned the windscreen, others would sell packets of tissues, *arbre magique* car-fresheners and cigarette lighters. Bangladeshi rose sellers were also a common sight early on. Tourists had become quite nervous of the gypsy flower-sellers who (rightly or wrongly) had become synonymous with pick-pockets, and the mild-mannered Bangladeshis were an immediate success. Initially selling only on the street, they soon entered into restaurants, bars and night clubs and would trawl through the parks in the afternoons. Umbrella-selling soon became the domain of Bangladeshis too. As soon as the Roman skies darkened, Bangladeshis would materialise, sitting on church steps with a sports bag full of umbrellas, waiting for the first drops to fall. In Rome the wait was often fruitless, but when the clouds obliged, the Bangladeshis would be there, everywhere, without fail, proffering their wares and uttering a now-familiar 'ombrel-lombrellombrell'.

As time passed and Bangladeshis became more familiar with the city and the habits and needs of its people in the passing seasons, so they penetrated further into the recesses of Roman life and diversified their wares. One still finds Bangladeshis at the cross-roads, but on Sundays and All Saints Day they will be selling flowers, and in the summer windscreen shields. You will find them in the underground stations selling contraband cigarettes and posters. Outside the supermarkets and in the open-air markets they sell oil, garlic and cigarettes. And in the summer, many hawkers leave the city and sell jewellery and sunglasses on the beaches. Some have taken their wares to Milan and Palermo, others to smaller towns in the Lazio region. Bangladeshis tailor their wares to the occasion: on International Women's Day each year, they sell mimosa and during the World Cup Football in 1994 they tapped into the patriotic fervour and sold hooters and flags all over the city. New ideas are generated each year. In 1994, a new craze called 'your-name-on-a-grain-of-rice' caught on as a less risky alternative to jewellery selling and in 1995 ductile balloon dolls filled with flour became a popular addition to the street-hawkers' wares, marking the city streets with tell-tale piles of flour where they burst.

Bangladeshi hawkers fit into a cosmopolitan street scene with its own social and ethnic hierarchy. During my fieldwork nowhere was this more evident than on the Spanish Steps, one of Rome's busiest tourist sites and thoroughfares. This eighteenth-century stairway leads from the church of the Trinità dei Monti and the smart Hotel Hasler, to Rome's most expensive shops in the Via Condotti, the Keats-Shelley memorial and Macdonalds. It links two exclusive areas of the city and provides the perfect photo-opportunity for film-stars and a sunny resting place for backpackers. Its accessibility by underground makes it the perfect pick-up joint for the Roman *pappagalli* who travel in from the suburbs in the afternoons to view legs and breasts from behind fake Raybans. Understandably it soon became a favourite pitch for hawkers.

Before the recent closure of the steps for restoration, the hawking hierarchy descended from the tops of the two upper stairways (the most lucrative spots) across the first terrace and down the wide lower flight to Piazza di Spagna below. First in the pecking order were the *Abruzzesi*, internal migrants from the Abruzzo region of southern Italy, who owned the licences for the *Gelati Bibite* refreshment vans parked at the upper entrances to the steps. Invariably, Bangladeshis were employed for a pittance to assist the seller. The *Abruzzesi* also ran Rome's chestnut stalls, one of which stood in Piazza di Spagna at the entrance to Via Condotti. These too were manned by Bangladeshis. The *Gelati Bibite* in front of the Hasler entrance invariably crowded onto the only other licensed pitch occupied in rotation by Jewish-owned souvenir stalls. Themselves former *abusivi*,[5] the Jews now monopolise one of the most lucrative trades in Rome, controlling licenses which change hands for tens of thousands of pounds. The stall holder usually paid one of the Bangladeshi rose sellers 5,000 lire in the morning to help him set out his wares. Descending the stairs below the souvenir stall, the tourist would pass a row of Italian (con) artists, complete with Panama hats and neckscarves, colouring-in ready-prepared views of the city.

The terrace between the upper and lower flights of stairs was home to a growing number of non-EU artists (usually rejects from the more

5 The term *abusivo* refers to an individual undertaking an unauthorised activity.

prestigious art pitch in Piazza Navona) who earned their living as cari-
caturists. Among them sat a Bangladeshi. Ranged aggressively along
the bottom of the steps were the Moroccan hair tressers whose speciality
was adding an extra '0' to the price for Japanese tourists and threatening
Bangladeshis who tried to copy them. The Moroccans had ousted the
Peruvian masters of colour and weaving who moved to sit slightly
higher up towards the central aisle of the lower staircase, selling plaited
bracelets and silver earrings. Jostling for a level place to spread their
wares on white sheets were hawkers of various nationalities including
Bangladeshis, Senegalese and Ghanaians. Bags, woven rucksacks,
peaked caps, sunglasses and jewellery were the commercial domain of
many nationalities and were bought from the ethnic businesses mush-
rooming around Piazza Vittorio. Perched on the steps at regular
intervals were the Bangladeshi rice-writers (I will enlarge on this market
niche presently). In high summer, they would arrive earlier than any
other sellers in order to get a pitch in the shade on the 'Hasler' side.
Between them the poster sellers spread out their wares.

Weaving in and out among the bodies, up and down the steps and
milling in the Piazza were yet more sellers: Bangladeshis touting roses,
umbrellas and good-luck beetles, a Senegalese be-decked with
sunglasses and a Chinese woman surreptitiously offering cans of coke
and fizzy orange from a carrier bag. Lurking in the nooks and on the
fringes, the drug dealers awaited their clients and watched them lolling
on the steps. And finally, with no alternative, *la bella gente* picked their
way from the 'Hasler' to Via Condotti. Every so often, with one motion
like a flurry of pigeons taking off, the sellers would grab everything they
possessed and scurry from the steps. To the amazement of bystanders,
they would scatter among the crowds in the Piazza, run into the underground tunnels or take refuge for a few minutes in Macdonalds,
sometimes pursued by tenacious customers. There they would wait for
the *vigili* – the municipal police – to disappear, before reassembling one
by one to an uneasy peace.

Perhaps street-selling began as a response to the precariousness of
the Roman labour market. Bangladeshis might sell during periods of
unemployment or to earn extra cash after work. Some undocumented
immigrants claimed that it was hard to find work without papers, and
that selling was the only alternative. However, there is no doubt that
street-hawking in Rome has generated its own momentum. It has flourished in a permissive climate and hawkers are drawn from both legal
and undocumented immigrants, from the educated and uneducated
classes. Earnings are potentially much higher than in employment,
although hawkers risk the confiscation of their goods, and, being highly
visible, are most vulnerable to police control, leading potentially to

deportation (though this was rarely a threat in practice). It is impossible to estimate the average earnings of a street-seller; they depend on the initiative, skill and luck of each vendor. It is as possible to earn nothing in a day and to lose all one's wares as it is possible to earn large sums of money, and the figures vary considerably. One rose-seller told me that the most he had ever earned was 100,000 lire on New Year's Eve, while a Bangladeshi rice-writer became renowned for his vast earnings. Street-sellers probably earn more per month than employees, but they work long hours, run many risks and their fortunes depend on the lenience of the municipal police.

Entrepreneurship

Since 1991 a significant self-employed sector has also developed in the Bangladeshi community as individuals set up shops, import/export businesses, market stalls and restaurants. Many of the businesses were set up as co-operative ventures. They provided work for two or three of the members and the others, in theory, shared in the profits. Almost without exception, the first businesses to be set up were run by Bangladeshi political activists who were the first to become familiar with Italian bureaucracy (Knights 1996c).

The majority of these businesses are located within a few hundred metres of each other near Piazza Vittorio Emanuele, behind the main railway station (figure 6.1). By early 1995 there were 7 general food stores, 4 video shops, 6 jewellery shops, 2 cultural circles cum bars, a clothes shop, a fish shop, a flower shop and an office services centre cum job agency. On Piazza Vittorio market there was a spice stall run by a Bangladeshi, who also ran a grocery store just off the Via Casilina. A restaurant had been opened in Via Principe Amedeo, but was not successful and was sold to some Indian businessmen. Most shops were orientated towards the needs of the Bangladeshi community: food, entertainment and supplies for hawkers. The only exception was a dry-cleaners opened just off the Via Prenestina and serving the local Italian community. In some cases the Bangladeshi shops performed functions which extended beyond their purely commercial role. In particular, two food shops run by leading figures in the Bangladeshi Association had multiple roles. While the Association was canvassing for members, the two shops would double as enrolment points. They also served as Embassy intermediaries: collection points for completed passport application forms and notification of passports available for collection.[6] The

---

6 Undocumented entry strategies obliged most new arrivals to apply for a passport on arrival (King and Knights 1994).

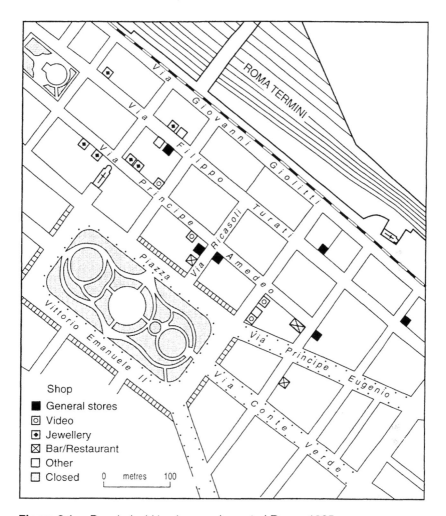

Figure 6.1   Bangladeshi businesses in central Rome, 1995

daily delivery service offered by the shops consolidated communications between the Bangladeshi households; news of demonstrations,
film-shows, concerts or visiting personalities from Bangladesh was
carried to the houses with the groceries. Towards the end of my fieldwork I discovered that one of the shops ran an informal banking service.

'Copy cat' hawkers and commercial overcrowding

One of the most striking aspects of the economic activities of
Bangladeshis was the apparently shameless way in which they copied

other people's successful ideas. It might be argued that there is nothing strange about this, especially in marketing, but what was singular about the Bangladeshi strategy is that it was not limited to practising the same economic activity in another place, but sought to replicate it in exactly the same place, or as near as possible to it! The practice was particularly evident among street-hawkers and entrepreneurs.

I observed one of the best examples of how ideas caught on among street-hawkers in the 'rice-writing' business. 'Your-name-on-a-grain-of-rice' consists in writing a person's name on a grain of rice, inserting it into a tiny glass test tube, attaching it to a piece of cord to be worn around the neck as jewellery. The wheeze was imported from Paris. It required minimal investment, was easily transportable and was for a time highly profitable. The first rice-writer on the Spanish Steps reputedly made $340 per day, and another claimed to have made $34,000 between June and August in the mass youth tourist resort of Rimini. An article appeared in a Dhaka newspaper claiming that one kilogram of rice was worth a large house in the Bangladeshi capital. Not surprisingly, the activity became a craze during the summer. Bangladeshis abandoned their habitual activities and headed off to the seaside with their pockets full of rice. In no time the Spanish Steps was lined with Bangladeshi rice-writers complete with cloned accessories, but all earning rather less than the pioneers.

'Copy-cats' were present in most other hawking activities and made Bangladeshis unpopular not only with the public but also with other sellers. No sooner had Bangladeshis started working at the cross-roads, than they had almost monopolised the business. Drivers on main roads into Rome, having paid once to have their windscreen cleaned, found themselves having to refuse the service at every single crossroads thereafter. In the summer heat, drivers and *lavavetri* sometimes came to blows! Diners in Roman restaurants can remember when they may have been approached by an occasional foreigner trying to sell a rose, but now complain of being bothered by Bangladeshis several times during a meal. A Bangladeshi starting out in the business told me how ashamed he felt as he waited outside a restaurant for the previous Bangladeshi to exit before entering himself and that when he left another Bangladeshi was waiting outside. By 1995, the rain in Rome was producing an epidemic of umbrella sellers. Tourists alighting from their coaches at the Roman Forum would be confronted by six or seven sellers all thrusting exactly the same umbrellas towards them and all saying 'ombrellom-brellombrell'. The proliferation of sellers all touting the same wares made Bangladeshis unpopular with other vendors. Not only did they depress prices, but they seemed to have no sense of space. Street-hawkers of other nationalities described (flabbergasted) how

Bangladeshis would stand by them for several hours watching them, and how the next day, when they returned to their regular pitch, they would find the same Bangladeshi (plus a friend) already there selling the same wares!

This same tendency is evident in figure 6.1 which shows how shops of the same kind are clustered within just a few hundred metres of one another. The same kind of concentration would not have been economically viable previously. All the shops adopted the same formula as the most successful one. Apart from general provisions for the houses, all the general stores supplied street-hawkers with garlic, tissues, windscreen shields, cigarette lighters and so on. All the jewellery shops were set out in the same way and bought from the same suppliers. The video shops rented out the same videos. And as soon as somebody initiated a new idea, someone would be sure to follow suit.

The intriguing aspect of the economic plagiarism described above is that although it appeared to deflate prices and to be detrimental to other sellers, it seemed to be a key component of Bangladeshi economic strategy. This paradox will be discussed further after the next section.

Why Rome?

The economic activities described above encompass three broad categories of individuals: 'risk-takers', 'law-abiders' and 'opportunists'. 'Risk-takers' were individuals, like hawkers, who maximised the risks associated with their migratory project in order to maximise their earnings. They probably do not intend to settle permanently in Italy, but are likely to stay for as long as they can make a good living, or to leave when they have earned enough to secure their future in Bangladesh. 'Law abiders', on the other hand, seek legal establishment. Usually employees, they aim to complete all the necessary bureaucratic procedures to acquire long-term rights in the country. The 'law-abiding' strategy may also apply to some undocumented migrants who prefer low-paid employment in the submerged economy rather than to compete with the hawkers and risk police controls. A third group, the 'opportunists', appear to have no clear economic strategy, but are ready to move towards opportunity. They may be documented or undocumented and have probably tried to leave Italy without success. While waiting for news of opportunity elsewhere, they support themselves, although their strategy seems to lead neither to great riches nor to long-term establishment.

Although these strategies may be attributed to individual Bangladeshis, it is still difficult to reconcile them with the group's concentration and rapid growth in Rome. And the habitual copying of other people's money-making ideas remains a commercial anomaly. Although it is understandable that undocumented, 'risk-takers' may be attracted to Rome's submerged economy, it is not clear why documented 'law-abiders' apparently prefer Rome to cities like Bologna or Milan, where industrial jobs in the formal economy are more readily available, employment conditions are better and wages are twice as high. It is not clear either why the majority of 'risk-takers' and 'opportunists' cluster in Rome. If 'risk-takers' seek to maximise their profits in the short-term, why remain in Rome where commercial overcrowding halves profits? Italy's submerged economy extends southwards towards Sicily and there is no reason why Bangladeshis should not operate in it in the same way as migrants from other ethnic groups do (cf. King 1993). Similarly, that 'opportunists' should remain in Rome where the opportunity of long-term settlement has expired and the short-term prospects of high earnings have been diminished is incomprehensible. Finally, how has Rome maintained its position at the top of the Bangladeshi classification table of opportunity in Europe throughout the 1990s? After all, the opportunity for long-term settlement expired in June 1990; *tangentopoli* (the nation-wide bribes scandal) induced a recession which hit Rome's service economy particularly hard, leading to redundancies and depressed earnings; and a combination of a shift to the right in Rome's administration and alarm about illegal immigration has led to increased vigilance by the municipal authorities.

My continuing failure to make sense of the overall economic strategy of Bangladeshis in Rome compelled me to look beyond the ways in which Bangladeshis participate in the Italian economy and to consider other, less visible forms of economic activity.

The 'network economy'

My interest in a potential covert economy was stimulated by my failure to provide coherent explanations of my initial findings. I was intrigued by the extreme rapidity of Bangladeshi assembly and organisation in Rome, and suspected that the community had previous experience of rapid mobilisation elsewhere. Levels of residential concentration seemed to be abnormally high. I was curious about the commercial overcrowding in Piazza Vittorio and the incestuous nature of entrepreneurial activities. I noticed too the obvious disparities in the earnings of (so-called) co-operative members. I could not reconcile the various economic strategies identified above to the Bangladeshis' preference for settlement in Rome. Why did the community keep growing when so many Bangladeshis complained bitterly to me about conditions there? And how did the 'copy-cat' hawkers fit in?

My observations revealed a vibrant, covert economy comprising a series of activities quite unrelated to the formal Italian labour market. I will refer to the combination of these covert activities as the 'network economy'. Unlike the overt economic activities discussed previously (employment, hawking and commercial enterprise) the 'network economy' is fuelled primarily by the act of migration itself rather than by post-settlement economic activity. This realisation shifted my attention away from the economic activities at destination and focused it on the economics of migration itself. *Adam bepari*, the primary 'motor' of the 'network economy' is discussed in the next subsection, while the secondary 'motor', comprising a range of specialised network services, will be described in section in the succeeding subsection.

Adam bepari

Adam bepari – literally translated 'the human traffic business' – has been referred to in connection with Bangladeshi migration to the Middle East by Osmani (1986). It is essentially a multi-national travel agency specialising in the movement of people around the world. It has agents of different nationalities in most countries and major Bangladeshi dealers in the main destination countries. It is a highly flexible business; nobody earns a salary but each earns commissions according to the number of migrants they are directly involved in 'processing'. The routes travelled by migrants are referred to as 'channels'. These vary depending on prevailing economic, political and legislative conditions in each transit country at any one time. Organising is called 'arranging', a word which carries a price-tag. The harder the journey is to arrange, the more valuable the services of the *adam bepari* dealer, and the higher the price. As immigration restrictions are tightened in receiving countries, so migrants rely more heavily on *adam bepari* brokers whose business flourishes. Europe is a case in point. Tougher immigration restrictions have driven the operations of *adam bepari* dealers into clandestinity, making them expensive for migrants. For researchers, it makes them difficult to observe or discuss.

   In the following account of *adam bepari* I have limited my disclosures about covert activities to those strictly necessary to explain those aspects of Bangladeshi migratory behaviour which the analysis of overt activities so far has failed to elucidate. These include: identifying the role of *adam bepari* in shaping the migratory dynamics of the network; making sense of the economic strategies of individuals and reconciling them to the overall economic strategy of the group; and finally, understanding why Rome should have remained such a major focus for Bangladeshi migration.

A Bangladeshi dealer in Italy will receive payment for arranging a 'channel' for a group of migrants from Bangladesh, or indeed from anywhere in the world, to Italy. He is paid per migrant and may receive payment (before or after migration) directly from each migrant, or from the migrant's contact in Italy. The price varies according to the deal. Arrangements are made for groups of migrants via the network of agents who arrange tickets, visas, accommodation, border crossings etc. The cost of migration from Bangladesh to Italy is around US $5,000. The cost from elsewhere varies according to the number of arrangements required to ensure safe passage. A single illegal border crossing in Europe can cost up to $1,000. For the majority of migrants *adam bepari* represents the only possibility they have of migrating.

Adam bepari is a highly profitable business and this has several implications for migratory behaviour. First, the commercialisation of migration means that the profit motive of *adam bepari* dealers is now a significant factor stimulating migration, since dealers are eager to sell their services as widely as possible. It also means that the choice of destination often depends more on the dealer's operations, or on the navigability of 'channels', than on the attributes of the destination itself. One might argue, for example, that Rome is an ideal destination for Bangladeshis, not because of the opportunities it holds for the majority of migrants, but because it provides ideal conditions for the operations of *adam bepari* dealers (submerged economy, lax controls, pliable administration etc.). Furthermore, as a commercial activity, migration is also subject to competition. In the case of Bangladeshi migration to Rome competition between *adam bepari* dealers has led to community growth irrespective of labour market conditions and of the absorptive capacity of the destination. Finally, only those who can afford to migrate do so, and their choice of destination is pre-determined by their means, resulting in the global, socio-economic segmentation of Bangladeshi migration in which some destinations (the Gulf, the Far East) are cheaper than Rome and others (Germany, North America) considerably more expensive. Many migrants begin their migratory project with a large debt which must be recouped against earnings. This reduces the attractiveness of low-wage employment and induces many to adopt high-risk strategies, such as the hawking described above, or other forms of covert private enterprise described in the next subsection.

From 'hundi' to the 'murghi' business

The secondary 'motor' of the 'network economy' is comprised of a range of covert services offered to migrants in the host country. The range and quality of services will obviously depend on the size of the Bangladeshi community. My research in Italy almost certainly did not uncover all the services on offer, but three examples are briefly described below.

Hundi is a well-established, international system enabling migrants to send remittances home from anywhere in the world via unofficial channels. Migrants pay a dealer in local currency and the dealer arranges for the equivalent payment, less commission, to be made to the family in the Bangladeshi currency, taka. The system was initially developed for rich people in Bangladesh who wanted to invest money outside the country despite currency controls. However, it has evolved into an extremely valuable service for migrants. In Rome, it has been especially important partly because there were no direct banking facilities operating between Italy and Bangladesh until 1994, and secondly because so many immigrants in Rome are illegal and hence are unable to use Italian banking facilities.

Another profitable business has been the operation of illicit telephone exchanges offering cut-price international phone calls to immigrants. These operations are generally set up with Italian collaboration and are run at the expense of telephone companies and subscribers around Europe. One such exchange, discovered by the police, was thought to be taking between 5 and 10 million lire per day, and the *Corriere della Sera* of 21 October 1992 reported the arrest of 15 Bangladeshis involved in the racket.

The *murghi* business refers to the common practice of sub-letting (*murghi* means 'hen' in Bengali). Although most Bangladeshis are obliged to share accommodation in Rome because it is so expensive, it is fairly common for contract-tenants (those who hold the contract with the landlord) to sub-let for profit. This had led to some severe cases of overcrowding. In 1995 I surveyed 30 flats which housed over 15 Bangladeshis. A few houses had as many as 40–50 Bangladeshis living in them. The average rent for an apartment in Rome fluctuates between 1.3 and 2 million lire per month. Each boarder pays approximately 200,000 lire per month for a bed and a further 150,000 lire for food. Bills, except the telephone, are inclusive. One Bangladeshi told me that some people take out several tenancies and become professional rent collectors. However, obtaining a tenancy also has its price in the 'network economy'. The same source related that in order to obtain a tenancy, it was often necessary to obtain a reference from the Bangladeshi Association, a favour which is allegedly 'arranged' in return for 10 per cent of the monthly rent collected. This, when multiplied several times, represents a handsome commission for Bangladeshi Association signatories and provides just one example of the financial benefits inducing entrepreneurs to compete for political power in Rome.

The covert economics of migration to Rome

This schematic analysis of some aspects of the 'network economy' enables us to understand those aspects of the Bangladeshi migratory project which were hitherto inexplicable. Since *adam bepari* is a transnational operation already specialised in sending migrants to the Far and Middle East and to Western Europe, the Italian episode in 1989 represented a minor branching out of the network and explains its ability to mobilise rapidly in response to opportunity in a new locality. The 'network economy' thrives on a concentration of Bangladeshis, since it would not be cost-effective to provide network services to a community scattered all over Italy. The economic viability of identical shops clustered close together may be explained by the affiliation of such shops to *adam bepari* dealers[7] The 'leader' of a shop may himself be an *adam bepari* dealer or he may be allied to one. And since customer fidelity is preordained (each customer base is composed of the various migration chains originating in different districts of Bangladesh), shops offering identical goods and services are as viable in a cluster as they are dispersed. Some of the overcrowded houses mentioned above were associated with specific migratory chains operated by *adam bepari* dealers.

The overriding suitability of Rome for Bangladeshi settlement lies in the fact that the 'network economy' has been able to flourish there because large numbers of migrants have been able to assemble and stay without papers. The economic activities of most Bangladeshis, especially undocumented ones, are inextricably linked to the 'network economy'. Identifying overt economic strategies of individuals and relating them to the Roman labour market is not sufficient to understand the overall economic strategy of the group. It cannot explain the continued growth of the Bangladeshi community in Rome, which instead may be partially explained by the large profits made by *adam bepari* dealers.

The new-found wealth of the dealer's family in Bangladesh would stimulate demand among neighbouring families to send a member of their family to Italy. Their transit creates more wealth for the dealer, further stimulating migratory demand among his neighbours and members of his social network. The initial opportunities existing in Italy in 1990 would enable the first migrants to obtain residence papers and legal work. Their establishment in turn creates still further demand.

The process is self-perpetuating. On the expiry of opportunity in

---

7   Although the shops are officially cooperatives, their unofficial management is hierarchical: almost all shops are known by the name of the cooperative leader rather than by the name of the cooperative. The leader is visibly richer than other members.

Italy, copy-cat tactics take over. Poor employment prospects and low pay in Rome's submerged economy make it difficult for migrants to recoup the substantial amount invested in migration to Italy without access to a highly profitable activity. As a result, some migrants will emulate the *adam bepari* dealers while others reproduce profitable network services. While the emulation of *adam bepari* dealers ensures a constant influx of new arrivals, the multiplication of network services relies on them. A communal interest in continued community growth develops, and the reliance of established migrants on new arrivals hinders negative feedback about conditions in the Roman labour market.

Meanwhile *adam bepari* dealers actively recruit new migrants among their peers and through their respective social networks, accounting for the differential regional emigration patterns identified in the next section of this account. In some cases, new *adam bepari* dealers process new recruits through established dealers, working on a commission basis, whilst in others they operate in competition with established dealers.

In this way the community in Rome grows despite the exhausting of opportunity and in the absence of adequate employment prospects. In Paris, the community experienced similar growth throughout the 1980s, but it went into decline in 1990 because Bangladeshis left for Rome. In the case of Rome, however, the dearth of opportunity in other countries has slowed the out-flow of Bangladeshis resulting in continued community growth.

Origins, settlement and economic activity

Having identified some of the covert economic dynamics driving the Bangladeshi migratory network, it is now possible to link them to other aspects of the migrant network, for example to its different regional strands (for more detail on these regional chains see Knights 1996a).

I found that both entrepreneurial activities and hawking were linked closely to the different regional migration chains making up the network, while the scarce employment opportunities in Rome tended to inhibit the formation of employment-led migration chains. Each chain comprises both entrepreneurs and hawkers, usually from the same district. The entrepreneurs include the *adam bepari* dealers, the leaders of co-operatives and those running network services. They occupy the top echelons of the hierarchy of each chain and compete with each other for political power in Rome. This means that both political and economic power in the community are often vested in the same hands so that each migration chain has its own leader who relies on a growing rank-and-file for both political support and profit (see Knights 1996c).

The hawkers are the 'rank-and-file' of the entrepreneurs. Evidence for this lies in the correlation between district of origin and specific hawking activities. For example, Bangladeshis from the district of Noakhali often work as flower or jewellery sellers. Umbrella sellers are most likely to come from Faridpur district, as are oil and garlic sellers. Bangladeshis from a town called Bhairub in the district of Kishoreganj work almost exclusively as *lavavetri*. In the cases of Noakhali and Shariatpur, district leaders have a commercial interest in the economic activity of their rank-and-file because they supply the items to be sold by the hawkers. In the case of Noakhali, the leader started off in Rome by selling the items which he now supplies to other hawkers. However this is not the case with the windscreen cleaners from Bhairub; it is much more likely that a newcomer from Bhairub is initiated to his economic activity by his flatmates. In this case, the reproduction of economic activity derives from the residential cohesion in Rome of individuals from the same district in Bangladesh. Discussions with people from other districts revealed that this is a common pattern.

This provides the link between the overt economic strategies of Bangladeshis and their differential settlement patterns in Rome. These residential patterns are, however, very fragile. On a national level, Sylhetis (who rely more on Italian labour market opportunity) seem to have acquired the greatest degree of autonomy with respect to the migratory network in Rome. In Rome, street-sellers from Noakhali and Faridpur are much more reliant on the established commercial infrastructure of the 'network economy'. They tend to live near their leaders/suppliers who are based near Piazza Vittorio. The windscreen cleaners from Bhairub, on the other hand, do not rely on suppliers and ideally need to live near their habitual cross roads. Although one might expect a more dispersed settlement pattern for this group, the Bhairubis are concentrated along the Viale Cristoforo Colombo and the Via della Magliana, which are main traffic arteries connecting Rome with Fiumicino airport and the commercial district of EUR. These specific settlement patterns contrast with those of Bangladeshis from Dhaka who are more evenly distributed over the city. These patterns suggest that the hawkers represent cohesive forces, binding the chains making up the network and reinforcing their identity. The employees, on the other hand (in the fragmented Roman labour market) are a dispersive force because employees, especially those working in the formal economy, are not so reliant on the community structures.

Signs of recession in the 'network economy' in Rome

So far in this chapter I have considered the economic mechanisms driving the Bangladeshi migratory network in Rome and explaining its rapid establishment and growth. In this section I will briefly consider some of the mechanisms leading to decline. I must stress, however, that these impressions are speculative and represent the situation as it appeared to be changing when I wound up my fieldwork in Spring 1995.

The Bangladeshi migratory network has been shown to be an efficient means of transporting migrants around the world (Knights 1996c) and the community flourished and expanded in Rome throughout the period of my fieldwork, except at the very end. However, the system seems to be driven by competition and the profit motive, while little consideration is given to the sustainability of the 'network economy' in the destination country in the long term. This oversight has been compounded by the ease with which migrants have been able to enter Italy. Furthermore, the permissiveness of the Roman authorities has enabled submerged economic activities to thrive and undocumented migrants to stay and work. The result has been that the Bangladeshi community has perhaps become too large for its own good.

Although the 'network economy' functions independently of the Italian labour market, it ultimately rests on the ability of Bangladeshis to earn money in Rome. Towards the end of my fieldwork there were signs that this economy was going into recession. Employment opportunities had decreased in Rome and employees, both in the formal and submerged economies, were earning too little to offset the substantial sum invested in their migratory project. Many had lost their jobs. Some moved from employment to street-hawking.

But the Roman public had become weary of street-hawkers. They were bored of having their windscreen cleaned every day and were refusing to buy roses for their wives, girlfriends and sisters. They simply stopped buying so much. Prices fell. Roses which cost 3,000 lire in 1992 were selling for 1,000 lire by 1994. Even the Italian flower stall at the bottom of the Spanish Steps was selling roses for 1,000 lire. The price of an umbrella had halved, from 10,000 to 5,000 lire. And you could have your name written on a grain of rice for half the price just weeks after the gimmick was introduced. I was once offered it at a tenth of the original price on the Spanish Steps by a dispirited Bangladeshi who had sat there all day without one customer.

The permissive climate which had prevailed in Rome was changing too. Post-*tangentopoli* austerity measures were beginning to have their effect and immigrants were becoming the scapegoats for general discontent with rising unemployment, a less buoyant informal economy, rising taxes, traffic congestion, pollution . . . indeed with all the ills of post-industrial, urban life. The election of the Green Party candidate, Francesco Rutelli, as the new mayor of Rome in 1993 ushered in a new era of efficiency in Rome's administration. Rutelli tore away at bureaucratic hurdles which had for years hindered the completion of municipal projects and, in an unprecedented move, he produced and publicised unending progress reports announcing among other things: the extension of the Rome underground; the creation of thousands of new car-parking spaces; the cleaning of public buildings; the introduction of information kiosks for tourists; the merger of bus and underground tickets into an integrated travel pass; further excavation of the Roman Forum; the restoration of the Spanish Steps and the long-awaited introduction of a special anti-pick-pocket patrol of bilingual *vigili urbani*! In short, Rome was being cleaned-up in preparation for the massive influx of pilgrims expected to accompany the forthcoming celebration of the Catholic Church's second millennium. Unfortunately for Rome's street-hawkers, they were not to be excluded from Rutelli's plans and this boded particularly badly for Bangladeshis.

Just as the Senegalese hawkers were flying in from Dakar to coincide with the first flush of Spring tourists, and the Bangladeshis were polishing their rice and dreaming of letting out their belts a couple of notches, the police blitzes on Rome's tourist sites began. A full-time patrol of *vigili urbani* was deployed at the Roman Forum from March 1995, and part of the perimeter walkway – an impromptu market for at least 50 sellers – was closed. The *Assessore* for commerce – Rome's highest authority for commercial affairs – personally visited Piazza Navona and the Spanish Steps in April and declared them areas of *degrado* – urban decline. The Spanish Steps – home to well over 100 sellers – was closed for seven months for restoration, and Piazza Navona was heavily policed. The right (and duty) to confiscate hawkers' wares was extended from the exclusive domain of the *vigili urbani* to the military police division, the *carabinieri*. In April, when I left Rome for the last time, the street-hawkers looked decidedly uneasy. The Senegalese no longer spread their wares on the ground but crouched with them in their hands and Bangladeshis had also adopted a more 'on-the-move' style of selling.

Tension rose in the overcrowded Bangladeshi houses leading sometimes to noisy disputes. From the Autumn of 1994, I was hearing reports of police raids on Bangladeshi houses (usually as a result of neighbours' complaints) and subsequent expulsion of undocumented migrants. Every week a few unlucky Bangladeshis were sent back on the weekly flights to Dhaka. The shelves in one or two of the Bangladeshi food shops were beginning to look quite empty.

Increasing restrictions all over Europe meant that there were few opportunities to pursue elsewhere, but nevertheless Bangladeshis were talking about moving away. One of my contacts returned to Bangladesh in the hope that his family could 'arrange' for him to go the USA (his sister had just married a cabinet minister in Bangladesh); another received papers from Canada from his wife who had moved there with her family. Some talked about trying their luck with the asylum legislation in Germany and Switzerland and others pondered about what Ireland might be like. A few had already left for Portugal where contract marriages were said to be cheap and you could get a Portuguese passport . . . and some had heard that there was a good living to be made on the beaches of Sardinia during the summer. Everybody was saving up!

Conclusion

In the account above, I have intentionally focussed on economic rather than social or cultural aspects of the Bangladeshi migratory network. This is not because I believe them to be any more important but simply that labour migration must have an economic rationale which must, in turn, be consistent with other cultural and social factors influencing the functioning of the migratory network.

In seeking an economic rationale for the Bangladeshi case I began in a fairly traditional way by considering the types of work done by Bangladeshis in Rome and the amounts of money they earned. However, when I set these results against the migration investment and potential earnings in Bangladesh the return on migration did not seem great enough to justify such a large concentration of Bangladeshis in Rome. Legally present Bangladeshis, for example, stood a much better chance of finding better-paid, longer-term and legal employment in northern and central Italy than in Rome while the more precariously placed street-hawkers might have earned more by spreading themselves more thinly over a larger area than by proliferating in the capital. Undoubtedly family and social ties, language and common cultural practice all help to explain the concentration, but even so I believed that there had to be a sound economic rationale underpinning these social and cultural reasons.

It was this conviction that prompted me to shift the focus of my observation from overt to covert economic activity. This produced results which were more consistent with my previous findings about the structure and functioning of the migratory network and the concentration in Rome.

I have shown that most clandestine economic activity revolves around the act of migration itself by facilitating movement and servicing the needs of migrants abroad. *Adam bepari, hundi*, the *murghi* business and the Bangladeshi co-operatives are all examples of economic activity generated by the migratory network; none of them are exclusive to Rome. I also found that different varieties of street-hawking are linked to regional migration chains. This suggests that hawking is not just a survival strategy and function of the Italian parallel economy but that it also derives from the migratory network itself.

My observations of clandestine economic activity enabled me to justify the community's existence in Rome. Although the Roman labour market does not provide attractive employment prospects, the feeble administration accommodates more lucrative parallel activity. Thus Rome soon became known as a place where Bangladeshis could live and work 'without papers'. This in turn created a demand to migrate there which *adam bepari* dealers responded to. Simultaneously, these dealers operated in Rome because lax controls also facilitated their business, enabling them to make large profits. Finally, the 'secondary motor' services depended on a concentration of Bangladeshis in Rome.

These findings show that the Bangladeshi migratory network is a dynamic economic entity. It enjoys a symbiotic existence with the Roman economy and administrative system, flourishing within them but not entirely dependent upon them. The Italian experience illustrates how quickly the Bangladeshi migratory network can mobilise in response to opportunity; and it demonstrates the flexibility with which at least one (and probably others) of Southern Europe's new immigrant groups can adapt to changing opportunities and constraints, sustaining their livelihood (but often only just) and perpetuating their presence.

References

Caritas di Roma (1992) *Immigrazione Dossier Statistico, 1992*. Rome: Sinnos.

Caritas di Roma (1994) *Immigrazione Dossier Statistico, 1994*. Rome: Anterem.

Gardner, K. (1992) International migration and the rural context in Sylhet, *New Community*, 18(4), pp. 579–90.

Gardner, K. (1993) Desh-Bidesh, Sylheti images of home and away, *Man*, 28(1), pp. 1–15.

King, R. (1993) Recent immigration to Italy: character, causes and effects, *GeoJournal*, 30(3), pp. 283–92.

King, R. and Knights, M. (1994) Bangladeshis in Rome: a case of migratory opportunism, in Gould, W.T.S. and Findlay, A.M., eds. *Population Migration and the Changing World Order*. Chichester: Wiley, pp. 127–43.

King, R. and Rybaczuk, K. (1993) Southern Europe and the international division of labour: from emigration to immigration, in King, R., ed. *The New Geography of European Migrations*. London: Belhaven, pp. 175–206.

Knights, M. (1996a) *Migration in the New World Order: the Case of Bangladeshi Migration to Rome*. Brighton: University of Sussex, unpublished D.Phil. thesis.

Knights, M. (1996b) Bangladeshis in Rome: the political, economic and social structure of a recent immigrant group, in Gentileschi, M.L. and King, R., eds. *Questioni di Popolazione in Europa: una Prospettiva Geografica*. Bologna: Pàtron, pp. 129–42.

Knights, M. (1996c) Bangladeshi immigrants in Italy: from geopolitics to micropolitics, *Transactions of the Institute of British Geographers*, 21(1), pp. 105–23.

Mahmood, R.A. (1990) Bangladeshi immigrants in the United Kingdom, *Bangladesh Public Administration Journal*, 4(2), pp. 75–98.

Osmani, S.R. (1986) Bangladesh, in Gunatilleke, G., ed. *Migration of Asian Workers to the Arab World*. Tokyo: United Nations University Press, pp. 22–65.

7

Citizenship Rights and Migration Policies: The Case of Maghrebi Migrants in Italy and Spain

Joanna Apap

In recent years, there have been significant changes in policies at national level towards labour migrants from the Maghreb in two new receiving states – Italy and Spain. Until the late 1970s, both countries were significant countries of emigration, and although both served as passage-ways to Northern Europe for migrants coming from North and sub-Saharan Africa, the need for immigration, rather than emigration policy, was highly limited. From the early 1980s onwards, however, with the tightening of visa restrictions in Northern Europe, coupled with an increase in prosperity in Southern Europe, both Italy and Spain have become receiving countries for long-term migrants. In response, by 1985–86, both countries had begun to develop legislation with respect to immigration into their territories. This legislation was initially quite similar, and appeared to be driven by a desire to match evolving policy at a European level under the Schengen agreement. More recently, though, legislation has evolved in different ways in the two countries, reflecting somewhat different patterns of immigration, and different local circumstances. In this sense, Spain and Italy provide an interesting dual case study, in which the relative strength of policy driven by European harmonisation on the one hand, and local and national factors on the other, can be compared.

The focus of this chapter is mainly centred upon policy as it concerns labour immigration from the Maghreb countries (Morocco, Algeria and Tunisia). Not only do Maghrebi migrants constitute a high absolute number and percentage of immigrants currently residing and working in the EU – about 2.5 million according to the European Commission (Commission of the European Communities 1994, p. 28) – but also migration from the Maghreb region has continued to increase in the 1990s. In part, this increase is due to an increase in poverty, unemployment and an uncurbed boom in population growth, which have inflated the pressure for emigration from the Maghreb region. Although there has been an increase in female education and family planning, and the birth-rate has already started to stall slightly, a significant fall in North African birth rates is unlikely in the next few years, even if it will not increase at the high rate predicted by some authors (Collinson 1993; 1996; Lopez García 1990; Spencer 1993). In contrast, it is certainly true that political, religious and ethnic conflicts have led to a world-wide increase in forced migration. This is particularly relevant in the case of Algeria, which has been a significant source of migrants to Spain and Italy. Nonetheless, forced migration does not account for the majority of migrants in either country (Werth and Körner 1991, p. 25), whilst there is little evidence that the proportion of forced migrants is increasing.

In this context, the main concern here is with policy towards legally resident migrant workers in the EU, and their families. This does not imply that the position of illegal immigrants, or of non-working migrants, is insignificant. Indeed, illegal immigrants, who enter receiving countries either clandestinely (on boats, through mountain pathways, etc.) or by overstaying their tourist or student visas, have had a significant impact on immigration policy development. However, whilst some attention has been paid in the academic literature to new arrivals of migrants (Collinson 1996; Tapinos 1993), of whom clandestine migrants are clearly an important part, much less attention has focused on the position of those who have remained in Southern European countries for a longer time period. And yet it is this move towards the establishment and settlement of immigrants that is perhaps most important in terms of a transition from 'country of emigration' status to being a 'country of immigration'. In turn, it is the position of legally resident migrant workers that has perhaps been most significant in the development of European policy towards migrants, a policy based on principles of free movement of persons within the Community, equal treatment under the law and social justice – including combating social exclusion.

Defining the terms 'immigrant' and 'immigration'

The term immigrant is at times used in the very broad sense of its root-word – *migrant*, a person who moves from one country to another.

However, a discussion of immigration policy development requires a more robust definition of the group this policy is aimed at, whilst at the same time, the nomenclature used is also quite revealing of the nature and purpose of policy development. For the purposes of this paper, an *'immigrant'* is therefore defined as someone who moves to another country and resides there for more than three months. In the case of non-EU nationals, this represents a cut-off point, beyond which a residence permit is required in all EU countries. Within this group, it is also helpful to focus on long-term resident migrants, who have been in the EU legally for five years or more, since the development of regulations concerning these migrants is both more fundamental and potentially more problematic for receiving states. In turn, *immigration* can be seen as the actual entry into a country by a person or group of persons with the intention of staying there for more than three months. However, this does not imply that these persons may not decide to return to their country of origin after a period of time; nor does it mean that they will necessarily work. In other words, immigration can lead to, but does not necessarily lead to, the creation of long-term immigrants and migrant workers.

Whilst this might be seen as a somewhat pedantic discussion, the issue of terminology is not simply an academic issue. For example, the terms 'immigrant' and 'immigration' are applied in different ways in different EU Member States, and related policies are equally shaped by each country's experience and the particular national needs. As Hammar (1992, p. 12) argues: 'There is an obvious relation between a country's immigration policy and its terminology'. Thus in Germany and Switzerland immigrants are 'foreign workers' (*Ausländische Arbeitnehmer* in Germany and *Fremdarbeiter* in Switzerland) and they are controlled by 'aliens bureaux' (*Ausländerbehörde* in Germany, *Fremdenpolizei* in Switzerland); the concept of 'immigrant', in the strict sense outlined above, is unknown. In contrast, France has always used the terms *les immigrés* and *l'immigration*, whilst Sweden has also used similar terms – *invandrare* and *invandring* – since the 1960s when it launched its new immigration policy. Britain has used the term 'immigrant' especially for non-whites, but it defines its immigration policy as *race relations*; whilst in the Netherlands, the new policy for immigrants is called *minorities policy* (Hammar 1992, p. 12). Terminology tends to influence the way in which immigration policy is conceived and understood in each country and these terms, initially instruments of description, then become fixed concepts limiting flexibility and creativity.

One can also go further, to differentiate between perceptions on the part of the host society with respect to different groups of migrants, perceptions which place some groups in a more precarious position than others. For example, if one considers the current situation in Europe, migration flows are coming from two main directions, Eastern Europe and North Africa. On the one hand, Eastern Europeans are often seen as related through blood to Western Europeans, and as such are seen as having always been 'in' Europe, albeit not in the EU. In this sense, they are often perceived as part of 'us', whereas North Africans are given a 'them' status. In contrast, suspicion of North Africans is such that they are often viewed more as a threat: an Algerian in France being seen by many simply as a potential terrorist.

Of course, the world of Islam is and always has been so lacking in monolithic qualities as to make the concept of an Islamic threat per se literally meaningless. But neither can there be any doubt that the member states of the European Union are confronting problems in their relations with the predominantly Islamic states of North Africa which raise issues about the whole future development of the EU. Thus Moisi (in Barclay 1995, p. 5) describes the emerging situation in Europe as that of 'a white, wealthy and Christian "Fortress Europe" pitted against a largely poor, Islamic world.' Such issues of terminology, and the way that the 'immigrant threat' is perceived in Italy and Spain, are returned to below.

Immigration and citizenship

In addition to the way in which immigrants are categorised and viewed by host country populations, the presence of immigrants in southern Europe also raises wider questions for government policy in the field of citizenship – as Zolberg (1987, p. 226) puts it, 'immigrants pose a challenge to traditional conceptions of states as self-contained population entities.' For example, with the arrival of immigrants, the traditional definition of membership in a community is no longer so self-evident, and one cannot directly relate such membership to formal citizenship. In an important sense, anybody inside a national territory, including illegal immigrants, is in some way a member of that particular community because he/she takes part in the life of the receiving society by, for instance, participating in the labour market (both formal and informal), sending children to school, being a neighbour and/or paying taxes (Levelt 1995).

Nonetheless, citizenship does mean more than simple presence in, or even membership of a community. Garcia (1993, p. 19) for example provides the following definition of citizenship:

> Citizenship in the modern world constitutes legal, economic, political and social practices which define social membership and which counteract social

cleavages. In this sense the practice of citizenship becomes a method of social inclusion which gives people who differ in age, sex, beliefs or colour of skin the same basic entitlements. It is this aspect of citizenship that has contributed to the legitimacy of the modern state. Citizenship has become also an element of legitimization for the new Europe. To what extent is citizenship going to be universalized in Europe, and to what extent are people going to be excluded?

There are various issues which arise in the European context with respect to the boundaries of citizenship. However, as Antje Wiener correctly states: 'Union citizenship needs to be distinguished from national citizenship' (Wiener 1996, p. 47). She goes on to argue that 'every citizen of the Union enjoys a first circle of nationality rights within a Member State and a second circle of new rights enjoyed in any Member State of the EU'. One of the main questions which arises in this regard is the extent to which the division between European Union citizens and third country nationals will increase, especially if further entrenchment of the idea of 'Fortress Europe' occurs due to 'deepening' of the Community.

Italy and Spain as new receiving states

As noted above, during the late 1980s the Southern European states – Spain, Italy, Greece and Portugal – were transformed from being countries of emigration to countries of immigration. The main stimulus for this transformation can be attributed principally to three processes, namely economic growth in Southern Europe; the 'stop' on immigration to Northern Europe; and a marked increase in push factors throughout the less developed world, but especially in North Africa. Thus for example, the control measures taken by the traditional receiving countries of North-West Europe led to an increase of immigration into Southern European countries, 'either because these were the traditional staging-posts for clandestine migrants routing to the north, or because Southern Europe was seen as a straightforward alternative to direct entry to Northern Europe' (King and Konjhodzic 1996, p. 50).

At the same time, migration studies and policy in Italy and Spain had, until the late 1980s, focused on emigration *from* as opposed to immigration *to* Southern Europe and both research and policy have been confronted with problems in the face of this transformation. For example, legislative procedures in the two countries tended to refer to the foreign tourist rather than the immigrant worker, whilst statistics were generally either absent altogether, or unreliable. It is also difficult to establish the exact number of immigrants over the last twenty years in Italy and Spain, due to an initial lack of legislation.

Nonetheless, in the recent years, a great effort has been made to gather statistics appropriate to the new situation and hence analyse more precisely and in greater detail immigration and its implications as well as furnish appropriate legislation which could cope better with the new problems involved. Thus recent estimates put immigration from outside the EU at around 1 million in Italy, with the number of illegal immigrants estimated at about half a million (*Il Manifesto*, 12 October 1996). For example, an official estimate made in 1989 by the Italian National Statistics Institute (ISTAT) put the figure at 963,000, although this may have been an overestimate due to an apparent failure to subtract the number of return migrants who were no longer on Italian soil. In turn, in Spain estimates vary between 450,000 and 657,000 with respect to number of third country immigrants known to be residing on Spanish territory, whilst the number of illegal immigrants in Spain is said to be about another 450,000 (*Migration News Sheet*, September 1996, pp. 6–7).

The predominance of push over pull factors, the limited capacity of the labour markets of the receiving countries and an increased migration for political reasons are all elements which, interacting with migration dynamics, have led to significant changes in migration policy and in attitudes towards migrants in Italy and Spain in recent years. New immigration flows are only partly absorbed in the hidden economy of the receiving countries and in sectors and jobs where the distinction between legal and illegal is minimal. This encourages the social exclusion of the immigrants as well as compromising their integration with the receiving society, not to mention the ethnic, cultural and religious divide which often separates the immigrant from the local population. In effect, the list of potential areas for policy development is vast.

Similarities between Italy and Spain

An initial point to make concerns the similarities between the way in which Spain and Italy have reacted to changes that have affected them. As stated earlier, both Spain and Italy have had past histories as sending countries and both countries in the early 1980s started experiencing the transformation from 'sending' country to becoming a 'receiving' country.

Both countries were used as a passage-way to the North of Europe; later on, after the tightening of visa restrictions in Northern Europe and an increase in the prosperity of the tertiary sector in Italy and Spain, both countries have now started experiencing the settlement of migrants on their territory. The differential of economic growth between the coun-

tries of Southern and North-West Europe has also narrowed considerably as EC membership has brought Italian and Spanish (and to a lesser
extent, Greek and Portuguese) wages closer to average EU levels.

In the midst of these dramatic changes, an initial lack of demographic
analysis of the situation, coupled with the lack of concrete migration
policy in Italy and to a lesser extent in Spain, have led to over-reactions
by the media and exaggerations in the numbers thought to be present.
Earlier surveys in Italy dealt with communities of immigrants coming
from the Philippines, Cape Verde, Somalia, Eritrea, Morocco, Tunisia,
Egypt and Iran; and recently the list has expanded to include immigrants from Algeria and other African and Asian countries such as
Senegal, Ghana, Sri Lanka, Pakistan and China. In the absence of a clear
direction from researchers or policy-makers, this apparently unending
immigration has led to sporadic acts of xenophobia being carried out
against individuals and immigrant communities.

However, in both countries a distinction is nonetheless drawn
between 'elite' immigrants, and other, more marginalised groups. In
both countries, the 'elite' (such as Americans and Japanese) are viewed
as 'investors'; whereas the term 'immigrant' is attributed to the poorer
groups of migrants. In Spain, the 'elite' includes Northern Europeans
who retire to Spain for its climate and lower cost of living, as well as
migrants from Spain's former colonies, who are usually very well qualified and manage to secure a standard of living similar to that of the
Spaniards, if not better. These groups have a substantially different
experience in Spain to the 'marginalised' group, composed of North and
sub-Saharan Africans, and to a certain extent poorer Portuguese and
Filipino immigrants. Meanwhile, the most marginalised of all in both
countries are the illegal immigrants.

The different demographic regimes between the two sides of the
Mediterranean basin act as a strong push factor for immigration which
is common to both Italy and Spain. Equally, an important and common
pull factor is the large informal sector of the economy and labour market
which is also significant in both Italy and Spain. Rapidly-rising official
wage-rates, a squeeze on productivity and, until recently, devaluation
of the lira in Italy (and to a lesser extent the peseta in Spain) have led
firms to recoup their competitiveness by tax evasion, reduced labour
costs and more flexible use of labour. In this context, informal and irregular demand for migrant labour in certain sectors such as agriculture,
construction, the tourist industry and domestic services is very high. In
fact, both Spain and Italy have a problem of sizeable and expanding
informal labour markets which absorb undocumented migrants.

In both countries the predominant group of labour migrants from the
Maghreb are from Morocco, and in both cases the distribution of

migrants within the receiving states is not homogenous. Reasons for the increase in the number of immigrants from North Africa entering Italy and Spain are various, but a principal one is geographical. The geographical proximity and 'openness' of both Italy and Spain, including their reliance on tourism, and their long coastlines, tend to make control of migrant inflows very difficult.

In terms of immigration policy development, both countries have had amnesty laws for illegal immigrants (Collinson 1996, p. 35): in Spain in 1985–86, 1991 and 1996; and in Italy in 1982, 1987–89, 1990–92 and 1996. In all of these regularisations, a lower than expected number of undocumented workers actually regularised their position in the host country, probably out of fear of being repatriated. In Spain, for example, the first legalisation process in 1985–86 resulted in 34,832 residence permits being issued (Izquierdo 1992), whilst as a result of the 1991 process, a further 109,135 work and residence permits were issued, well below the estimated number of undocumented workers.

Differences between Italy and Spain

Although there are similarities in the position of Italy and Spain with respect to their experience of immigration, differences prevail too. Differences are particularly evident in terms of the types of migrants that are present in Italy and Spain; the interpretation given to the word 'integration'; and the extent to which there is integration of the immigrants within the host societies. There have been important implications for changing attitudes towards migrants and hence the evolution of immigration and citizenship policies in Italy and Spain, issues dealt with in the next section.

One reason for this difference might be the variations in the spatial distribution of immigrants in the two countries. In Italy, immigrants are spread throughout the country, although they are found particularly in the Centre-North and certain areas of the South (Sicily and Campania) which are easy landing places for migrants coming by sea from the Maghreb. In contrast, in Spain, the majority of the immigrants are in either Madrid or Catalonia, where most job opportunities can be found. Southern regions such as Andalusia have also received a number of seasonal workers, who look for jobs in the tourist sector or in the agricultural harvest, although this conflicts with the interests of the locals who themselves look to the tourist and harvest seasons for extra income from part-time work. As a result of the spatial concentration of immigrants in Spain, one does not find such well-pronounced regional policies as one does in Italy, since the numbers of immigrants are not very high in most regions, and where numbers do increase dramatically, this usually occurs during the summer period, for a short time, after which the immigrants return back to their country of origin.

Changing attitudes towards migration in Italy and Spain

The Italian public has grown increasingly interested in the question of migration, both because of greater numbers involved and due to episodes, often quite serious, of intolerance which have caught the attention of the mass media and the general public. Nonetheless, with some local exceptions, the impact of migration on Italy is still quite modest in comparison with other European countries, in particular because migrants' access to social and welfare services remains limited – particularly if they are illegals. This, however, has not prevented the outbreak of various forms of racism (Treves 1989; Vicarelli 1994).

Meanwhile, a number of opposing reactions to immigration have emerged from Italian society. On the one hand, one can find 'solidarity' towards migrants as expressed by various Catholic voluntary organisations, such as Caritas, by some political parties, and by trade unions. On the other hand, in Italian, as in other European cultures, a form of ethnocentrism does exist which, under certain conditions, gives rise to xenophobic or racist behaviour, although to date, for various reasons, this has had less occasion for expression than elsewhere. In a survey reported by Bonifazi (1992), it was interesting to note the over-estimations given by respondents of the number of immigrants present in Italy, and that these over-estimations grew between 1987/88 and 1991 (table 7.1). It is perhaps this, as much as actual growth in the number of immigrants, that has led to the feeling that there are 'too many' immigrants in the country (table 7.2)

Table 7.1   Evaluation of the number of foreigners living in Italy

	1987–88 (%)	1991 (%)
Low (a)	13.6	9.8
Medium (b)	18.8	15.3
High (c)	17.6	19.7
Very high (d)	13.7	20.9
Don't know	36.2	34.3
Total	100.0	100.0

Notes:
(a) 1987–88: under 750,000; 1991: under 700,000;
(b) 1987–88: 750,000–1,500,000; 1991: 700,000–1,500,000;
(c) 1,500,000–3,000,000;
(d) over 3,000,000.   *Source:* Bonifazi (1992, p. 40).

Table 7.2   Opinions on the number of foreigners living in Italy

	1987–88 (%)	1991 (%)
Too many	49.7	74.5
Neither too many nor too few	35.7	19.1
Not many	1.7	1.1
Don't know	12.8	5.4
Total	100.0	100.0

Source: Bonifazi (1992, p. 40)

Spain's immigrant population accounts for less than 2 per cent of the country's total population and the immigrant proportion of the official labour force is even smaller (about 0.7 per cent – Colectivo IOE 1990, p. 123). Nonetheless, especially in the period 1988–92, the press and government encouraged the belief that immigration is one of Spain's most serious political and social problems by exaggerating numbers and pointing to its negative effects on the labour market and its implications for petty crime, terrorism and drug trafficking.

As in Italy, the sensationalism of the press concerning increases in the number of migrants caused people to panic about the numbers actually present. In response, in 1992 the government modified the *Ley Corcuera*, a piece of public order legislation, granting wider powers to the police to crack down on the supposed link between immigrants and crime.

However, following the murder of a Dominican woman in 1992 and statistics showing a lower level of immigration than previously thought (Cornelius 1994), the government accepted that they had overstated the situation, and in 1994 a social policy was established with respect to migrants working and residing on Spanish territory which sought to soften some of the stricter regulations of the foreigners' law (*Ley Extranjería*) and to avoid further demonstrations of xenophobia. In turn, the press practically stopped writing about the issue and the situation calmed down considerably.

As in Italy, there have been surveys of public opinion about immigration in Spain, with a survey by Colectivo IOE (1986), although now rather dated, showing quite a differentiated pattern of opinions depending on social class. From their survey, five distinct attitudes emerged:

• *Nationalism:* a view which supports the rights of Spanish citizens and can be found across the entire spectrum of Spanish society; however, this is most prevalent, unsurprisingly, in the right-wing press, amongst many employees, and the unemployed, but least strong amongst middle-class women and civil servants. As in Italy, those holding a nationalist view tended to overestimate the numbers of third-country nationals present on Spanish territory, and this view was particularly dominant in the poorer southern regions of Spain, where Spaniards feel more in competition with immigrants for work in the tourist industry and in manual labour, due to higher levels of unemployment.

- In contrast, company directors tended to put *economic* considerations first and foremost, in keeping with Spain's constitutional commitment to the market economy. They tend to accept the presence of foreign workers on the grounds that Spanish workers increasingly reject certain forms of employment, or impose demands on their employers that are simply too costly to fulfill.

- A *Christian universalist* view defends the concepts of equality and fraternity and supports the weak and needy – in this case, immigrants. Middle-class women were found to be the most staunch defenders of this view, although they accepted elements of the 'nationalist' view, notably in believing that Spanish people should be given first preference for employment.

- A *workers' universalist* viewpoint which opposes exploitation of foreign workers, but also arguably has more to do with nostalgia for the past than with concrete alternatives for the present.

- A *practical view* which stresses the need for better border controls, but also accepts the need move towards legalising the status of most of the country's foreigners. This view is dominant in government departments and NGOs, although the former place more emphasis on immigration policy to control illegal immigration, whilst the latter stress improvement in legal and social conditions for immigrants already in the country.

These variations in public perception of immigrants, and what should be done by the government in response, help to explain why in both countries, although there has been legislation with respect to immigrants, there is little, as yet, in the way of wider-ranging policy. This distinction between legislation and policy reflects Roger Scruton's distinction, in the Dictionary of Political Thought, between legislation as 'the "making" of law ... (which) will always stand in need of subsequent interpretation by the judiciary', and policy, which encompasses 'the general principles which guide the making of laws, administration, and executive acts of government in domestic and international affairs.' (Scruton 1992, pp. 262, 358) Indeed, policy implies consistency over time which is not necessarily the case for legislative measures: and certainly inconsistency could be seen to characterise Italian and Spanish policy, as discussed in the following section.

Immigration, policy development and citizenship

The above sections have discussed a number of important similarities between the situation of immigrants in Italy and Spain, in terms of their numbers, patterns of arrival and public perceptions, although there are also certain differences, notably concerning their geographical distribution. However, when one turns to the development of legislation and policy, differences between the two countries become more evident; indeed, it can be argued that although policy development is at a very early stage, the two countries are progressively moving towards quite different models with regard to long-term resident migrants.

In Italy, the most significant legal norms to date referring to immigrants from outside the EU are represented by two laws, the first passed in 1986 (Law 943: *Norms on the employment and treatment of immigrant workers from outside of the EC and the prevention of undocumented migration*) and the second in 1990, the so-called 'Martelli Law' (Law 39: *Special measures on political asylum, entry and residence for non-EU national and stateless citizens already present in the country*). Both laws stipulate criteria, procedures and time-limits for regularisation of the status of those immigrants who were in an irregular or illegal position, and it is this aspect of the laws that have perhaps received most attention. Law 943 upholds the principle that non-EU workers already present in the country should enjoy the same treatment and rights as Italian workers. The law is divided into separate administrative provisions, such as the granting of an entry visa being dependent on the existence of an authorisation to work (Article 8). Work and residence permits normally last two years and may be extended. Meanwhile, the law envisages three categories for entry: asylum seekers, family reunification for immigrants legally resident and fully employed, and labourers called individually by employers who guarantee both employment and adequate housing.

However, in addition, both laws go further. For example, the 1986 law also provided for the setting up of regional immigrant advisory councils, new representative bodies of immigrants, and task-forces at the Ministries of Labour and Foreign Affairs to foster immigration policy for employees, while the 1990 law stipulated new norms for entry, sojourn and expulsion and approved funds to the Italian regions for the creation of primary reception centres for immigrants. Meanwhile, since the publication of the Martelli Law, the Italian government has issued a number of decrees and amendments to the law, which further regulate flows of new immigrants and conditions for those already in the country. This system is seen as a pliable instrument, able to meet labour market demands, although some have described the changes as xenophobic (*Migration News Sheet*, December 1995, p. 3).

Across these various decrees, a pattern is clear: of the development of a 'preventative' policy with regards to new immigration, and attempts to assimilate immigrants already in the country. Thus, for example, in Italy measures taken include the allocation of immigrants' children in a dispersed fashion to Italian schools, partly in order to maintain a majority of Italian children per classroom and hence prevent the development of 'immigrant ghettos' in certain neighborhoods. In this sense, Italy can be seen as moving towards the French model of 'assimilation', which Solé (1988, p. 60) describes as 'the melting pot idea'. This implies the cultural, social and political subordination of one group to the other, and the partial or total loss of immigrants' identity as they merge with the majority group. It can be contrasted with 'integration', in which the indigenous population and a minority group gradually move towards equality on the socio-economic, cultural and political levels, becoming a single population unit (Solé 1981).

With regard to citizenship, there has also been some legislative development. Italian citizenship is now based on a new law, approved in 1992, which abolished the previous law that dated back to 1912. In essence, this early law favoured return migrants of Italian origin, but made the achievement of citizenship difficult for third-country nationals. In contrast Italian citizenship can now be obtained:

- *jus sanguinis*, i.e. by having Italian parents, including by adoption;
- *jus soli*, but only where the parents of a child found in Italy are unknown ;
- by *decree*, to a foreigner whose father or mother was an Italian citizen by birth; to an adult foreigner adopted by an Italian citizen; to a foreigner who has served for at least five years as an employee of the Italian state; or to a foreigner who engages in military service in Italy;
- by *marriage* to an Italian citizen, after residing legally in Italy for at least 6 months, or after three years of marriage; and
- by *naturalisation*: on some conditions, as service rendered to the Italian state for a period of five years, even if abroad, or through residence in Italy for ten years.

However, naturalisation, a decree of the President of the Republic, only comes into effect when loyalty has been sworn to the Republic of Italy and to its President, and is not easy to obtain (*Migration News Sheet*, December 1995, p. 3). In turn, citizenship can be refused in the case of a prison sentence of more than one year and for an attempt to undermine the security of the Italian Republic. Italian citizenship may also be lost if a new citizenship is acquired.

In Spain, the basis for migrants to obtain citizenship is very similar to Italy. For example, in both cases, preference is given to descendants of emigrants; in the Spanish case, these are mainly Ibero-Americans, who are citizens of Spain's former colonies in Latin America, whilst in the case of Italy, which had few such colonial ties, the main target group is descendants of former Italian emigrants or those married to Italians in the United States, Northern Europe and Australia. However, differences do begin to open up when one considers the broader spread of immigration policy, rather than the detail of citizenship law. Thus to a certain extent, the emerging situation in Spain with respect to longer-term resident migrants can be described as more akin to the German model, whereby immigrants are viewed as temporary guests. For example, the Foreigners' Law (*Ley Extranjería*) of 1985, which was the first Spanish law ever to regulate directly the rights and responsibilities of foreigners in Spain (Bodega et al. 1995), was very much based on the German legislation for migrants, reflecting Spain's active participation in the Schengen Agreement, for which Germany was the driving force (Cornelius 1994; Santos 1993).

The need for such a law, as noted earlier, arose from continuing migrant pressure, and the pressure of public opinion, within Spain. The main objectives of the law were fourfold and can be summarised as:

- to systematise entry and residence procedures for foreigners in Spain;
- to protect the national job market;
- to guarantee acceptable working conditions for foreigners, as well as to assist them to integrate, avoiding illegality and marginalisation;
- to harmonise Spanish legislation with that of other EU member states, working within the framework of the European unification process, and especially the Schengen agreement.

However, three articles of this law were found unconstitutional in July 1987 and in itself the law was very difficult to implement in many cases, because of its technical complexity and the deficient infrastructure of a 'country unfamiliar with the administrative actions of immigration' (OECD report cited in Bodega et al. 1995, p. 308). Most of the criticisms of the law were centred upon its discriminatory character, although in reality Spain was only following European immigration policies which facilitate freedom of movement *within* EC member states, but restrict the entry of third-country nationals, especially those from the Third World. Within Spain, meanwhile, although discrimination is directed towards various ethnic minorities, some groups, notably Ibero-Americans, Portuguese, Filipinos, Andorrans, Equatorial-Guineans and the original inhabitants of Gibraltar are given preferential treatment. This is not simply a question of former colonial and other historical ties – for example, no such treatment exists for Moroccans coming from the region which was a Spanish protectorate until 1956.

With respect to immigration policy, Spain has tightened its borders in full compliance with Schengen, and has moved towards the regularisation of foreigners already living in Spain. Thus 1996 saw the onset of two very important processes for immigrants in Spain: first, a new regularisation process aimed at some 50,000 foreigners without residence permits; and secondly, a modification of the regulations of the *Ley Extranjería*, making it slightly less strict. For example, one of the amendments of the *Ley Extranjería* allows immigrants to obtain visa extensions of two years after their first year of residence and then of longer duration until they are considered permanent residents, where previously they had to renew their visas each year. However, even though it is the only country in the Southern European region which can claim to have moved a step further towards an immigration policy in its broader sense, rather than just passing legislation on an *ad hoc* basis, the social and juridical dimension of this Spanish policy are still not so well established. Of course, it could be argued that having no defined policy is also a policy, since it gives the state the flexibility to respond to rising needs (Cornelius 1994).

One important development in Spain has been the establishment of a quota system for those who apply for a work and residence visa. This system allowed 20,600 migrant workers to obtain visas in 1993, 29,349 in 1994, and 20,600 in 1995, and included the possibility for workers who were already residing in Spain illegally to regularise their situation (see Mendoza, Chapter 3).

In both Spain and Italy, autonomy of the regions is evident, but one further difference is that in Spain, the region of Catalonia is working on its own policy of integration of immigrants, independent of the rest of the country. In Italy, some regions have taken more initiative than others to demonstrate their support towards the immigrants, as is discussed in the following section. However, there is no region with such a developed policy of integration of immigrants as Catalonia. Here, the regional government – the Generalitat de Catalunya – has enacted a plan of integration for migrants (*Pla Interdepartmental d'Immigració*), in collaboration with the trade union CITE and other local organisations based in Barcelona and neighboring towns, in which theoretically, it implements the politics of *jus soli*. According to this principle, the children of immigrants are considered as Catalans, and receive compulsory schooling in Catalan, and measures to promote their integration (a principle that also applies to other Spaniards). This reflects the fact that the Catalan government is working towards asserting Catalonia as an autonomous entity with its own language, as well as perhaps a greater degree of open-mindedness to diversity, and tolerance of immigration, in a relatively rich part of Spain that has long been a recipient region of migrants – especially other Spaniards. Of course, the development of this policy has its limits: for example, the application of the politics of *jus sanguinis* versus *jus soli* is ultimately left to the jurisdiction of the central state in Madrid, and Catalonia at the moment has no power to apply the principle of *jus soli* to third-country nationals residing upon its territory. Notwithstanding Catalan calls for more autonomy, at present it can only decide how to integrate immigrants, rather that give them legal status.

Regional, local and private initiatives

In Italy, regional initiative is more extensive and relevant than Spain, not least because immigrants are much more widely dispersed around the country. Nonetheless, there is a significant gap between the planned norm and the concrete initiatives undertaken (Bonifazi and Gesano 1994). In practice, Italian regions are highly differentiated in the extent to which they have managed to activate concrete policies on immigration. The first initiatives regarding immigrants were launched in the early 1980s in some of the larger cities of Central and Northern Italian regions. In Lombardy, Umbria, Piedmont, Liguria, Emilia Romagna and Tuscany, there is arguably a high degree of sensitivity as far as planned measures and concrete initiatives are concerned. For example, in Brescia, the city authorities have not only organised their own structures, but have also coordinated the activities of other bodies. In 1989 an *ad hoc* local service was created in Brescia: the Reception and Orientation Office for non-EU foreigners, and it at once assumed an important role in orientating immigrants in the use of public services. The Office keeps a register of users, as well as helping them find work and accommodation. Initiatives in this field have included the restoration of old buildings, an agreement with hotels, and the formation of housing co-operatives. There has also been an increase in the number of immigrants' associations, for which the local authorities act as coordinators. The industrial sector has organised an occupational training course for metal-workers (Treves 1989). Meanwhile in Turin, unions and businesses have both been active in promoting occupational training for immigrants. Local authorities have played an important part in job finding, placing immigrants in public building projects or in other areas of public interest. There have been some interesting initiatives in the area of education: apart from literacy courses, school integration and middle-school certificate projects, there is also a multicultural training course for teachers on the agenda. Nonetheless, the meeting of social needs, and especially accommodation needs, has arguably been less successful.

Elsewhere in Italy, however, the situation of immigrants is not as good. Apart from a general lack of preparedness, delays in dealing with immigrants have been attributed to the slowness of administrative procedures. A regional Council for Immigration Problems (with the participation of some co-opted or elected immigrant representatives) has been set up in almost all regions, but this body only appears to work in a third of these regions. In principle, its responsibilities cover cultural and educational initiatives, social welfare, economic assistance, reception centres, domestic help, accommodation, health care, and initiatives encouraging the formation of associations 'for' and 'of' non-EU immigrants, although these are not always acted upon, or necessarily successful (see Però, Chapter 8). In particular, in the South of Italy, public measures have not been so successful and social forces and the voluntary sector have acted in a climate of general indifference. Meanwhile, there has also been an absence of any real commitment on the part of the public institutions.

In Spain, the number of immigrants is lower and there is a quota system which to some extent controls entry, such that the number and variety of regional initiatives for immigrant integration is much lower. Beyond the example of initiatives of the Catalan government mentioned above, however, there are some well-known organisations which are involved in voluntary work with immigrants across the whole of Spain, and especially in Barcelona, Baleares, Canarias, Málaga, Andalucia and Madrid, where the majority of the migrants reside. These organisations include the *Comisiones Obreras*, a trade union which helps migrants through its specialised information centre (CITE), as well as *SOS Racismo*, the *Centro d'Informacio e Documentacio de Barcelona* (CIDOB), the *Asociación de Solidaridad con los Trabajadores Immigrantes* (ASTI), CARITAS, Jama Kafo, and the *Colectivo IOE*. These organisations arrange tours of Barcelona and neighboring localities, hold classes in vocational training to help immigrants achieve qualifications which are recognised by Spanish employees, and help with finding jobs.

Most of the organisations mentioned above support the maintenance of migrants' own cultural identity, as a better way to allow integration in Spanish society in the short term, and allow the possibility of return migration in the longer term. This is based on the premise that expecting an immigrant to renounce almost completely his or her previous identity could cause serious conflicts and a sense of insecurity within the individual, especially if they find it difficult to achieve citizenship rights in the host country. Such organisations are trying to help the migrants to integrate in Spain but are also holding evening classes on Arabic and Arabic culture, for example for North Africans, so that the children of Maghrebi migrants will always feel they have the choice of returning to their country of origin if they choose to.

Conclusion

Individual European countries' migratory policies have featured restrictive and coercive elements in recent years. In the light of this, a basic need for coordination has often been felt. Yet, neither the EU nor any other international organisation have so far managed to make effective progress in this direction. The attempt to standardise the practices of some European countries (e.g. in Schengen) does not seem to have overcome problems caused by viewing the issue of immigration in purely conjectural or local terms. In fact, in spite of the same economic crisis, the same social problems and – what seems to be the most important – the same targets (more or less agreed upon), each country still seems to be reacting in its own way: even when a comparison of the solutions adopted (especially restrictive ones) could lead one to think that there might be room for a European agreement on migratory policies.

What can be seen quite clearly from the situation in Southern Europe is the extent to which immigration of workers from poor countries can be described as a direct response to specific demands for cheap labour articulated by employers and their representatives in the political and administrative process; or whether the migration process is essentially supply-driven by factors of poverty and demography (King and Konjhodzic 1996, p. 74). It is still unclear to what extent competition exists between immigrants and national workers. Initiatives to integrate legalised immigrants and decisions with respect to the extent that migrants can achieve citizens' rights are still at very early stages. Even in the areas where migrants have secured certain rights, the gap is still very wide between these rights and what is truly done to help them benefit from these rights.

One thing is more certain however: there are various disequilibria prevailing between the Northern and Southern banks of the Mediterranean which will continue to persist for some time. Too strict immigration policies will only help fuel an increase in clandestine

entries. In this sense, as Collinson (1996, p. 98) states, 'the central issue
. . . is development, not migration. Migration is likely to continue in
some form or another, and may even increase, whatever the outcome of
future economic cooperation between the EU and the Maghreb.' EU
member states, including Italy and Spain, have placed much reliance on
traditional forms of immigration regulation, as reflected recently in the
Barcelona declaration of November 1995. So far, migration has been
treated as 'a problem with straightforward solutions, rather than as a
continuous structural component of international interaction and integration, to which there may be no solution as such, but which continues
to pose a challenge throughout all levels of domestic and international
policy-making' (Collinson 1996, p. 95). Rather than preventing and
regulating migration, which may represent a short-term solution, states
such as Spain and Italy may need instead to cooperate, to study what
kinds of interventions would tackle the root causes of the new immigration flows.

References

Barclay, G. St. J. (1995) The European Union and the Maghreb: a clash of civili-
sations? *Australia and World Affairs*, 25(4), pp. 5–17.
Bodega, I., Cebrian, J.A., Frenchini, T., Lora-Tomayo, G. and Martin-Lou, A.
(1995) Recent migrations from Morocco to Spain, *International Migration
Review*, 29 (3), pp. 800–19
Bonifazi, C. (1992) Italian attitudes and opinions towards foreign migrants and
migration policies, *Studi Emigrazione*, 105, pp. 21–42.
Bonifazi, C. and Gesano, G. (1994) L'immigrazione straniera tra regolazione dei
flussi e politiche di accogliamento, in Golini, A., ed., *Tendenze Demografiche e
Politiche per la Poplazione, Terzo Rapporto*. Rome: IRP, pp. 259–89.
Colectivo IOE (1986) Los immigrantes en España, *La Documentación Social*, 66,
pp. 22–40.
Colectivo IOE (1990) Spain's illegal immigrants, *Contemporary European Affairs*,
3, pp. 117–37.
Collinson, S. (1993) *Beyond Borders: West European Migration Policy Towards the
21st Century*. London: Royal Institute of International Affairs.
Collinson, S. (1996) *Shore to Shore: The Politics of Migration in Euro-Maghreb
Relations*, London: Royal Institute of International Affairs.
Commission of the European Communities (1994) *Strengthening the
Mediterranean Policy of the European Union: establishing a Euro-Mediterranean
partnership*. Brussels: Communication from the Commission to the Council
and the European Parliament (COM (94) 427 final).
Cornelius, W.A. (1994) Spain: the uneasy transition from labor exporter to labor
importer, in Cornelius, W.A., Martin, P.L. and Hollifield, J.F., eds., *Controlling
Immigration: A Global Perspective*, Stanford, California: Stanford University
Press, pp. 331–69.

Garcia, S. (1993) *Europe's Fragmented Identities and the Frontiers of Citizenship*, London: Royal Institute of International Affairs, Discussion Paper 45.

Hammar, T. (1992) *European Immigration Policy*, Cambridge: Cambridge University Press.

Izquierdo, A. (1992) *La Inmigración en España 1980–1990*. Madrid: Ministerio de Trabajo y Seguridad Social (Collection "Informes Serie General", 17).

King, R. and Konjhodzic, I. (1996) Labour, employment and migration in Southern Europe, in van Oudenaren, J., ed., *Employment, Economic Development and Migration in Southern Europe and the Maghreb*. Santa Monica, California: RAND, pp. 7–106.

Levelt, U. (1995) The European Union as a political community through the lens of immigration policy, in Martiniello, M., ed., *Migration, Citizenship and Ethno-National Identities in the European Union*. Aldershot: Avebury.

Lopez García, B. (1990) L'Espagne entre le Maghreb et l'Europe: imaginaire et interférences de l'opinion dans la politique Maghrébin de l'Espagne, *Annuaire de l'Afrique du Nord*, 29, pp. 23–37.

Santos, L. (1993) Elementos juridicos de la integración de los extranjeros, in Tapinos, G., ed., *Inmigración e Integración en Europa*, Barcelona: Fundacion Paulino Torres Domenech, pp. 91–125.

Scruton, R. (1992) *A Dictionary of Political Thought*. London, Richard Clay.

Solé, C. (1981) *La Integración Sociocultural de los Inmigrantes en Catalunya*, Madrid: CIS.

Solé, C. (1988) *Catalunya: Societat Receptora d'Inmigrantes*, Barcelona: Institut d'Estudis Catalans.

Spencer, C. (1993) *The Maghreb in the 1990s*. London: Adelphi Paper 274.

Treves, C. (ed.) (1989) *Sindacato dei Diritti e Società Multietnica*, Rome: Ediesse.

Tapinos, G. (1993) La integración y su medida, in Tapinos, G., ed., *Inmigración e Integración en Europa*, Barcelona: Fundacion Paulino Torres Domenech, pp. 17–32.

Vicarelli, G. (1994) *Le Mani Invisibili*. Rome: Ediesse.

Werth, M. and Körner, H. (1991) Immigration of citizens from third countries into the southern member states of the EEC, *Social Europe*, Supplement 1/91, pp. 1–134.

Wiener, A. (1996) Rethinking citizenship: the quest for place-oriented participation in the EU, *Oxford International Review*, 7(3), pp. 44–51.

Zolberg, A. (1987) Keeping them out: ethical dilemmas of immigration policy, in Myers, R., ed., *International Ethics in the Nuclear Age*, Lanham, Maryland: University Press of America, pp. 261–97.

8

Immigrants and Politics in Left-Wing Bologna: Results from Participatory Action Research

Davide Però

———

The main general aim of this contribution is to provide some insights into what goes on in relation to immigration in what is considered to be the most progressive city in Italy, Bologna. Parallel to this, there is the additional aim of making available to the many people operating within the immigration sector one of the still rare experiences in using participatory action research (PAR) in the context of migration in Italy and in Southern Europe more generally[1]. This will be done by drawing on an extensive period of field research there[2]. The examination of the life conditions of a group of 'regular' (i.e. 'legal') male Moroccan workers residing in one of the major council housing schemes for immigrants, as well as an outline of the particular socio-political fabric in which the housing scheme is located, will constitute the case-study presented in this chapter. The research process and the results to which it has led will also be the object of critical reflection.

The chapter is organised as follows. I start with a general portrait of Bologna touching on some of its most characteristic traits. That will be

———

1 Another useful account of participatory research with immigrants in Turin is given by Maher (1995). Of interest is also the account of action-research concerning immigrants and local communities in Emilia-Romagna presented in Pepa (1996).
2 This field research is part of my D.Phil. in Anthropology at the University of Sussex. My fieldwork in Bologna lasted from December 1994 to October 1995 and also involved a number of subsequent visits. I dedicate this chapter to G. Mohammed, E. J. Omari, M. Ahmed, K. Said and the others.

followed by a general review of the immigration phenomenon in the city, paying particular attention to the question of housing. Then, after providing a concise account of the principles of participatory action research, the PAR case study with the residents of one 'centre of first shelter' (*centro di prima accoglienza* or CPA) will be presented, starting with a general description of the housing project, its location and its early goals. This will be followed by an account of some of the local views of such a residential structure. These views will be subsequently compared and contrasted with the actual situation found in the CPA. An examination of some the main differences existing within the group of residents will be then carried out (also in order to question some of the dominant institutional views which see or want them as a *community*). Particular emphasis will be given to the differences in the residents' migratory projects. Then the chapter will move on to a brief description of the lifestyle within the centre and of the kind of social relations which seem to exist with the 'outside'. That will be followed by an analysis of the political-institutional relationships, that is to say the kind of relations existing between the residents and the council authorities administering the CPA. Here particular attention will be paid to the immigrant residents' own views on the matter. An account of the participatory action will end the presentation of the ethnographic case study. Critical considerations about the project and the local institutional practices will constitute the conclusion.

Bologna: some general features

Bologna is a town located in North-Central Italy. It is the capital city of Emilia-Romagna, the region which extends south of the Po river. The population residing in Bologna numbers roughly 400,000, while that of its province numbers 900,000 (including Bologna), and that of Emilia-Romagna 3.9 million.

In order to describe the main economic, social, cultural and political features of the town, I will draw on a local popular expression which describes Bologna as 'la Rossa, la Grassa e la Dotta', which in English would sound approximately like 'the Red, the Fat, and the Knowledgeable'. Let us start with the *Fat*, which symbolises the good food of its exuberant and prodigal *cucina*, and at a more general level the city's abundance and wealth. Bologna belongs to the richest area in Southern Europe (see King and Konjhodzic 1995, p. 34). The economy of the town is based on the tertiary sector and an extremely well-developed structure of small and medium industries. Its province and region also have a very strong agricultural sector. The region's most typical productive unit is the *co-operative* (some 25 per cent of the whole productive system). Bologna (and its region) also has one of the lowest unemployment rates in Southern Europe (cf. King and Konjhodzic 1995, p. 40). Bologna is said to be *Knowledgeable* because it hosts the oldest university of the Western world, founded in 1088. Currently Bologna University has over 90,000 students and is one of the largest in the country. Finally, Bologna could be described as the *Red* because, besides the typical red colour of its traditional buildings, it has a long-established left-wing administration. In fact, since the end of World War II the town, as well as the region, has been continuously governed, first by the PCI, the Italian Communist Party (the second largest party in cold-war Italy), and then, since 1991 by the Democratic Party of the Left or PDS.[3] The PDS is now the largest party of Italy, and by far the largest in Bologna. The work of the Bologna council has always involved providing social services which were outstanding by Italian standards (Ginsborg 1990; Jaggi et al. 1977; Kertzer 1980). Experimental and innovative policies have always characterised and distinguished the local administration of Bologna, for example in relation to the working classes, women, old people, homosexuals, and (with many reservations) Third World immigrants.

Immigration in Bologna: the quantitative dimension

General features and employment

Unlike the northern European countries, immigration in Italy is a fairly recent phenomenon, as we saw in Chapter 1. Indeed, Italy until not long ago was itself a country of emigration, and it was only since the early 1980s that it became a receiving or immigration country on a large scale. The reasons for Italy's attraction as a country of immigration were also outlined in Chapter 1 and are further discussed in a wide range of sources (see e.g. Barsotti and Lecchini 1994; King 1993).

In the mid-late 1980s, the immigration of people from developing countries to Bologna and its province underwent a significant acceleration. Recent official figures estimate the actual number of both 'regulars' and 'irregulars' at around 15,000–16,000, corresponding to 1.5–2 per cent of the population of the province.[4] This number is slightly higher than the national average, but is much lower than the percentage of

3 The PDS is what the PCI became in 1991, after a long process of transition during which, no longer Communist and not yet PDS, the Party was publicly called 'la cosa' or the thing!
4 These figures and others which follow in this account are taken from a local publication *La Società Multietnica*, no. 1, published by the Osservatorio Metropolitano sulle Immigrazioni di Bologna, 1995. These statistics are broadly consistent with recently published, more aggregated data on *permessi di soggiorno* (Caritas di Roma 1996). These latter figures show that on 31 December 1995 the province of Bologna had 17,256 permit-

foreigners in European countries with long-established immigration such as Germany (7.3 per cent), France (6.3 per cent), Great Britain (3.5 per cent) etc. Thus on the whole it can be said that the metropolitan area of Bologna has a rather limited migrant presence, in relation to the other major European countries. It is, however, more typical of the phenomenon of the 'new immigrant presence' in Southern Europe. Regarding the nationality of the immigrants from developing countries residing in the town at the end of 1994, Moroccans constituted by far the largest group (1,028; of which 828 were men and 200 women), followed by Filipinos (660), Chinese, Tunisians, ex-Yugoslavs, Pakistanis and Albanians.

Given the relative facility to find regular and stable employment, the Bologna area (and Emilia-Romagna more generally) has for many immigrants come to represent a sort of second destination in their migratory route within Italy. Often, in fact, such routes start off in the south of the country with illegal and extremely exploitative work conditions, usually in agriculture and (less frequently) fishing. This is related to the fact that many North African migrants arrive in the south, often crossing to Sicily by boat, and work there for a time before moving northwards to find better jobs.

The kinds of jobs available in the Bologna regional labour markets which are most commonly taken up by immigrants are those usually classified as unskilled labour (even though the demand for skilled labour is growing, but apparently not enough training courses are being run to enable immigrants to meet this sector of demand). The sectors which absorb most male immigrant labour are the building industry (*edilizia*), agriculture, and manufacturing industry (mechanical, food, and so forth). Immigrants are also often found in jobs requiring night work (bakeries, or hotel porters etc.). Women, especially Filipinos, are usually employed in domestic and care work. It must be highlighted that all such sectors of the labour market have become rejected by the indigenous population, which prefers skilled employment in the tertiary sector. Consequently the recurrent prejudicial claim that 'immigrants take *our* jobs' sounds particularly unfair, especially in Bologna. In fact it must be acknowledged that not only do immigrants not take what are supposedly indigenous jobs, but they actually contribute quite significantly to the high standard of wealth and quality of life for the indigenous inhabitants in the area.

holders, of whom 14,023 were non-EU nationals. For the wider region of Emilia-Romagna, the total number of immigrant permit-holders was 76,354, of whom 66,641 were non-EU nationals; the main nationalities were Moroccans (12,811), Tunisians (5,753), Senegalese (3,937), Albanians (3,754), ex-Yugoslavians (2,592), Ghanaians (2,307), Chinese (2,195) and Filipinos (2,105).

An important characteristic of the immigrant population in Bologna province is its high unionisation: approximately 2,800 have joined one of the three major unions: CGIL, CISL and UIL. These figures are to be evaluated positively especially in consideration of the rather low rate of unionisation which characterises the small-industrial sector which dominates the economy of the province, and the general avoidance of unions by immigrant workers in Italy.

Housing

If the labour market does not seem to constitute a problem for the immigrants, the same cannot be said for the housing market. Finding decent accommodation at a reasonable price is, even for the indigenous working-class, extremely difficult these days, as in Bologna there are no flats available for less than $700–750 per month (exclusive of other costs such as heating etc.). For the immigrants, because of racial discrimination, the situation is even worse. Housing, in fact, has immediately constituted the major problem that the immigrants have faced in the city and its surrounding area since their substantial arrivals during the mid-1980s. By the late 1980s the situation developing around the lack of housing for immigrants, in Bologna as well as in the rest of Italy, was commonly addressed as *emergenza* (emergency). Thus, immigrants have been forced to sleep and live outdoors, in fields, cars, abandoned houses, old caravans, in situations of extremely poor hygienic conditions; others found accommodation in situations of dubious regularity, where ruthless landlords (sometimes their own employers) took advantage of their need. In 1989, the then Social Policies Councillor of Bologna wrote in an official report: ' . . . the need [of housing] is increasingly urgent, as is unfortunately testified by the high number of illegal immigrants and workers who sleep in absolutely subhuman conditions' (Bartolini 1989, p. 6; my translation).

The illegal occupations of public housing, which were carried out by immigrants at the time, contributed to both bringing the question of housing to the attention of public opinion, and pressing for a more incisive intervention by the local administration. In a conversation on the topic, one of the original leaders of the immigrant occupations in Bologna pointed out what happened. He stressed how the 'squatters', who were 'legal immigrant workers', only occupied houses which had not been assigned to the local population and indeed which had been closed down for years by the authorities because they were sited in an 'unhealthy' location, that is in proximity to tobacco manufacture. Moreover, he expressed the view that not only did the occupations press the local authorities to intervene, but they taught the immigrants the following lesson: 'rights are something that one takes, and not a gift [*regalo*] that somebody else makes to you'.

In the meantime, although with significant delay with regard to the situation that had developed, the immigration law 39/90 (widely known as the Martelli Law) was at last approved by the Italian parliament. Even if, according to many commentators, it was far from being free from vices, it did have some merits.[5] One of its merits was that it contributed to addressing, albeit partially, the question of housing. This was done by providing the regional authorities with funds to be allocated to the realisation, through the local council authorities, of 'centres of first shelter' or CPA. Around 1990 and 1991 in Bologna there were about 1,000 'first shelter' beds distributed in eight CPAs. The CPAs, according to Law 39/90, were meant to offer *accoglienza* (shelter) to the immigrant for 60 days. However, because after such a period the general situation of the immigrants with respect to housing was virtually unchanged, the Council authorities decided to extend it for another six months. However, by December 1991 it was clear that the immigrant housing policy in response to the Martelli Law had failed to promote the transition to the *seconda accoglienza* (the second shelter), so the administration decided to extend the duration of the 'shelter' for another two years! In October 1993 the newly appointed relevant councillor, in her presentation statement about immigration, acknowledged that not only had most CPA residents by then lived in such structures for two or three years, but they currently did not have any realistic possibility of a way out into a better residential condition. In other words, the CPA structures which originally came into being with the intent of providing a highly temporary service, were now officially acknowledged as permanent (Del Mugnaio 1993).

Before turning to a close examination of one of the CPAs, it is worth looking at the *management policies* of the centres of first shelter, as later they will be subject to scrutiny too. The first element to point out in this regard is that the management styles to which the CPAs have been subjected by the local administration have been two (at least until mid-late 1995), one quite different from the other. The first management approach adopted to govern the newly-instituted CPAs in early 1991 prescribed: i) a 24 hour porter's lodge service with the function of controlling the residents' passes, checking their rent payments, and co-ordinating with the security service; ii) a night security service (operating from 10.00 p.m. to 6.00 a.m) with the function of controlling the people within the residential structure, and checking their respect for the structure itself and its equipment; and iii) educators with the

5   For accessible critiques see Vasta (1993); Veugelers (1994).

function of promotional-educative intervention also in relation to residents' access to local resources and services (Comune di Bologna 1990).

However, in 1993 this centrally-directed management style was replaced by *'autogestione'* (self-management) in five of the CPAs. With such a move, the council administration tried to establish a new relationship with approximately 500 client-users of its residential structures. Such a passage from 'strong' management (with armed surveillance) to self-management was also intended to mark the boundary between the phase of *first shelter* and that of *second shelter*. *Autogestione*, in the eyes of the administration, would also have constituted the first significant step towards the goal of achieving localised 'centres of community' (*centri di comunità*) (cf. Del Mugnaio 1993).

The new management policy of *autogestione*, i.e. the creation of a *centre of community*, revealed itself to be quite problematical in terms of its implementation in a number of CPAs. One of the attempts to overcome such difficulties was that of steering towards the promotion of *autogestione* a participatory action research (PAR) project which a local NGO, funded by the Bologna city council, was about to carry out *'on'* (sic) the ethnic minority communities of the town. In other words, in order to implement the *autogestione* (which for the local authorities represented the first step toward the creation of a centre of community), an NGO with a specific project of PAR was brought in.

Before turning to a close analysis of one of the CPAs recipient of both *autogestione* and PAR, I would like to provide a concise account of the general priciples of participatory action research. Such a basic account aims at facilitating the understanding of the case-study being presented, and makes no claims to exhaustiveness. Deshler and Ewert (1995) provide the following operative definition of PAR: 'a process of systematic enquiry, in which those who are experiencing a problematic situation in a community or workplace participate collaboratively with trained researchers as subjects, in deciding the focus of knowledge generation, in collecting and analysing information, and in taking action to manage, improve, or solve their problem situation'.[6]

They also highlight how the term *participation* indicates a 'democratisation thrust' in the social research process. In fact, in PAR those who in conventional research are 'objects' of study become active and essential participants in the production of transformative knowledge (see also Gaventa 1991; Nelson and Wright 1995; Whyte 1991). With regard to *action*, Deshler and Ewert (1995) stress the crucial concern for the research process to directly and concretely impact on important social, political, economic or cultural questions which negatively affect the

6   Another effective definition is provided in Whyte (1991, p. 5).

(non-trained) participants. Thus, unlike conventional research, for PAR it is crucial to produce immediate changes which are beneficial for local people. *Research* points to the 'systematic effort to generate knowledge' primarily for local, specific and immediate use, rather than for the production of generalisable knowledge (Deshler and Ewert 1995), even though such a more abstract or universal type of knowledge (e.g. academic) may well come from PAR (Però 1996).

The CPA and the participatory action research

At some point in early 1995, while I was already in Bologna conducting fieldwork for my D.Phil. on the politics of identity of the Left in relation to immigrants, I got involved in the aforementioned project of 'participatory action research *on* the ethnic minority communities' (my emphasis). At first the project appeared to me as a great opportunity for fostering the process of 'learning the ropes' (Shaffir and Stebbings 1991), that is the process of gaining a more and more 'intimate familiarity' with the specific sector of social and political life that I was studying. My involvement in the PAR project looked very appealing to me for two other important reasons. The first was that it enabled me to have the chance to strengthen the transformative impact of my fieldwork, in terms of the creation of a more socially just local environment. The second reason was that my PAR involvement potentially contributed to a democratisation of my fieldwork, by balancing the 'extractive' character typical of more conventional field-research with a more active participation of the marginalised in the research process.

My recruitment, like that of most of the other professional action researchers, took place when the project was about to enter its empirical phase. The research group consisted of eight people coming from various disciplinary backgrounds (economics, political science, sociology, philosophy, education, and anthropology as in my case) and traditions of research training (Italy, the Netherlands, and Britain). Our task was that of contributing to the final planning and execution of the empirical part of the project in the field.

Until the beginning of the empirical phase, the project officially had a multiplicity of general and specific aims, which included: contributing to the development and empowerment of the 'ethnic minority communities', including fostering their role as collective actors; preventing and combating the exclusion of such 'communities' from urban life; constructing a 'map' of the immigrant communities involved in the project through self-representations of their history and experience; and achieving knowledge about the internal resources and the needs of such groups, their system of values and mechanisms of internal solidarity.

Despite the rather long list of official goals (of which the above are just a few), in practice two appeared to be privileged during the period preceding fieldwork. The rationale for the following two goals was strongly correlated with the type of immigrants who, in the meantime, had been selected for the project: Moroccan male workers living in two CPAs. Such a choice was, to a large extent, due to the fact that Moroccans constituted by far the largest group of immigrants in town, as well as the most heavily (709 out of 1,028) reliant on the residential structures of the council.

The first of the two goals which became paramount was that of helping to promote the new style of CPA management, i.e. *autogestione*, which council policy had recently prescribed but could not manage to implement. Such a policy would have marked the transition from the *first* to the *second shelter*, as well as the first step towards the creation of a *centre of community*. It must be said that the aim of achieving *autogestione* turned out to be somewhat controversial, and raised some perplexities within the research group, especially with regard to the practical feasibility of the project. In fact, it seemed unrealistic that we, who knew so little about these people's culture and lives, would have succeeded in enabling the creation of a sense of community through the implementation of *autogestione*. At a more personal level, the idea of trying to implement such a goal seemed to me at least questionable and moreover raised many ethical issues. How was it possible that such a radical research approach as PAR was being deprived of its most essential features – such as the participation of the marginalised in the action-research process so that the negative impact of the oppressive mechanisms of the establishment could be confronted – to become, in practice, a means through which the 'establishment' attempted to discipline and order the people at its margins? In other words, how was it possible that from being a tool of empowerment of the oppressed, PAR was basically being turned into a disempowering one? However, at that stage of the project the key question for me was the following: what was I going to do in relation to all that? Quitting or staying in? Taking into consideration the fact that probably I would be more helpful to the cause of the immigrants if I stayed, my eventual decision was to stay in and 'study up', as Laura Nader (1974) would put it, that is studying where the power is. Thus, I decided to continue on with the PAR and simultaneously carry out an ethnography of the establishment (benefiting from my official role as an NGO researcher), a little like Judith Okely did with the *gorgio* authorities in her study of the traveller gypsies in Britain (Okely 1983; 1994). And with regard to the objective of promoting *autogestione* and the creation of a 'centre of community', at the end it was decided that this should remain the main goal, at least until the empirical acquaintance with the CPA might suggest or force a re-direction.

The second goal which, in the period prior to fieldwork, appeared to be stressed alongside that of the promotion of *autogestione*, was a more generically cognitive one. This concerned the gathering of detailed qualitative data on various aspects of the life of immigrants living in the CPA structure, including connections between the migrants and the social fabric of the neighborhood. As we will see further on, the actions that actually took place under the second goal eventually resulted in a divergence from the first of the two initial goals.

Four researchers were mainly be concerned with one CPA, and four with the other. Meetings between the two research groups were arranged periodically in order to exchange experience and suggestions, as well as to compare the data collected. Below I provide an account of the PAR carried out in one of the two CPAs. This was the CPA I was myself involved in, and which was sited in the district of Bologna I knew best, the area in which I had been carrying out my doctoral fieldwork for some months already.

The CPA which I studied was opened in early 1991. Territorially it belonged to the borough in which I was living and conducting most of my ethnographic research on the politics of identity and the Left. The area of the district where the CPA is located could be described as 'first urban periphery'. However, within such an area, the CPA could be said to have a 'special' place. Such specificity consists of a quite evident isolation from the rest of the local residential area. In fact, the large car parking area for commuters, the heavily congested four-lane highway, another road edged by the high wall of an operating factory, and the uncultivated fields that constitute the immediate surroundings of the CPA, are quite effective in providing a powerful sense of disconnection from the nearest residential areas.

The CPA consists of 18 prefabricated metal bungalows plus two other buildings made of a similar material (the mosque, the office of the operators). Internally each of 18 bungalows is subdivided into two double rooms of about 2 x 3 metres separated by a bathroom of approximately 1.5 x 1.2 metres containing a sink, a shower and a toilet. The metal bungalows are positioned in squares of six so as to form three internal courtyards, from which the six bungalows can be accessed. Figure 8.1 is a map of the layout of the CPA and its immediate surroundings.

From the main road, the CPA, although visible, is certainly not eye-catching. Given the low height of the buildings and their greyish colour, it is likely to pass unobserved by most of the drivers in transit. Because the courtyards are basically invisible from the outside, most would not even think of it as a residential structure. At first sight in fact the bungalows, because of their close resemblance to portacabins, suggest more the idea of a building yard. After all, given that the customary residential pattern of the indigenous population consists of flats and houses, why should one think otherwise?

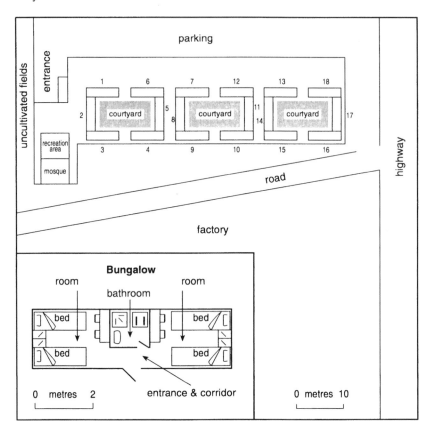

Figure 8.1   The CPA housing project for Moroccan immigrants, Bologna

However, as emerged from surveys conducted in the area prior to our entrance into the CPA, the Italian residents of the district would normally know that in there live *extracomunitari* (extra-communitarians, as the non-EU citizens from the Third World are commonly referred to); but that is all that most of them are likely to know, at least accurately, about the CPA, its inhabitants and their life conditions. Yet, much more than such a minimum knowledge is what the locals *believe* to know, as emerged from the conversations, descriptions, talks and representations gathered in the surveys. For example, somebody said that in the CPA lived over 200 people, somebody else described the living conditions of the centre as 'good'. Another thought that the living conditions in the centre were actually 'too good', especially given that 'they do not pay anything for living there, but we do'. Somebody else said that they were illegal/irregular (*'lavorano in nero'*) workers or pushers and blamed the council for housing such persons. Someone else thought they were Tunisians, and another thought they were gypsies. One of the two nearby bars which the immigrants frequented was, because of this reason, derogatorily renamed 'Tunisia' by some unsympathetic locals.

Entrance into the CPA and some features of the residents

After the surveys in the area surrounding the CPA, we entered the centre. This was facilitated by the help of two former *'operatori'* (staff) who introduced us to the residents. Once inside, one of the first things which we became aware of was the general aversion of the residents to abstract and wordy meetings, perceived as 'useless talks', which they had developed over the years. Accordingly, in order to overcome their initial legitimate diffidence we made an extra effort to emphasise the distinctiveness of our presence there in terms of concrete and practical orientations.

Here follows an ethnographic account covering some aspects of the life in the residential structure designed for hosting immigrant workers. The residents, all Moroccan men, officially numbered 72. However, the actual number was revealed to be somewhat higher, given the constant presence of guests and squatters, whose sex not always matched the relevant requirements of the regulations. As required by the regulations, the official residents were all 'regular' or legal immigrants, they were all residing in Bologna and they were all workers (mainly employed in the industrial and building sectors as unskilled labour), even though a few remained temporarily unemployed. With regard to the presence of 'irregular' residents, these features were much less to be taken for granted.

Although all the residents of the CPA were from Morocco, they were far from being a homogenous group, let alone a 'community' (as in various cases they have been portrayed or referred to). Many were the *differentiations* existing within the group. One differentiation concerned the *educational level*, which ranged from a few illiterates who usually had a rather poor knowledge of spoken Italian, to a few graduates who fluently spoke Italian as well as English (and of course French). The majority were somewhere between these two extremes; a significant portion had the equivalent of A-levels, and quite a number of these had attended university without accomplishing the entire course of study. The older residents tended to be less educated than the younger.

With regard to their *age*, most residents were in the bracket going from late twenties to early forties. The residents were also differentiable in terms of *marital status*, even though none of the married men was able to have his wife there; roughly half were married and half were not. Sharp differences existed also with regard to the place of origin, as approximately half of them came from a rural location in Morocco.

An important element of differentiation among the residents (especially in relation to the social policy of *autogestione*) was their *migratory project*. Some of the residents in fact were only temporarily resident there, and had no intention to settle down permanently in Italy. In most cases these people had left their wives and children in Morocco, whom they eventually intended to rejoin once the economic target that they had set for themselves had been considered as achieved. On the whole, this was the category of people that seemed to accept more easily their life conditions in Bologna. (This was probably due to their awareness that they were experiencing a situation of only temporary discomfort, of psycho-physical and cultural deprivation which would only last for a limited period, as sooner or later they would return 'home'). For them, usually emigration represents the way to find the resources to improve further an economic activity already established at 'home', or the means of starting a new one, such as a small business. These people seemed very hard workers, and avid savers: just the strictly necessary was spent on food, clothing etc., and virtually no money was spent on leisure activities, except tobacco. Their days were strictly spent between the workplace, commuting time and the residence. These were 'target migrants', oriented to an eventual return home, and usually in their late thirties and forties.

The remaining migrants could be further subdivided into those who intended to settle down in Italy, and those who had mixed feelings. For the latter, their experience of 'permanent liminality' – i.e. the awareness coming from the prolonged experience of having left Morocco a long time ago and not having quite 'arrived' yet in Italy – increasingly made them sceptical about the actual possibility of a proper settlement. All the former were still living in the CPA after four years because of the difficulty in finding proper accommodation. For those who were married and wanted to bring their wives over from Morocco, the situation was even more difficult as the law prescribed that they had to be renting a flat *on their own* for a certain number of months before they could bring their family to Italy. And in Bologna, as previously mentioned, there are no flats cheaper than $750 per month (excluding bills), a sum which is likely to be over two-thirds an immigrant's monthly wage. How can they possibly survive and support a family with the remaining sum of approximately $270? Given such conditions it is more convenient to keep on living in the CPA which only costs one-sixth the rent of a small flat. The housing market thus strongly conditions them towards keeping on staying in the CPA.

The consequences of such a *de facto* imposed residential pattern, especially when it is prolonged over the years, are multifaceted and difficult to assess with some precision, but certainly they reinforce the dynamics of exclusion, marginality, resentment and displacement (no longer there, not yet here). Such a situation of *residential apartheid* seems to have played a great role in making some of the immigrants reconsider important ideas, convictions and beliefs, including political and religious ones, that they had at the moment of their arrival and for some time after. With regard to politics, for example, some immigrants who located themselves on the Left of the political spectrum, confessed that their experiences in Bologna have made them increasingly disillusioned with progressive politics. In some cases, the vacuum that such disillusionment creates seems be filled by an increase in sympathy or support for extreme strands of the Islamic religion.

The lifestyle in the CPA and its relationships with the outside

Most of the daily non-work activities of the CPA residents take place in their metal bungalow, and in particular inside the double room which each of them shared with another fellow resident (see figure 8.1). Such a small room contained two beds, plus a few small pieces of furniture some of which were used as wardrobes and others as cupboards for the storage of various objects and food. Most rooms also had a fridge (sometimes two) which had been installed by the residents themselves. The location of the fridge varied according to the location and shape of the rest of the furniture. Sometimes it had a place of its own, in other cases it was placed on top of the cupboard or wardrobe. A small low table was often placed between the two beds; one of its main functions was to serve as a surface for the preparation of food. Suitcases and shoes were kept under the beds together with various other objects (e.g. sports equipment). Most rooms had a hi-fi stereo as well as a television. The TV set was often connected to a satellite dish so that Moroccan and other Arabic programs could be watched in addition to the Italian ones. The narrow corridor that led from the main door of the bungalow to the two rooms and the bathroom was usually the location of a small electric cooker and a cupboard for the storage of pans and crockery.

In winter, when the average temperature in Bologna is close to freezing, the evening and weekend cooking usually involves moving back and forth between the bedroom (where the food is stored and prepared), the corridor (where the actual cooking takes place), and the bathroom (for the supply of water and for washing-up). Eating the meal takes place in the bedroom and usually involves four or six people. In Spring, the warmer weather enables the residents to take advantage of the space outdoors. Thus some of the above activities are carried out in the courtyard just outside the bungalow. In summer cooking and eating outdoors is no longer a choice but becomes a necessity, given that the temperature inside the metal bungalows becomes hardly bearable. For the same reason, at this time of the year a number of residents move their mattresses to the courtyards and sleep outdoors.

Cooking is however just one of the most common daily activities which the structure of the CPA turns into an awkward task to accomplish. Ironing, for instance, is another. Given the lack of space for a proper table, ironing is often done on one's own bed. The extra difficulty constituted by the wobbling ironing surface – i.e. the mattress – is overcome by the high skills that the resident has developed over various years of practice. Washing is mostly done by hand in the bathroom sink, even if it is not uncommon to see the few washing machines which some residents bought and placed in the courtyard at work (especially at the weekend).

The turning of what for most people in Bologna are rather straightforward daily activities into awkward tasks is not the worst outcome that the CPA structure can produce. In fact, there are common activities which simply cannot take place at all in such a residential scheme, like sex or studying, to name but two.

In addition, there are questions of hygiene and health, which in such a place cannot be other than poor, despite the cleaning by residents. One example which is often quoted by the residents when discussing these matters (as well as easily observable if one enters the bungalows) is the massive presence of cockroaches and black beetles all over the place: 'they are between the walls. No matter how much insecticide you spray, you just can't get rid of them'. One resident, I was told on a couple of occasions, had to rush to the hospital during the night because a cockroach ended up in his ear and he could not get it out. Another example of the dubious hygienic conditions, perhaps more difficult to observe by the occasional visitor, is the presence of rats. Other health problems experienced by the occupants of the CPA include two cases of tuberculosis and many instances of recurrent nosebleeds; the latter problem is thought to be related to the electric heaters used in the bungalows.

Once, rather naively I asked one of the operators who worked in the CPA about the *abitabilità* ('habitability') of the centre, that is to say whether the centre complies with the health and safety standards and regulations set by the government, hence if it had been granted the 'habitability-licence'. His answer was: '*Abitabilità?* . . . in such a place?

... you must be kidding!', and he went on to explain to me that CPAs are 'exceptional residential structures' for which the regulations about habitability do not apply. In other words, even from the point of view of health and safety regulations, the CPA constitutes an exception to the rule.

Let us now move on to a brief examination of the relationships that exist between the residents of the CPA and the indigenous population. Generally speaking, the main contacts that the residents have with the locals are those which take place at work during working hours. It could be said that such relationships are those which the necessity to work renders inescapable. However, once the working-time is over, it is rare for social contact to continue into leisure time. It is very rare to see Italians in the CPA, especially Italian women. Similarly, it is rare to hear of residents who go out with Italians on a regular basis.

An absence of rapport is also observed between the CPA and the local civil and political society, at least until the beginning of the empirical phase of the participatory action research. In fact, with the exception of one local Caritas volunteer, nobody from the local party branches, civic associations and similar organisations was found to have on-going relationships with the CPA, and therefore knew at first-hand the difficult conditions of life in there. However, it must be acknowledged that the members of these groups seemed on balance to be more correctly informed about the CPA than the 'ordinary' citizens we met during our surveys in the surroundings of the centre.

In relation to the places in Bologna which the residents of the CPA would point out as most significant to their life there are the *Servizio Immigrazione* of the Council (for most administrative and bureaucratic questions including housing), and the immigration offices of the two main trade unions, the CGIL and CISL (mainly for matters concerning work).

The most common relationships with the 'outside' during the leisure time seem to be those involving other Moroccan immigrants or relatives, either in the Bologna area (often living in another CPA) or elsewhere in the country. In fact, for the residents it is rather common to spend one's weekend visiting one's sister's family in Genoa, for instance, or a brother in Perugia, especially if these people live in 'proper' houses. For the youngest residents, a lot of intra-community social relationships pivot around recreational activities like sports, in particular soccer games which often involve the older members in organisational roles (e.g. coaches, referees, supporters).

To conclude this brief overview of the relationships between the CPA and the 'outside', I would like to touch upon the question of communications. Until mid-1996 not even one public payphone was available to the residents of the CPA, who at present still cannot receive incoming calls, with all the negative consequences that one can imagine. This is particularly striking in consideration of the city council's important efforts to 'telematize' the town in a democratic way, offering to all its registered residents a free subscription to the internet. With regard to postal communication, the situation is not much better either. The frequency of undelivered and lost mail has forced some of them to join a few others and open a post-office box, which, once more, represents something different from the local custom.

In sum, this sub-section has shown how in the CPA even the most common and apparently simple daily activities actually become awkward tasks. It has also provided a picture of the poor hygienic and health conditions of the centre, as well as an impression its deep isolation from the local society in many basic respects.

Internal and politico-institutional relationships

Once inside the CPA, it immediately became clear to the research group that – in addition to the 'ordinary' difficulties involved in living in such a structure, and the lack of significant social contact with the indigenous society – both the social relationships inside the centre (and hence its overall 'atmosphere'), and the politico-institutional ones, that is to say the relationships between the residents and the council administration, had very much deteriorated. Even though I had been previously warned about that, witnessing such situations in person was quite another thing.

Thus, right from the start, when I first entered the CPA, it emerged that life in there had become unsustainable, as well as physically dangerous. For instance a number of stories that I was told at the time about the difficulties of living in the centre all pointed out how, since *autogestione*, the control of the centre had increasingly been taken over by a group of squatters who had in the meantime moved in, together with some of the gypsies who were illegally camping at the edges of the CPA and some visitors who came in at any time of the day as well as of the night. These 'outsiders' were all persons who turned the complex into a centre for selling and buying stolen goods and drugs (which often were also consumed there).[7]

The actual taking over of the CPA by such uninvited persons meant

---

7 However, it must be stressed that not all the squatters or illegal residents were involved in such illegal activities. A number of them, in fact, were just unauthorised occupants or guests of the legal residents, and had nothing to do with criminal activities.

that even the most basic service that the centre provided to its legitimate residents (who were actually paying a rent for it), that is the function of a *dormitory*, had become negatively affected. In fact, the lifestyle of many of the unauthorised persons, which was made up of often deliberately noisy and annoying nocturnal practices (largely connected to the abuse of alcohol and drugs), strongly clashed with both the legitimate need of the workers to rest, and more generally with their frugal lifestyle, which was strongly characterised by hard physical labour, self-imposed economic restrictions, savings and so forth.

As it is easy to imagine, such a situation created tensions between the legal residents and the illegal persons, which resulted in the former being bullied, harassed and physically assaulted. Cases of residents having to be taken to hospital for knife wounds, being beaten up, having to sleep in the nearby park because their room had been squatted, or having to go and sleep in friends' houses during the weekend so as to avoid becoming the target of violence, constituted some of the situations which I recorded.

A common trait to the stories and the descriptions of the regular residents was the resentment and anger towards the local administration which was held largely responsible for the deteriorated climate in the centre. What had happened? Why were they so upset with the local administration? Some of the stories, in fact, pointed out quite openly that the reason for such a degraded environment was to be attributed to the policy of *autogestione* (self-management) that the administration had adopted (in a top-down manner) as the management policy for the centre.

Such a policy was commonly interpreted and perceived by the residents as a deliberate act of abandonment and neglect on behalf of the council authorities. Under such circumstances, nobody was therefore minded to try and implement a policy such as that of *autogestione* which had been enforced upon them from above. Moreover, this would have been extremely hard in such a situation of precariousness, and given the lack of adequate support by the authorities it would also have been physically dangerous. By a council official's own admission: 'we do not have anyone taking up the responsibility of representing the centre, because others would throw stones at him'. If the illegals had been expelled, they would have returned the following day or even during the same night as nobody was there to protect the centre, and the perimeter wire fence had a number of 'emergency exits' or 'holes' through which anybody at any time could have easily entered the centre.

With regard to the *forze dell'ordine* (the police forces), the residents' own experience of them suggested that it was better not to count on them either. Indeed, I was told a number of cases of far from exemplary behaviour by such forces, when emergency calls for protection were made to them. In most cases the *polizia* or *carabinieri* were said to have never arrived, or if they did they had to be called several times and, of course, when eventually they did get there it was too late for any intervention in defence of victims, but not too late to harass them. '*Andate a farvi le pugnette*' ('go and wank yourselves') was what apparently had been shouted at those who had called them because one of their friends had been stabbed by one of the illegal squatters. Thus, the residents of the CPA not only found themselves in the practical impossibility of satisfying the council (top-down) prescriptions of *autogestione*, but they actually found it quite irritating.

However, the current situation in the centre, and the policy of *auto-gestione*, were not the only arguments used in residents' criticisms of the council. References to the past, that is to the living conditions in the centre under previous management policies, were often made. With regard to the past two interconnected arguments were often pointed out to me. The first was that the council had always been incapable of guaranteeing good management, and that residents had always been experiencing an oppressive life in the centre as a result of this. A number of conversations with the immigrants touched upon the fact that before the *autogestione/abandonment*, the situation was completely different, but still far from good. A situation of harassment, once again, was reported to have characterised the previous period. This time, though, the harassment was not coming from the illegal persons, but from those who were supposed to keep order, that is to say the armed guards of the security team. The previous management in fact has been rightly self-described by the authorities as *strong* management ('*gestione forte*'). The complaints concerning the armed surveillance described some of the guards as racist and harassing. Examples of their behaviour consisted of various abuses of their power, such as unjustified sudden entries into the bungalows at night, various objects being engraved with swastikas etc. Besides, some of the security guards were said to consume drugs while on duty.

A second line of critique which emerged from discussions with the residents was the absolute lack of continuity between one management style and the next (i.e. strong management and *autogestione*). The inconsistency of moving from an unwanted situation of strong authoritarian management to another of unwanted *autogestione* (which in practice meant chaos) was perceived as a lack of genuine concern towards them on behalf of the administration.

Another element of distrust was due to the clear perception of being at the bottom line of an administrative system which, despite its official claims (of efficiency, transparency and democracy) of being in support of the immigrants, actually seemed to neglect them. Hierarchically made up of different centres of interest often pursuing goals of their own rather than providing a good and integrated service to the immigrants, and with some centres placed at the same time in horizontal competition with each other,[8] the system ended up providing a poor service. The Moroccans' clear perception of such an organisational structure, achieved also through their direct and painful experience of its inconsistent outputs, significantly contributed to infuse their sense of deep distrust towards the local administration.

A strategy often adopted by the residents in their attempt to overcome the dysfunctions of the system was to try to deal directly with the top of the hierarchy (i.e. the councillor for immigration), thus jumping the intermediate level supposed to implement the policies. This strategy was not very successful (despite having sharply identified one of the nodal areas of 'dysfunctions'), also because the political figures had necessarily to rely on their administration in order to implement anything. However, the refusal to deal with the intermediate levels of administration seemed to be an effective strategy of resistance.

To sum up. In this section I have explored the relationship existing between the immigrants and the local administration and how it has developed over the years. We have seen this from the point of view of the immigrants, that is of the marginalised and powerless. From the descriptions given above it has emerged that the immigrants are very upset, disappointed and disillusioned with the local institutions which they held responsible for the very oppressive life conditions in the centre; and they consider at best as inconsistent the switch form 'strong management' to *autogestione*.

The participatory action

The personal and direct witnessing of the situation in the CPA, of which the previous section is a synthesis, in the end made the research group agree at least on the impossibility of pursuing the *autogestione* in terms of PAR; as well as on the necessity of directing the action elsewhere, possibly with the participation of the residents. Thus, the original idea to promote the implementation of *autogestione* became progressively replaced by two other interrelated goals. The first was that of 'bridging' the CPA with the progressive part of the local civil and political society (with which, as we saw earlier, there existed no links). The second was

8   For example, the strong competition taking place among a number of co-ops and NGOs over resources, contracts and appointments.

that of pressing for the re-establishment of a minimum of order and security within the CPA (which was one of the main concerns of the residents). Indeed the 'bridging' with the local civil and political society, besides being an end in itself (i.e. improving the very poor socio-political inclusion of the residents in the district), was also instrumental to the second aim. If some members of the local civic and political organisations could be convinced to support the cause of the immigrants, it would then be easier to obtain from the administration the commitment to bring back the security and order that the CPA residents needed.

It is in this phase of 'bridging' to the local civil and political society that the research takes on proper participatory connotations. Thus, the idea that came from one CPA resident of forming an intercultural association involving some of the other CPA residents, some of the researchers and some people from the neighbourhood (and which largely coincided with the strategy that the researchers were increasingly reckoning as the most appropriate and feasible), was immediately taken on board and implemented.

Thus, with the active participation of some CPA residents, it was decided to create such an association and to do it quickly, and to look for some outsiders, preferably residing in the area, who were genuinely concerned with the living conditions of immigrants and possibly in possession of some rudiments of interculturalism. While only a few people initially reckoned to be able to give the appropriate support and commitment that joining the association would have demanded, a significant approval and concern started to grow among the progressive part of the local political society and voluntary sector in the borough, also in response to our campaign of publicity and discussion. Largely as a result of this, the immigrants, for the first time ever, joined some of the relevant *commissioni di quartiere* (the borough commissions) such as that for 'culture' and that for 'social security'. Although the commissions only have an essentially consultative function, especially when, as in this case, it is the Right which runs the borough, the act of joining them did have an important symbolic dimension. Such a decision also made it harder for the ruling political forces to continue neglecting the existence of the immigrants in the territory, and actually forced them to come to terms with their presence.

The process of choosing the *name* of the intercultural association and writing up its *charter* was characterised by a great deal of enthusiasm among the group which celebrated the event with a typical Moroccan Cous-Cous dinner. But it was the organisation of the *festa* (party) for the official presentation of the association to the town which received the highest degree of participation. One of the local Social Centres immediately agreed to make available, free of charge, its building and personnel for the initiative, which turned out to be a success both in terms of 'fun' and in terms of the quantity and quality of the participants. In fact, not only did many people turn up (approximately one hundred) but a number of them were even 'politically' significant (the newly-appointed town councillor for social policies and immigration, various officials of the Immigration Service of the council, the person responsible for immigration of the largest trade union – CGIL, town and local party cadres, many members of the voluntary associations dealing with immigration and social exclusion, and so forth). Of course the presence of such people was very important for the recognition and legitimation of the newly-born association in the public eye. All that was further strengthened by the presence of a journalist from the major local newspaper (and the subsequent article he wrote). Finally over ten people declared themselves interested in participating in the future activity of the association.

As a result of the meetings which took place in occasion of the above event, a few days later a large delegation of the main left-wing coalition in the borough visited the CPA in order to get a more direct idea of the conditions of extreme discomfort of the Moroccan workers. From that moment the CPA consolidated its presence on the political agenda of the borough, a presence which had started with some immigrants joining the borough commissions.

As regards this chapter, the story ends with the definitive abandonment of the *autogestione* management policy of the CPA on the part of the council, which re-introduces the *operatore*. The people illegally living within and around the CPA who played such a great part in worsening the already hard living conditions of the regular residents are expelled. Despite the fact that the association will never fully take off in terms of organisation of intercultural activities, partly because of the regrettable withdrawal of a number of its members, the bridge into the local political society was there to stay.

Conclusion

This chapter has provided an account of the situation of immigrants from the 'Third World' in the wealthy and progressive city of Bologna, with special reference to a group of Moroccan workers living in a council housing scheme for immigrants. Most importantly, however, this account has addressed what is usually left out in much immigration research, at least in Italy: that is to say, how the establishment can actually operate to the disadvantage of the immigrants, even in those areas which in most respects are undoubtedly progressive, such as the Bologna region. Telling the 'political story' of the mis-usage of the radical research tool of PAR by the local institutions has constituted the

main rhetorical device through which some of the inconsistencies of the
establishment view in relation to immigration have been highlighted.
In my work I developed a critical methodology which has combined an
anthropological concern to hear people's own criteria of relevance with
a participatory approach which involved them in the planning and
implementation of action. In so doing, I have produced material which
seems to point to a new direction for policydevelopment. Thus, instead
of expecting immigrants to be able to organise themselves as a 'community' which is self-contained, this work suggests the importance of
creating links via the surrounding civil society into the local political
system, so that the immigrants can represent themselves and get their
own issues on the political agenda. Accordingly, political integration
rather than a segregated 'community' seems to be the way forward, if a
greater social inclusion is to be achieved. If this is not attempted in
Bologna where there is a well-developed and progressive civil society
and a more sensitive political environment, where else could it be?

Acknowledgments

I would like to thank John Gaventa, Russell King, Jeff Pratt and Sue Wright at
the University of Sussex for their helpful comments on an earlier draft of this
chapter. I would also like to thank Adriana Bernardotti, Pietro Pinto and
Alessandro Zanini for their help in Bologna. Finally I am especially grateful to
Elisabetta Zontini for her suggestions and support both in Bologna and at
Sussex.

References

Barsotti, O. and Lecchini, L. (1994) Social and economic aspects of foreign immi-
    gration to Italy, in Fassmann, H. and Munz, R. eds. *European Migration in the
    Late Twentieth Century: Historical Patterns, Actual Trends and Social Implications.*
    Aldershot: Edward Elgar, pp. 81–92.
Bartolini, S. (1989) *Progetto Immigrazione: relazione dell'assessore Silvia Bartolini.*
    Bologna: Comune di Bologna.
Caritas di Roma (1996) *Immigrazione Dossier Statistico.* Rome: Anterem.
Comune di Bologna-Assessorato alla Sanità e all'Immigrazione & Assessorato
    alle Politiche Sociali (1990) Proposta di regolamento per l'accesso e la perma-
    nenza nelle strutture alloggiative di prima accoglienza del comune di
    Bologna, in *Progetto per l'Immigrazione.* Bologna: Comune di Bologna.
Del Mugnaio, A. (1993) *Documento programmatico della giunta comunale sulle
    politiche per l'immigrazione: relazione dell'assessore Anna Del Mugnaio.* Bologna:
    Comune di Bologna.
Deshler, D. and Ewert, M. (1995) Participatory Action Research: Traditions and
    Major Assumptions, in *ToolBox, PARnet.* http://munex.arme.cornell.edu/
    PARnet/tools/tools _1. htm#evaluation, December 1995.
Gaventa, J. (1991) Toward a knowledge democracy: viewpoints on participatory

research in North America, in Fals-Borda, O. and Rahman M.A. eds. *Action and Knowledge*. London: Intermediate Technology Publications, pp. 121–31.

Ginsborg, P. (1990) *A History of Contemporary Italy*. London: Penguin.

Jaggi, M., Muller, R. and Schmid, S. (1977) *Red Bologna*. London: Writers and Readers.

Kertzer, D.I. (1980) *Comrades and Christians*. Cambridge: Cambridge University Press.

King, R. (1993) Recent immigration to Italy: characteristics, causes and consequences, *GeoJournal*, 30(3), pp. 283–92.

King, R. and Konjhodzic, I. (1995) *Labour, Migration and Employment in Southern Europe*. Brighton: University of Sussex Research Papers in Geography 19.

Maher, V. (1995) Participatory research on non-European immigration to Italy, in Nelson, N. and Wright, S. eds.. *Power and Participatory Development*. London: Intermediate Technology Publications, pp. 105–13.

Nader, L. (1974) Up the anthropologists: perspectives gained from studying up, in Hymes, D. ed. *Reinventing Anthropology*. New York: Vintage.

Nelson, N. and Wright, S. (1995) Participation and power, in Nelson, N. and Wright, S. eds. *Power and Participatory Development*. London: Intermediate Technology Publications, pp. 1–18.

Okely, J. (1983) *The Traveller-Gypsies*. Cambridge: Cambridge University Press.

Okely, J. (1994) Thinking through fieldwork, in Bryman, A. and Burgess, R.G. eds. *Analysing Qualitative Data*. London: Routledge, pp. 18–34.

Osservatorio Metropolitano delle Immigrazioni di Bologna (1995) Introduzione, in *La Società Multietnica*, 1(1).

Pepa, L. ed. (1996) *Immigrati e comunità locali. Azioni, interventi e saperi dall'emergenza al progetto*. Milan: Franco Angeli.

Però, D. (1996) Political anthropology of Italy in action, *Anthropology in Action*, 3(3), pp. 36–8.

Shaffir, W.B. and Stebbings, R.A. (1991) Learning the ropes, in Shaffir,W.B. and Stebbings,W.B. eds. *Experiencing Fieldwork*. Newbury Park, CA: Sage, pp. 83–6.

Vasta, E. (1983) Rights and racism in a new country of immigration: the Italian case, in Wrench, J. and Solomos, J. eds. *Racism and Migration in Western Europe*. Oxford: Berg, pp. 83–98.

Veugelers, J.W.P. (1994) Recent immigration politics in Italy: a short story, in Baldwin-Edwards, M. and Schain, M. eds. *The Politics of Immigration in Western Europe*. London: Frank Cass, pp. 33–49.

Whyte, W.F. (1991) *Social Theory for Action*. Newbury Park, CA: Sage.

9

De Facto *Refugees in Portugal and Spain: State Policy, Informal Strategies and the Labour Market*

Jorge Malheiros and Richard Black

This volume has concentrated on analysis of the situation of labour migrants – many of them undocumented and in precarious employment and housing conditions – in Southern Europe. Such a concentration is justified by their weight of numbers, as well as by the important links between labour demand, demand for work (by migrants) and evolving policy at a national and local level across Southern Europe. However, in addition to labour migration, Southern Europe has also been affected in recent years by another form of migration of growing importance worldwide – that of refugees and asylum-seekers. For this group, the emphasis placed in Chapter 1 on structural conditions promoting immigration is arguably less relevant. However, whilst the individual motives of migration of asylum-seekers differ from those stressed in Chapter 1 – though fitting into the diversity of circumstances revealed in subsequent chapters – this chapter seeks to stress how labour market factors, in combination with other political and social elements, are still relevant in explaining and responding to new immigration flows.

Asylum-seekers have received increasing attention from the Iberian authorities during the 1980s and 1990s. During this period, their growing numbers, diversity of origins, and a temporary rush of candidates from Eastern Europe, especially Poland and Romania, have caused considerable concern to the Internal Affairs ministries of

Portugal and Spain. However, in addition to asylum-seekers – who are looking for formal refugee status in Iberia – there are two groups of *de facto* refugees which are also of considerable importance in policy terms, namely refugees from East Timor (Maubere) in Portugal and from the Western Sahara (Saharauis) in Spain. The presence of both groups is associated with the decolonisation process Spain and Portugal started in the mid 1970s, in both cases a process that is still unfinished. Meanwhile, although they are a minority among the foreigners living in Iberia, the particular status they possess and the specific context of their situation justify a differentiated approach. Moreover, the recent arrivals of Timorese students in Portugal as well as the visibility of this community in the international media are contributing to greater international concern about questions related to East Timor.

Based on the experience of Portugal and Spain in dealing with these two groups, this chapter seeks to demonstrate that two situations with similar origins were managed quite differently by the Portuguese and Spanish authorities. Differences in the political position of Portugal and Spain towards the questions of East Timor and the Western Sahara have led to important differences in the policies of reception and resettlement of the refugees coming from these areas. In turn, these differences in reception and resettlement policies have had important effects on the livelihood and the integration process experienced by Maubere and Saharaui refugees. With the help of information collected in in-depth and focus group interviews as well as a survey of the experiences of the Maubere and Saharaui refugees in Portugal and Spain, an overview of the problems experienced by these groups is presented.[1]

In particular, attention is paid to labour market questions, which are seen as central to the future position of the two communities. For example, policy towards the 'integration' of Maubere and Saharaui refugees is torn between the objectives of giving assistance towards integration in 'local' labour markets in Iberia, and facilitating potential return to the territory of origin, given that the two groups' presence in Iberia is considered temporary. Of course, such a question is not unique to these two groups of *de facto* refugees, but is relevant more widely in asylum and refugee policy across Southern Europe and beyond. However, the particular dynamics of the Timorese and Saharaui situations throw up a number of interesting questions, which are examined in the light of wider experience.

1   This chapter is based on work conducted during a Fellowship held by Jorge Malheiros at King's College London, funded by the 'Human Capital and Mobility' programme of the Commission of the European Communities.

Background: labour market integration and refugees

It is not intention of this chapter to consider in detail the theoretical relationship between labour markets and the integration problems of refugees. However, it is useful to start from a simple framework that can work both as an interpretative tool and as a guideline for the analysis of the case-study of the Maubere in Portugal and the Saharauis in Spain. Such a framework contains three fundamental elements:

- First, it is assumed that the employment vulnerability of asylum-seekers and refugees is higher than the vulnerability of the locals and even of the majority of immigrant populations. This leads us to look beyond the employment problems felt by locals and immigrants, at specific features that make the condition of asylum-seekers and refugees more precarious.
- Secondly, this framework only presents factors/measures directed to reduce the labour market problems of refugees (as a vulnerable foreign group in general and specifically as refugees). This leads us to exclude discussion of solutions to global labour market problems, as outside the range of this research.
- Thirdly, it is assumed that the majority of the asylum-seekers who join the labour market in developed countries, and specifically in Southern Europe, work in unskilled, precarious and poorly-paid jobs.[2] This leads us to consider specifically issues of labour market segmentation, and ways of overcoming it, although it is noted that some large and relatively organised refugee groups (e.g. Vietnamese in the United States and in France, or Cubans in the United States) do present trends of upward professional mobility, sometimes associated with the reproduction of class distinctions brought from the country of origin (Finnan 1981).

According to dual labour market theory, the concept of a secondary labour market corresponds to the segment of employment which is characterised by vulnerability in terms of salary, contractual terms and possibilities of a professional career. Thus, when looking for a job in developed countries, immigrants have to face many formal restrictions (visa restrictions, limitations to issuing of working permits, etc.). To this they add their own disadvantages (lack of understanding of the

2   Several studies confirm this situation for a number of countries in Europe. Interesting examples are provided in the studies of Black (1992) on refugees in Greece, Hauff and Vaglum (1993) on Vietnamese refugees in Norway, and della Donne (1995) on refugees in Italy.

language, lack of familiarity with labour market circuits) and also the prejudice or even the hostility of some members of the local population. Each of these obstacles tends to push immigrants towards secondary labour markets.

The role of migrant networks is fundamental in overcoming these limitations, because they act as privileged channels of contact between immigrants and employers (although they may also further segment the labour market because of the dominance of ethnic networks). Moreover, they provide information and initial material and social support to the newcomers (Malheiros 1996; Pohjola 1991). Even when considering the restrictive effects of networks (for instance, preventing broader social contacts with members of the host society), authors assume their fundamental role in reorganising migrants' lives after the move (Pohjola 1991, p. 440). However, although labour market segmentation may make immigrants a useful part of the national labour force as a whole by generating additional employment opportunities (Castles and Miller 1993), the extent to which this will happen will depend on the ability of migrants to provide or acquire the skills required by the production process of developed countries.

In order to get such skills, and achieve levels of productivity which are required by local labour markets, immigrants need access to language and professional training.[3] The idea is not to protect immigrants but to provide them with the conditions to fulfil their roles in the best way possible. This benefits immigrants directly, contributes to reducing the possibility of marginalisation, and might also have potential positive effects on local economies. Concerning the question of training, the role of public institutions, NGOs and immigrant associations is fundamental. Meanwhile, the negative image of immigrants often held by the populations of host countries is one of the major hindrances that migrant communities have to face. It is not only a question of competition for jobs and social services but also the development of an image which portrays immigrants, especially if coming from African or Asian countries, as an unskilled population with primitive or threatening cultural and social practices. In order to change this image, local authorities, migrant associations and local societies sometimes seek to spread messages about the local advantages of the presence of migrants, and contribute to the establishment of new relations between locals and migrants. In academic terms, there is a need for studies of the

3   This does not imply that immigrants' training should be privileged. As a useful part of labour force, immigrants should have access to training on the same basis as nationals, unless particular situations (e.g. language problems or the existence of a marked local concentration of unemployed immigrants) merit training directed specifically at immigrants.

interaction and reciprocal images of immigrants and locals in European cities (cf. Bach et al. 1993, for US cities).

Only in a few respects does the image of certain refugee groups privilege them in relation to ordinary migrants. For example, the stigma of their hard plight (experience of conflicts and non-respect for the human rights in their own countries together with a difficult journey), especially when well-documented and explored by the mass media, may help to generate a feeling of sympathy among the population of the host country. However, in general, refugees and asylum-seekers present features which make their participation in labour markets harder than in the case of other migrants. Their migration is not pre-planned and therefore they often arrive at their destination without capital and contacts. They frequently suffer from psychological problems, such as war trauma, which may affect the process of integration in the labour market (Hauff and Vaglum 1993). Also, the problem of inadequacy of professional skills seems to be more frequent among refugees, since the occupations held by asylum-seekers in their home countries (lawyers, peasants, non-Christian priests, politicians, artisans, etc.) often involve skills which are non-transferable to the host countries. Good examples are provided by Cambodians and Laotians in Quebec City (Dorais 1991) and some refugees from Sri Lanka in Denmark.

Due to these constraints, the actions of NGOs, governments and local authorities are particularly relevant in the process of labour market integration of refugees. The first question to be addressed concerns the position of professional training goals within the framework of global training policy. If it is assumed that refugees are a short-term burden, then training should be based on providing refugees with skills that will be useful when they return to their home country. However, this approach requires both money and foresight as to what will be the future requirements in refugees' home countries. Since these conditions are not easily met, some countries prevent refugees from working and do not offer special training programmes. In practice, the idea is to keep refugees from becoming involved in the host society and to send them home as soon as the conditions change in their country of origin.

In other cases, the authorities assume that refugees may stay for a long time. If this is the case, the need for training and language courses that contribute to the participation of refugees in the host society is normally accepted. However, if the possibility of return arises, a discordance may occur between the skills possessed by the refugees and the needs of the home country.

A third possibility relies on an interactive approach which is not easy to develop. The idea is to provide specific qualifications to refugees that may help both the labour market participation in the host country and a potential reintegration when and if they return. Despite the interest of this perspective there are several limitations to its implementation. Frequently, the qualification requirements of the host and home country labour markets are not matched and therefore the organisations in charge of the training programmes opt for a more immediate strategy and start programmes directed to help the functional integration of refugees locally. However, in countries which have established programmes to help the integration of refugees in the labour market, such as Denmark or the Netherlands, the success of these initiatives has been relatively limited (Melchior 1993). Even in these countries, high rates of unemployment and high levels of job insecurity are found.

Programmes implemented in several countries (e.g. Denmark, the Netherlands, the UK and Spain) demonstrate that the success of initiatives directed to integrate refugees in the labour market (e.g. language and professional training) depend much on co-operation between private and public institutions both at local and national levels (Melchior 1993). What is necessary is co-operation between local populations, municipal authorities and refugees at local level whilst maintaining funding and advisory support provided by national governments or nation-wide private institutions.

Methodological issues

To examine some of the questions discussed in the previous section, a case-study involving a group of Timorese in Lisbon and a group of Saharauis in Las Palmas de Gran Canaria was developed. The central aim of the case-study was to evaluate the process of adjustment of these refugees to labour market conditions in their respective host countries. Additionally, the study sought to evaluate the logic and the effects of language and training courses implemented in particular by the Portuguese authorities for the Timorese. The existence of constraints and solutions to the adjustment process was a fundamental issue guiding this research. In this regard, three principal research hypotheses were considered:

- Among the study groups, a high level of job vulnerability (unemployment, downward professional mobility, job instability) was expected to be found.
- Informal solutions, ranging from the intervention of migrant networks to illegal employment practices, were expected to play an important role in the relationship between asylum-seekers and the labour market.
- Institutional solutions (language courses, professional training, etc.)

directed to help the process of integration of refugees in the labour market were expected to be insufficient and/or of limited success.

The process of adjustment to the labour market was not expected to be uniform in the groups selected for the case-study. Not only does each group of forced migrants present specificities in this process but even within each group, important differences were expected. For instance, white-collar professionals, such as journalists or accountants, are likely to experience higher integration difficulties than blue-collar workers (cf. Stein 1979).

To test these hypotheses, a methodological sequence was developed which included three stages:

- *data collection*, using in-depth group interviews and a semi-open questionnaire applied to a larger sample of the target groups;
- *preliminary data analysis* based on the discussions held at the focus group sessions and on responses to the questionnaires;
- *discussion of initial results and group debate*, using a second round of adapted focus group sessions with the same people as were present at the first round of interviews.

A closed approach to target groups was adopted in order to follow up the adaptation process of the group members over several months. It was not an objective of the research to have a representative sample of the communities of forced migrants from Timor and the Western Sahara and therefore the target groups were relatively small.[4] The present research tends to abandon the narrow positivist position towards data collection and analysis which stresses questions of validity and reliability. As much as possible, this project tries to follow an interactionist approach (Silverman 1993), where subjects give a deep insight into their experiences and the research results are discussed between interviewer and interviewees.

The first-stage focus-group discussion aimed to uncover the factors lying behind the migratory movements and the process of adaptation to the labour market. It also contributed towards the choice of questions to incorporate in the questionnaire. According to Ford and Warnes

---

4   Thirty-two Timorese living in the Lisbon Region, and 11 Saharauis living in Gran Canaria participated in the study. Although the total number of Saharians living in Gran Canaria is relatively small (between 250 and 260, according to the data of the POLISARIO member responsible for the preparation of the Western Sahara referendum census), the validity of the results obtained with this group is clearly limited. The focus-group sessions normally had three participants, apart from the researcher(s).

(1993, p. 5), 'focus group discussions can produce accounts of behaviour operationalised at many different levels: generating "objective" reports of experienced events; description of the motivations for behaviour; and explanations of underlying expectations and needs'. In the present case-studies, the first-stage sessions corresponded, more or less, to the first level. Participants gave a report of their migration pattern and of their experiences in Iberian labour markets following a semi-directive interview pattern. The final part of the session was always directed to a discussion of the future intentions of individuals concerning potential migrations and work. With this methodology it was possible to uncover dimensions, which resulted from the simultaneous presence of the individuals, which may not have been revealed in ordinary individual semi-structured interviews.

Focus group sessions were complemented by semi-structured questionnaires applied to a larger sample of members of the target groups and covering the same fields as the first stage of focus group interviews. These questionnaires, drawn up with the help of the information gathered in the focus groups, resulted in more extensive and comparative data which enabled a quantitative analysis. Again, it is stressed that even this questionnaire does not intend to be a representative sample of Maubere and Saharaui refugees. Rather, it sought to cover the range of situations that can be found among the groups of forced migrants represented in the case-studies. Respondents were selected through a modified snowballing technique, in which individuals were asked to suggest other potential respondents whose circumstances were different to their own.

The second-stage focus-group sessions resulted in an extremely interesting debate between the researchers and interviewees. At this stage it was possible to share preliminary 'results' with respondents and to confront the 'constructed researcher view' and conclusions with the subjects' own experience. A rich focused interaction was reached, stimulating adjustments in interpretation and an increased level of participation of the subjects in the research process. The second stage sessions were more open and more interactive, although they followed a distinct procedure. The session started with a presentation, by the researcher, of a brief summary of the main conclusions (general patterns of migration, working trajectories and labour market problems, suggestions of potential solutions for the problems found). Afterwards, group members were asked to comment on the conclusions and a discussion was promoted around the themes presented. As the conclusions were different from group to group and the interaction level was high, the sequence of issues and the specific themes registered some change from one group to the other.

Political issues

Situation in the places of origin

Despite the enormous distance between the territories of East Timor and Western Sahara and the different characteristics (ethnic and cultural backgrounds, religious behaviour, etc.) of their peoples and geographies, the colonial history of these places reveals a number of similarities. In both cases, Iberian rule was disputed by other European powers (The Netherlands in the case of East Timor and France in the case of Western Sahara) which administered neighbouring territories (Indonesia, French Morocco, Mauritania) of larger dimension and stronger economic importance.

Also the attitude of the Spanish and Portuguese administrations towards these colonies shared common features: until recently (the 1960s in the Western Sahara and the early 1970s in East Timor) attention given to these territories was very limited and both economic and demographic investment were very reduced. According to Price (1979), Spanish policy in the Western Sahara was weak and interest in this territory was only generated after the early 1960s, firstly with the loss of other colonies in the region (Spanish Morocco, Ifni) and then with the discovery of phosphates at Bou Craa (Gonzálvez Pérez 1994). Similarly, to the Portuguese fascist regime, East Timor was the least interesting of their colonies. The so-called African provinces, namely Angola and Mozambique, were the real focus of interest of Portuguese colonial administration, not only due to their economic relevance but also because of the problems caused by the colonial war. Separated from the metropolis by 16,000 km., East Timor was an isolated and forgotten half-island which only experienced some development in the fields of agriculture, education, water supply and road building in the early 1970s (Pires 1994).

Another common feature lies in the diversity of the peoples inhabiting both territories. The Western Sahara was inhabited by several nomadic groups sharing the Islamic religion and some forms of political organisation. Historically, these groups had strong relations with the Southern region of Morocco, and some influential Moroccans claim to have family origins in the Western Sahara (Lacoste 1985). However, the Spanish colonisation over the 20th century contributed both to sedentarisation of nomadic groups in the territory, and to a strengthening of ties between the peoples living under Spanish rule in Saguia-el-Hamra and Rio de Oro (the former name of the Western Sahara territory). The development of a Saharaui common identity is a relatively recent feature developed in the framework of Spanish colonialism and re-enforced in the liberation wars against Spain and Morocco.

Also in East Timor, a large diversity of ethnic groups speaking different languages and dialects could be found, some of them similar to dialects spoken in parts of Western Timor (AGU 1970; Marcos 1995). Although the population of this island has always been sedentary, Portuguese rule contributed to a concentration in certain towns, and especially in the capital, Dili, although this process was more limited than in the Western Sahara. Also, as was the case with Spanish rule in the Western Sahara, the Portuguese presence in East Timor helped to unify the peoples of East Timor (the Maubere) creating specificities which differentiate them from their neighbours (notably through education, language, the legal system, and especially the Catholic religion). Thus, it is not surprising that a significant number of the first members of the Timorese political parties were administrative officials in the Portuguese administration, a privileged group, with higher levels of education than the ordinary population (Pires 1994). After 1975, the Indonesian occupation and disrespect for human rights in the territory has clearly contributed to the development of solidarity and nationalistic feelings among the Maubere people.

Overall, it is important to remember that we are dealing with peoples holding a common identity, who have developed a recent (within a few decades) but strong nationalistic feeling, built on the conditions of Spanish and Portuguese colonialism. Meanwhile the withdrawal of the Portuguese and Spanish administrations was completed at the same time (the end of 1975) in a context of political confusion and instability, leaving the door open to subsequent occupations which led to the oppression of local peoples and to serious conflicts, as yet unresolved. The presence of important natural resources in the territories (phosphates in the Western Sahara) and national waters (Saharaui fish bank and oil in the Sea of Timor) of both nations have complicated the geopolitical context of both situations.

Current political positions of Portugal and Spain

The attitudes of the Portuguese and Spanish authorities towards each group of *de facto* refugees have distinct differences, which relate in part to differences in political positions respectively towards East Timor and the Western Sahara. Thus Portugal has never recognised the Indonesian occupation (diplomatic relations between both countries were broken and never re-established), whereas Spain agreed (and later confirmed) the transfer of the administration of the Western Sahara to Morocco and Mauritania. Portugal, especially recently, has made a direct effort to find a solution for the problem of East Timor. Under the supervision of the UN Secretary General, occasional meetings have taken place between the ministers of foreign affairs of Portugal and Indonesia. Although improvements brought by these meetings have been limited, they represent advances towards solving the problem of East Timor.

This involvement of Portugal in the political question of East Timor, coupled with continuing arrivals of East Timorese students in Portugal, contributed to the creation, in 1995, of a special inter-ministerial body to deal with the problems of Timorese refugees. Two major tasks have been identified: a major survey of the members of the Timorese community in order to identify their key problems; and an effort to co-ordinate existing initiatives that aim to support the insertion process of the Timorese community.

In contrast, the Spanish authorities are not major actors in the Western Sahara, although they have expressed on several occasions their support for peace and a referendum on the future of the territory. However, in order to maintain good relations with its southern neighbour and to defend its interests in North Africa (which include the enclaves of Ceuta and Melilla and fish banks off the coast of the Western Sahara), the attitude of the Spanish administration is frequently closer to the Moroccan position than to the Saharaui one. It is important to mention the economic co-operation between the two countries as well as the importance of the sale of Spanish weapons to Morocco. Another example of the attitude of the Spanish central government towards POLISARIO was the closing of the offices of this organisation in Spain in 1985, after an incident between POLISARIO, a fishing boat and the Spanish navy.

Consistent with this political position, on the question of asylum-seekers, Spain has refused to accept some requests made by Saharauis. An extreme example occurred in 1985 when the government refused entry to a group of 21 asylum-seekers coming from Morocco (AAPS 1994). Despite this attitude of the central government, several NGOs and some regional authorities have offered support to the Saharauis, providing study grants or accepting the presence of POLISARIO representatives. Other initiatives include the reception of Saharaui children in summer holiday camps and the collection of aid packages for the refugee camps in Tindouf, Algeria.

Besides the specific attitude of the Portuguese and Spanish governments towards the two territories, there are other relevant socio-political questions that have influenced the distinct contexts of reception of the Maubere and Saharaui refugees. One example concerns the strong cohesion of the Saharauis around POLISARIO, which contrasts with the fragmentation of the Maubere between several movements with different ideologies and different positions on the question of the future status of the territory. Moreover, the average level of politicisation among the Saharauis is apparently much higher than that of Timorese. The experience gathered in the organisation of the lives of thousands of people in the Tindouf refugee camps (Thomas and Wilson 1996) certainly contributes to reinforcing group identity among Saharauis as well as their identification with the cause of self-determination.

Finally, a solution for the Western Sahara problem is, at least apparently, in a more advanced stage than a solution to the question of East Timor. The prospect of a democratic, free and honest referendum in the Western Sahara (whatever result it produces, assuming it is respected by all parties) might be an important learning process for other similar situations such as the case of East Timor.

Migration patterns and territorial links

For the Saharaui refugees, geographical proximity between places of exile (Canary Islands, Algeria and even Mauritania) and the country of origin (Western Sahara) has led to the construction of a network that involves frequent flows of people circulating between Tindouf (Algeria), several places in Mauritania, El Aaiun and Dahkla (Western Sahara) and the Canary Islands (especially Gran Canaria and Lanzarote). The nomadic tradition of the peoples of this region, as well as long-established commercial ties between the Western Sahara and the Canary Islands, help to re-enforce the links between these places. The country of origin acts as the reference point for the network, despite limitations on movement introduced by the Moroccan occupation. In fact, for the exiles, to circulate around the Western Sahara is easier than to circulate through it.

The evidence of such territorial links arises from various pieces of information. First, all the interviewed persons had relatives in the Tindouf camps and the majority (7 out of 10) also had family in Mauritania. Secondly, the Saharaui population in Mauritania is dominated by single males[5] and among the married men who were interviewed (8 out of 9), most said their wives were in Mauritania or in Tindouf. Thirdly, the routes chosen to leave for the Canary Islands involved, frequently, passage through Mauritania, or a sojourn in the Tindouf camps.

5   There is no exact information about the sex composition of the Saharaui population in the Canary Islands. According to the information of POLISARIO representatives, there are fewer than 50 women among the estimated 500 Saharauis living in the archipelago.

Migration patterns among Maubere refugees present a more diverse context. There is a specific network system linking East Timor with Australia, which received 2,000 Timorese directly in 1975/76, and a concentration in the town of Darwin, the nearest to East Timor. This network is also connected to Portugal 16,000 km away, since many of those who have arrived in Lisbon as asylum-seekers after 1976 have used Portugal as a platform to emigrate to Australia. This migratory network (Timor-Portugal-Australia) started in 1979 with the first departures under ordinary migration schemes. Since then, Australia has created a Special Migration Programme for Timorese with the purpose of helping the process of family reunion in Australia. In the global context of emigration to Australia, Timorese were, until 1990, a privileged group, because the concept of a 'relative' was interpreted quite broadly, including direct and distant relatives, and also because the Maubere were allowed to enter the country without a valid contract for work (Viola 1986). After 1990, this favourable context experienced some restrictions. On the one hand, the relations between Portugal and Australia deteriorated and the latter country closed its diplomatic mission in Lisbon. On the other hand, some of the special provisions mentioned above, which benefited Timorese who wanted to emigrate to Australia, were revised and became more restrictive.

However, onward movement to Australia remains a major feature of the spatial behaviour of the Maubere settled in Lisbon. Although the percentage of people who wished to emigrate to Australia was not high among those interviewed and was apparently less important than in previous years, the number of young Maubere who want to emigrate is still significant.[6] The reasons for this lay strongly in the perception of better support for integration in Australian society at all levels (training, work, housing). In the words of M:

> When people arrive in Australia they have to learn English for six months. A man and his family are entitled to a subsidy. Then the government finds a job and a dwelling that people pay for with their salary. These conditions don't exist here. (Authors' translation of taped interview in Portuguese)

Moreover, the larger opportunities in the Australian labour market also act as an inducement to emigrate to Australia, especially when considering the problems that young Maubere have in the Portuguese labour

6 According to data collected by Viola (1986) in the Australian Embassy in Lisbon, more than 90 per cent of the Timorese families sojourning in Portugal in 1984 wanted to be resettled in Australia. Our interview data for 1994 show that 11 wanted to stay in Portugal, 16 intended to return to East Timor, and 8 intended to emigrate from Portugal.

market (see below). Also the geographical proximity between Timor and Australia combined with the possibility of obtaining Australian nationality (a situation that makes an eventual visit to the homeland safer) are factors that pull people to Australia. The words of S. illustrate this:

> The proximity of Timor is also important because they think they can obtain a visa to go there sightseeing and to visit their families. Some people have obtained Australian nationality after three years of settlement. (Authors' translation of taped interview in Portuguese).

Especially after 1981/82, this geographical pattern of Timorese migration has been largely supported by institutional agreements between Portugal, Australia and Indonesia with the important intervention of the International Red Cross working inside East Timor to promote family reunification. This institutional intervention combines with informal networks only in the second migration stage, that is, in the move from Portugal to Australia. Also some Timorese believe that the informal support given by the settled community to the newcomers is stronger in Australia than in Portugal. It is important to stress that more than 90 per cent of the families who were contacted during field work had relatives in Australia, compared with just 17 per cent having relatives in the European Union, and 14 per cent in the US and Canada. The result of this migratory chain has been a progressive reduction of the Timorese community established in Portugal (from more than 2,500 in 1986 to around 1,500 in 1995) and a significant increase in the number of Maubere in Australia (around 5,000 in 1983, 10,000 in 1986 and 16,500 in 1995).

Besides the specificity of the geographical links established by Saharaui and Maubere refugees, there are other relevant features which contribute to distinguishing the migration patterns of both groups. First, the composition of the migrant groups is significantly different; in the case of Saharauis single males dominate, whilst for the Timorese family movement, whether atomised or in groups, is more important. However, these generalisations hide several nuances. For instance, there are some Saharaui families living in the Canary Islands and since 1993 more than 90 per cent of Timorese arriving in Portugal have been single men. Secondly, the presence of the two groups in Portugal and in Spain is not justified by the same kind of reasons. Whereas in the case of Saharauis geographical proximity (associated with knowledge of the language), as well as the opportunity to find work, were cited fundamental issues, the settlement of Timorese in the Lisbon region is largely justified by the affective and *de facto* links between them and the

Portuguese nation. Such links include the fact that the majority of the Maubere settled in Lisbon worked for the Portuguese Administration in Timor and have been re-deployed in the national administration; whilst some of them have Portuguese family or Portuguese ancestors and they identify more with Portugal than with Indonesia, despite their Timorese self-consciousness. For the latest arrivals of young men, political activities in East Timor in support of self-determination provide a motive for moving to a country in which they expect to find political sympathy, a favourable reception context, and the support of a settled community.

Another major difference between these two groups concerns the level of political and ideological cohesion of each communities. In the case of the Saharauis, POLISARIO emerges as a symbol of union and organisation in exile, aggregating practically everybody around its proposals and reinforcing the contacts between those who remain in the Western Sahara and those who are in places of exile. For almost all Saharauis, self-determination is the only possible solution to the problem of the Western Sahara. In fact, all those interviewed declared they wanted to return to the Western Sahara, if Morocco ceases its occupation. Even those who wanted to keep a temporary migration status in Gran Canaria, wished to continue their lives in both territories. As A. says:

> POLISARIO has been, since the occupation, the single political structure of the Saharaui people. There are very few dissidents. I know people in POLISARIO who share different opinions: communists, fundamentalists, liberals . . . We believe new political forces will appear when we have succeeded in our fundamental goal. (Authors' translation of taped interview in Spanish).

Concerning Timorese, the level of ideological fragmentation of the community is much higher and the definition of common strategies presents some limitations, despite some recent reconcilation between different groups. In the words of P:

> 'There were always fractures among Timorese. Before, the ties were more close. There were also political divergences . . . There is the Nationalist convergence of UDT and FRETILIN . . . the Nationalist youth, also the Independence Secretariat of Ramos Horta which are in dispute with FRETILIN. There is also the Movement of 12 November, the Reunification movement, and specific associations like ART (Associação dos Refugiados de Timor) and CRT (Comissão dos Refugiados de Timor), the latter being a reaction to the former. (Authors' translation of taped interview in Portuguese).

These divisions of the Timorese organisations in exile lead to important difficulties in the definition of common strategies. This is aggravated by the wider process of social disaggregation of the community, reinforced by successive departures to Australia and also by a spreading of community members from initial reception centres in Quinta do Balteiro in Oeiras municipality through other parts of the Lisbon Metropolitan Area since 1981. Subsequently, the main concentrations of Timorese residents have emerged at Laveiras (Caxias) and, south of the Tagus estuary, at Bela Vista in the municipality of Setúbal. Moreover, ethnic differences between members of the community (not only between the diverse Timorese ethnic-base groups, but also between these and Timorese of Chinese origin) may act as an additional splintering factor.

Labour market integration

In common with the context of reception outlined above, labour market problems experienced by Maubere and Saharaui refugees are also different, whilst within each group there are categories of people who experience specific situations. Concerning the Saharauis, questions of unemployment and downward professional mobility do not assume a central position. The majority of those interviewed were either administrative/semi-skilled service workers or industrial workers (skilled and unskilled). There were no former farmers or pastoralists among those interviewed, although these were important activities in the Western Sahara, according to the 1974 Census. However, the sedentarisation process of the last years of Spanish rule had led many young people to settle in the major towns and to look for jobs outside the traditional sector (in administration, industry, construction, etc.). The results were an increase in the proportion of the local population in 'modern' activities, and an ageing of the active population in the traditional sector (Gonzálvez Pérez 1994).

After the Moroccan occupation, the sedentarisation process accelerated, not only due to the concentration of people in the Tindouf camps, but also due to the increase in population flows towards the main Western Saharan towns. The consequences for the structure of the active population were an increase in situations of dependence (those who live in the camps rely largely on external aid), an acceleration of the decline in the agricultural sector, and an abandonment of jobs in administration, industry, construction and the former colonial army by much of the Saharaui population.

As in other situations, in the case of the Saharauis there has been a process of 'selection' of the refugee population in Las Palmas de Gran

Canaria, which is dominated by males (young adults and adults) with some professional experience outside the traditional sector, and having, in several cases, a relatively high level of education (more than 10 years of study). Nonetheless, comparison between former professions in the country of origin and jobs held currently does not reveal a clear pattern of downward professional mobility. Also, unemployment is rare; it is important to stress that all those interviewed had found a job less than six months after their arrival in the Canary Islands. Two factors have major importance in this process of finding jobs and limiting professional devaluation. First, the activation of informal mechanisms which involve both the Saharaui group members and the local population – it is important to remember the age-old relations of the populations of both territories – has a major role in the process of overcoming the problems of unemployment (table 9.1). Secondly, a concentration in temporary employment, frequently of an illegal nature, leads to a process of long-distance and long-duration commuting. Saharaui men often adjust their presence in the Canary Islands to periods of heavy demand for employment in agriculture, fishing or even the tourist sector. Even those who live more permanently in the islands alternate periods of work with periods at home, especially if they develop activities in sectors such as fishing.

Despite the relatively favourable situation of Saharauis in the Great Canaria labour market, it is important to stress their reliance on temporary jobs and lack of legal documentation (table 9.2) which reveals the precarity of the situation of some members of this group. Also recent problems within the Spanish fishing sector may result in rising unemployment of Saharauis in the Canary Islands. In practice, the Saharauis are aware of the difficulties of the Spanish labour market, as demonstrated by the fact that the 'unemployment crisis' was mentioned by several respondents as a major problem.

Table 9.1 Sources of information about employment for Maubere and Saharaui refugees

	Maubere	*Saharauis*
Through locals	+/–	+
Through family members or kinship ties	++	++
Through QGA/QEI (programmes for re-deployment in Portuguese administration)	++	–
Self-employed/through advertisements	–	+
Through professional training	–	–
Other situations	–	+/–

Source: Focus group interviews, Lisbon and Gran Canaria, 1994.

Table 9.2 Main problems cited by Maubere and Saharaui refugees

	Maubere		Saharauis	
	no.	(%)	no.	(%)
Global unemployment crisis	8	(18)	4	(31)
Lack of professional skills/low level of literacy	12	(27)	1	(8)
Lack of initial contacts	3	(7)	0	(0)
Documentation	0	(0)	6	(46)
Language	9	(21)	0	(0)
Discrimination	2	(5)	1	(8)
Others	3	(7)	0	(0)
No answer	3	(7)	1	(8)
None	4	(9)	0	0)
Total respondents	44	(100)	13	(100)

Source: Authors' survey, 1994.

This description of labour market involvement of Saharauis in the Canary Islands is almost exclusively limited to men. In fact, the number of women in the whole of the community is low, and their presence in the labour market is practically nil. Their role in Saharaui society in the Canary Islands corresponds almost exclusively to the administration of the domestic sphere and to assisting dependent members of the family (aged, handicapped, children). This lack of participation in the labour market is partly due to language problems – men had more access to foreign influences at home – but especially to the traditional socio-cultural features of Muslim Saharaui society, where the participation of women in the labour market is still hardly accepted. However, life in refugee camps as well as the participation of men in the war against Morocco have given to Saharaui women a new role in the management of Tindouf camps, strongly reinforced by the education efforts developed by Saharauis in exile (Perregaux 1993). It will be interesting to follow up the evolution of the participation of Saharaui women in the Canary Islands labour market, to see the influence on younger generations of education in Tindouf. The attitudes of the few girls of Saharaui families who were educated in Spanish schools and have spent all their lives in Gran Canaria may also play some role in a potential process of change.

As far as the Maubere are concerned, the majority of the members of the community settled in Portugal have some direct or indirect links (through relatives) with the former Portuguese administration of the territory. Therefore, many of them benefited from special re-deployment measures under the Quadro Geral de Adidos and its successor, the Quadro de Efectivos Inter-departamentais, which enabled them to find, after a transition period (frequently of more than one year), similar government positions to those held in Timor. More serious, however, are the problems faced by women (table 9.3) and young Timorese who want to join the labour market in Portugal. For women, the lack of transferable experience brought from East Timor as well as some language difficulties limit possibilities of employment, even in domestic service which plays a major role for migrant women in general.

Table 9.3   Employment situation of Maubere refugees one year after arrival in Portugal

Employment situation	*Men*	*Women*	*Total*
Employers/independent workers	0	1	1
Employees	10	1	11
Unemployed	5	4	9
Non-active	1	7	8
Total	16	13	29

Source: Authors' survey, 1994.
Note: These data exclude those who arrived as students and continued their studies in Portugal.

Nonetheless, an increase in the numbers working in domestic service after arrival in Portugal was reported by some respondents, reflecting the changing attitude of some women towards work. This may be against the wishes of men: for instance, while speaking about employment problems of his family, P. said that his wife could not work, not only because she had to look after their five young children, but also due to questions of principle – 'In Timor it is not common for women to work outside their homes'. The trend to a stronger participation of Timorese women in the Portuguese labour market reflects the loss of family assets during forced migration and the need to combine two salaries in the family budget. In some cases, the death of the husband or separation of the couple leaves women alone with young children and obliges them to find a job.

Young Timorese experience a situation which is even worse than the situation of women. Most of the unemployed in table 9.3 are young people, who contribute to an unemployment rate among those interviewed of almost 30 per cent, which although based on a small sample, is much higher than the Portugese average (around 7 per cent). Despite the frequent use of institutional support in finding employment, especially among the young (table 9.4), professional training or employment advice rarely results in a place in the labour market. The strong mobilisation of institutional resources by this group reflects a traditional reliance on state institutions and also a specific sympathetic context which leads the Maubere to training programmes prepared by the regional delegations of the National Social Service and some NGOs.

Table 9.4   Use of institutional support by Maubere refugees to obtain employment, by age group

Age group	Used institutional support	Did not use institutional support
15–24 years	9	2
25–44 years	4	6
>44 years	3	8
TOTAL	16	16

Source: Authors' survey, 1994.
Note: These data exclude students and women or retired persons who have never sought a job in Portugal.

However, the Timorese recognise that this training is not sufficient to overcome the narrowness of the Portuguese labour market, a problem that affects all Portuguese youth. Moreover, limited initial training and literacy, as well as language problems, especially for those who were educated in East Timor after the Indonesian invasion, are disadvantages that this group faces while competing in the Portuguese labour market. The practical results of incentives given to the latest wave of young Timorese in order to provide them with access to academic qualifications remains to be evaluated. However, since one of the major ways of finding jobs among the Maubere (through re-integration in public service) does not apply to young people, the remaining solutions are the mobilisation of family contacts and, eventually, the acceptance of low-skilled tasks (in construction or in domestic service, for example) or emigration to Australia.

It is fair to say that the labour market integration of Timorese in the Lisbon Metropolitan Area presents more problems than the integration of Saharauis in the Gran Canaria labour market (table 9.5). However, direct comparison has several limitations. First, Saharaui refugees in Gran Canaria are a smaller and less diverse group (mostly men, aged 20–40), conditions that limit the range of problems experienced. Furthermore, the geographical proximity of the key territories (Canary Islands, Mauritania, Western Sahara and Algeria) enables circular migration that lessens problems such as unemployment or downward professional mobility. The strategy of circulation, associated with the impossibility of obtaining Western Saharan documentation as well as a systematic refusal to accept Moroccan papers, leads to a number of situations of illegal work and residence in the Canary Islands. Since obtaining Spanish nationality is almost impossible for these people, the question of legality is probably the hardest problem of Saharauis in the Canary Islands, a point reinforced in the focus group sessions.

Table 9.5   Labour market situation of Saharauis and Maubere: problems and strategies

	Maubere	Saharauis
Problems		
Unemployment	+	−
Lack of job opportunities	+	+
Downward professional mobility	+	−
Skills mismatch	+	−
Language	+	−
Strategies		
Formal support	+	−
Integration assistance	+	−
Informal support	+	+
Illegal work	−	+
Emigration (or circular migration)	+	+

Source: Authors' survey, 1994.

Concerning Timorese, their strong reliance on institutional solutions has not been very effective in the question of labour market integration, especially in the case of young people. However, many Timorese still think like P. who says that 'institutions give more guarantees than temporary work or work found through friends'. Finally, the diversity of the community in terms of socio-economic status, ethnic origin, gender and age as well as the geographical distance between place of origin and place of settlement make the problems of this group of people more complicated. Emigration to Australia emerges normally as the chosen solution.

Conclusion

This chapter has reviewed the experience of two little-known groups of refugees in Spain and Portugal, who despite owing their migration to similar circumstances, have reached remarkably different situations in the more than twenty years since the decolonisation and the subsequent takeover of their countries of origin. In conformity with the first of the hypotheses outlined above, both groups have experienced considerable job insecurity in their host country, although this has varied, from a situation of unemployment and transitional downwards professional mobility for the Maubere in Portugal, to a greater importance of job instability, and the illegal nature of available work, for the Saharauis living in Gran Canaria. However, more generally, it is difference rather than similarity which marks comparison between the two groups. Thus whereas the Maubere have relied more strongly on institutional support, including professional training, and the re-integration programme for professionals formerly employed in the Portuguese administration of East Timor, Saharauis have been forced much more into reliance on informal solutions, in which migrant networks have been crucial in ensuring insertion in the labour market.

These differences reflect the specific characteristics of the two refugee groups, but most importantly the different contexts of reception produced by the attitudes of Spain and Portugal towards the political situation in the Western Sahara and East Timor respectively. In the absence of favourable government policy, informal solutions have been necessary for Saharauis living in Gran Canaria, and have left this group highly vulnerable in terms of their illegal situation; although ironically it has left them better able to survive within parts of a segmented labour market. In contrast, a highly favourable reception context for the Maubere in Lisbon has not prevented problems of unemployment particularly for younger generations, and a widespread desire to move onwards to the larger Timorese community in Australia. In this sense, the development of institutional solutions largely orientated towards insertion in the domestic labour market has failed to achieve this objective; although this may reflect in part the strength of the Maubere social network on an international level, and the orientation of this group towards their home country, or since this is not yet a possibility, towards a location that is at least closer to home.

References

AGU (1970) *Timor: Pequena Monografia*. Lisbon: Agência Geral do Ultramar.

AAPS (1994) *El Referendum en el Sahara Ocidental: Libro Blanco*. Madrid: Associacion de Amigos del Pueblo Saharaui.

Bach, R. et al. (1993) *Changing Relations: Newcomers and Established Residents in US Communities*. New York: Ford Foundation.

Black, R. (1992) *Livelihood and Vulnerability of Foreign Refugees in Greece*, London: Department of Geography, King's College London, Occasional Paper 33.

Castles, S. and Miller, M. (1993) *The Age of Migration: International Population Movements in the Modern World*. London: Macmillan.

della Donne, M. (1995) Difficulties of refugees towards integration: the Italian case, in della Donne, M., ed., *Avenues to Integration: Refugees in Contemporary Europe*, Rome: Ipermedium, pp. 110–44.

Dorais, L-J. (1991) Refugee adaptation and community structure: the Indochinese in Quebec City, Canada, *International Migration Review*, 25(3), pp. 551–73.

Finnan, C.R. (1980) Occupational adjustment of refugees, *International Migration Review*, 15(1), pp. 292–309.

Ford, R. and Warnes, T. (1993) *Residential Strategies in Later Life: Focus Group and Interview Study Results*. London: Department of Geography, King´s College London, Occasional Paper 38.

Gonzálvez Pérez, V. (1994) Descolonización y migraciones desde el África Espanola (1956–1975), *Investigaciones Geográficas*, 12, pp. 45–63.

Hauff, E. and Vaglum, P. (1993) Integration of Vietnamese refugees into Norwegian labor market: the impact of war trauma, *International Migration Review*, 27(2), pp. 388–405.

Lacoste, Y. (1985) Les embrouillements géopolitiques des centres de l´Islam, *Hérodote*, 36, pp. 7–45.

Malheiros, J. (1996) *Imigrantes na Região de Lisboa: Os Anos de Mudança. Imigração e Processo de Integração das Comunidades de Origem Indiana*. Lisbon: Colibri.

Marcos, A. (1995) *Timor Timorense*. Lisbon: Colibri.

Melchior, M.(1993) Refugees: problem or challenge as a work force? *Migration*, 18, pp. 77–95.

Perregaux, C. (1993) *Gulili: Mujeres del Desierto Saharaui*. Tafalla: Txalaparta.

Pires, M. (1994) *Descolonização de Timor: Missão Impossível?* Lisbon: Publicações Dom Quixote.

Pohjola, A. (1991) Social networks: help or hindrance to the migrant? *International Migration*, 34(3), pp. 435–44.

Price, D.L. (1979) *The Western Sahara*. Beverly Hills: Sage Policy Paper.

Silverman, D. (1993) *Interpreting Qualitative Data. Methods for Analysing Talk, Text and Interaction*. London: Sage.

Stein, B. (1979) Occupational adjustment of refugees: the Vietnamese in the United States, *International Migration Review*, 13(1), pp. 25–45.

Thomas, A. and Wilson, G. (1996) Technological capabilities in textile production in Sahrawi refugee camps, *Journal of Refugee Studies*, 9(1), pp. 182–98.

Viola, M.A. (1986) *Os Deslocados de Timor: formas associativas na colectividade Timorense da Quinta do Balteiro*. Lisbon: Dissertação de licenciatura em Antropologia, Universidade Nova de Lisboa (unpublished).

The Contributors

Joanna Apap is a D.Phil. student in the Sussex European Institute, University of Sussex.

Richard Black is Lecturer in Human Geography in the School of African and Asian Studies at the University of Sussex.

Victoria Chell is Honorary Research Associate in the Migration Research Unit, Department of Geography, University College London.

Anthony Fielding is Professor of Human Geography in the School of Social Sciences at the University of Sussex.

Theodoros Iosifides has recently completed a D.Phil. at the Sussex European Institute, University of Sussex.

Russell King is Professor of Geography in the School of European Studies at the University of Sussex.

Melanie Knights works at the Latin America Department of the UK Foreign and Commonwealth Office.

Jorge Malheiros is Lecturer in the Centro de Estudos Geográficos, Universidade de Lisboa, Portugal. In 1997–8, he is Visiting Researcher in the Sussex Centre for Migration Research.

Cristóbal Mendoza is European Research Fellow in the Department of Geography, King's College London.

Davide Però is a D. Phil. student in the Sussex European Institute, University of Sussex.

Index